The Economic Transformation
of American Cities

The Economic Transformation of American Cities

Thierry J. Noyelle
and
Thomas M. Stanback, Jr.

Foreword by Eli Ginzberg

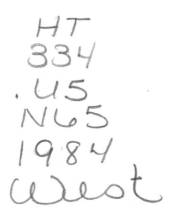
Rowman & Allanheld
PUBLISHERS

ROWMAN & ALLANHELD

Published in the United States of America in 1984
by Rowman & Allanheld, Publishers
(A division of Littlefield, Adams & Company)
81 Adams Drive, Totowa, New Jersey 07512

Library of Congress Cataloging in Publication Data
Noyelle, Thierry J.
  The economic transformation of American cities.

  Bibliography: p.
  Includes index.
  1. Metropolitan areas—United States.   2. United
States—Economic conditions—1945–   —Regional dis-
parities.   3. Urban economics.   I. Stanback, Thomas M.
II. Title.
HT334.U5N65   1983   330.973   83-21292
ISBN 0-86598-144-2

84 85 86   /10   9   8   7   6   5   4   3   2   1
Printed in the United States of America

This publication was prepared partly under contract #ERD-712-G-79-47 from
the Division of Economic Research, Economic Development Administration,
U.S. Department of Commerce. The statements, findings, conclusions,
recommendations, and other data in this report are solely those of the
authors and do not necessarily reflect views of the Economic Development
Administration.

Contents

Tables

Foreword

One of the curses of modern economics, as Nobel prizewinner Wassily Leontieff has observed, is the preference of economists for building models and their aversion to undergoing the drudgery involved in collecting, sifting and organizing the data, without which the validity of their models can never be tested. Logical consistency and mathematical sophistication are not substitutes for hard data, and it is more and better hard data that modern economics most needs.

These obiter dicta help to explain my great enthusiasm for Noyelle's and Stanback's new book. They have taken Leontieff's charge to heart. They plowed through and organized large bodies of data relating to the changes that the principal metropolitan areas have undergone in the post–World War II period, particularly in the decades of the 1960s and 70s.

Conventional wisdom about what has been happening to the U.S. economy in the post–World War II era with particular reference to structure and location would stress the following:

the retrogression of the snowbelt economy and the strikingly rapid advances of the sunbelt economy;

the movement of manufacturing out of the older urban centers to the suburbs and smaller non-urban communities;

the increase of services, usually defined in terms of retailing and consumer services, with their lower than average productivity;

a mounting unease with the rapid growth of the governmental and nonprofit sectors without any clear perception of their role in contributing to output and employment;

the growing concern that with U.S. manufacturing in decline, the preeminence of the U.S. in the world's economy is in serious jeopardy.

One could continue but the foregoing are among the key themes that have gained wide currency.

The important point to stress is that the foregoing propositions have tended to be supported by, at best, scattered evidence and that, up to the present large-scale study, no broad systematic effort has been made to see the picture whole and to let the facts—not theory—lead the way.

Let us look more closely at each of the beliefs outlined above, with the data that Noyelle and Stanback have pulled together and analyzed.

To begin with, Noyelle and Stanback do not question, much less deny, that, taking the entire region as a unit of analysis, the economy of the Sunbelt has been expanding much more rapidly than the Snowbelt. But once they probe more deeply and look at the array of different types of cities in both the South and the North—using a typology that they have developed based on a structure reflecting sources of employment and output—then the simple areal generalization begins to fall apart. To oversimplify: they indicate that most, though not all, of the major cities in the Snowbelt have been able to compensate for some or all of the losses that they have experienced as manufacturing wandered off first from core to the suburb, later from the suburb to other areas, particularly to the South.

Two further strong findings emerge: putting New York City to one side, there has been a reshuffling of the cities where large companies are headquartered, but for the most part the northern cities have done quite well—losing some, gaining others, but definitely continuing to dominate the national landscape.

Further from the important new data that Noyelle and Stanback have worked up with respect to regional and divisional headquarters of large and medium sized corporations, the conclusion emerges that the center of control for subsidiary corporate activities continues to be in the North. There is no basis for Noyelle and Stanback to denigrate the gains of the South or to assume that they are nearing an end. But there is also no basis for them to write off the North where many cities have made good progress in compensating for their loss of manufacturing and are gaining strength from the continuing growth of services.

The second contention deeply embedded in contemporary thought about the relocation of manufacturing, first out of the central cities and latterly away from the suburbs to free standing small non-metropolitan communities, comes closest to being substantiated by Noyelle and Stanback's analysis. But even here the authors make an important but generally neglected point: that manufacturing itself is being transformed with internal and external services playing increasingly important roles, that these "producer services" tend to cluster in good-sized cities and, that most of these cities remain in the Snowbelt.

Drawing heavily on earlier work on which they collaborated, Noyelle and Stanback challenge the widespread conviction that the expansion in services has been mostly in retailing and in meeting other consumer needs, and that the services basically provide only low wage, low productivity jobs that cannot be viewed as compensating for the losses of good blue collar employment. While there are many low wage, low productivity service jobs in retailing and in other service sectors there are also a great number of high wage, high productivity jobs in finance, advertising, accounting and other producer services.

One of the more intriguing sections of Noyelle and Stanback's book is Chapter 7 where they present detailed information on the distribution of selected producer services with heavy emphasis on banking and insurance but including others as well, all of which point to the continuing ability of most of the larger northern cities to hold their own.

While the authors explore in somewhat less detail the role of government and nonprofit institutions in the restructuring of the U.S. economy, they provide, inter alia, a critical chapter (9) which shows the importance of higher education and research in quickening the pace of transformation in selected northern and southern cities.

While Noyelle and Stanback's data and analyses do not directly speak to the widespread concern that, with a weakening of its economic base, the U.S. international competitive position is being eroded, by implication there is much in their treatise to raise serious questions about such oversimplification. They point repeatedly to the transformations underway that have reduced the relative share of manufacturing employment till it accounts for fewer than one out of every four workers. But they do emphasize that in terms of dollar output, manufacturing remains critically important. What needs to be remembered is the impact of these domestic transformations not only on the U.S. commodity trade but also on its balance of payments position. We know from other sources that services have begun to loom ever larger as a proportion of total U.S. exports.

A single work that calls into question five deeply entrenched views of the U.S. economy, views that are held by businessmen, economists, government officials, is clearly on that criterion alone an important contribution. But Noyelle and Stanback have done more. They have provided much of the data and the framework for analysis that will enable others to develop valid views about the economic transformations that are underway in the U.S. with particular references to how they are affecting different regions of the country and specifically its older and newer cities. As such they have made an important contribution to dynamic economics, a sadly neglected arena.

Eli Ginzberg, Director
Conservation of Human Resources
Columbia University

Preface

When, back in the late 1970s, Eli Ginzberg urged several of us at the Conservation of Human Resources Project to take a closer look at the structural transformation that had been affecting the United States during the previous two or three decades, we chose to do so from the standpoint of the economy's shift to the services, an area in which the Project staff had already accumulated considerable expertise over the years. Several studies were eventually conducted under this broad agenda, among which this is the third coauthored by us.

In *Services/The New Economy* (1981), written in collaboration with Peter Bearse and Robert Karasek, we set out to map the principal directions of the sweeping transformation that had been at work through much of the postwar decades and had been accelerating during the 1970s. Our analysis made clear that the shift to the services had resulted not only from changes in what the economy produces (final output), but also from changes in how it produces (greater use of services as intermediate inputs). In addition, we pointed to major changes in the structure of metropolitan economies and in the composition and functioning of labor markets.

In *Cities in Transition* (1982), we examined the impact of the shift to the services on the labor market of seven medium-sized cities. We were able to take the analysis a few steps further by observing differences in patterns of adjustments to changing metropolitan roles and by providing evidence of an emerging tendency toward increasing labor market dualism.

The present book examines the impact of the shift to the services on the structure of the U.S. metropolitan system. While a few economists and geographers (reviewed in Chapter 3 of this book) had done earlier work on the impact of the postwar development of corporate headquarters, producer service firms and other strategic services on the economic structure of metropolitan places, we felt that a system-wide analysis was needed. Such an analysis would treat a wide variety of economic activities and extend beyond the largest places to a broad spectrum of metropolitan economies. The task turned out to be far more ambitious than we had anticipated, requiring exploration of a large number of previously untapped data sources as well as analysis of more-conventional materials. The thesis developed in this book is, we believe, an important one: that the advent of the service era has given rise to a system of cities fundamentally different from that which structured the economic geography of the United States during the previous manufacturing era. Urban analysts need to reconceptualize their understanding of the system of cities in the light of these historical changes, to rethink their notions of economic development and growth diffusion, and ultimately to review the directions urban policy is taking. While we recognize that our contribution to this agenda is modest, we hope it marks a step in the right direction.

In concluding this preface, we wish to thank two groups of individuals who made important contributions. First are Marc Glassman, David Kung, Wenny Lin, Eileen Nic, Terry Stanley, Bob Watts, and Tom Wong, who provided clerical assistance or technical expertise at various stages of the research. Second are Heidi Jones, Fedor Kabalin, David Harris, Ellen Levine, Penny Peace, and Shoshana Vasheetz, who demonstrated both patience and skill in preparing the various drafts of this manuscript.

October 1983   Thierry J. Noyelle
Thomas M. Stanback, Jr.

CHAPTER ONE

Introduction

As America moves into the last decades of this century, it is clear that both the nation and its cities have been caught up in a major transformation which may well rival the earlier industrial revolution in terms of wrenching changes and developmental opportunities. Between 1970 and 1980 close to 19 million jobs were added to the American economy, of which over 90 percent were in the service sectors, while manufacturing employment stagnated through much of the decade. Moreover, in goods as well as service producing industries there was a shift toward white collar occupations, which brought the share of such jobs to about 80 percent of the total workforce. Closely associated with these developments were changes in institutional arrangements, featuring increasing prominence of large corporations, nonprofit and public sector enterprises, along with major changes in technology, the location of activities, and the nature of work.

In city after city, the results were dramatic. In New York City, the decade brought the loss of roughly 400,000 jobs in manufacturing, and a growth and reshuffling of employment in the complex of corporate headquarters and allied business and financial services (hereafter *complex of corporate activities*), in nonprofit institutions and in the public sector, which together, today, account for roughly two thirds of the city's labor force. Most importantly, New York steadily strengthened its position as a world center, as evidenced by its rising prominence in the Eurodollar market or by the rapid buildup of foreign banking, trading, and other business facilities within its limits.

Likewise, in less than three decades Atlanta, Denver, Miami, and other Sunbelt cities rose to become key business centers, at the same time that some of the older northern cities such as Boston, Minneapolis, or even Philadelphia were breaking away from their former dependence on manufacturing employment and strengthening their positions as major regional centers, attracting scores of offices from large corporations as well as major facilities of the nonprofit or public sectors.

Yet the prospects are by no means favorable everywhere. Even if some troubled places such as Cleveland[1] or Akron[2] succeed in firming-up their position in the hierarchy of cities, once their respective industries have adjusted to the new conditions of world competition, it may well be that other cities like Buffalo,[3] Youngstown, or Flint will remain under considerable stress in years to come. Moreover, it is clear that the difficulties met by cities in adapting to the nation's new economic order need not be restricted to the older, northern cities in the years just ahead (e.g., the experience of Birmingham).

In short, the picture that is emerging is at once confusing and complicated. While there is widespread recognition that urbanization is undergoing a very fundamental transformation, there is little agreement as to either the major forces at work or the manner in which the urban system is being restructured. In large measure this is due to a general tendency to focus attention on growth and ignore underlying processes of change. Experts and laymen alike have tended to view major regional and urban developments almost entirely as a reflection of differential rates of employment and population growth, failing to look beneath the surface for complex and even offsetting trends. We have spoken of the "rise" of the Sunbelt and the "decline" of the Snowbelt cities, forgetting a basic lesson of economic history: that change is usually two-sided, implying both growth and development. Quantitative changes in the scale of the economic system typically bring about qualitative transformations in the way such a system operates, with changes in the organizational structure of the economy opening up opportunities for moving to an even higher scale of operation.

This book is an attempt to identify linkages between urban growth and development by examining the changing structure and economic role of the 140 largest metropolitan centers in recent decades. The analysis indicates that the major changes undergone by the nation's economy, as it has moved increasingly from a goods to a service orientation, have been both induced and reinforced by a dramatic transformation of the urban system.

Since the developments that have taken place are complex in nature and require a fairly extensive and elaborate analysis, it should be helpful to present here an overview of the main thesis of the book.

An Overview of the Main Thesis of the Book

Recent changes in American urbanization have been characterized not simply by the growth of the Sunbelt metropolises, but also by a widespread transformation of the economic base of cities in both the northern and southern regions of the country, along with a reorganization of functional linkages that exist among metropolitan centers of the urban system. Lying back of these changes is the transformation of the nation's economy in recent decades, a transformation featuring rapid growth of services, the rise of white collar work, and relative stagnation of production employment.

The rising importance of services in the U.S. economy during the postwar period is principally associated with the growing role of activities of the corporate complex (e.g., banking, insurance, advertising, legal counsel and the service-like functions carried out within the central offices of corporations) as intermediate inputs in the roundabout processes of production and with the rise of public sector and nonprofit (health and education) services to fulfill the demands of an increasingly complex and human capital intensive modern society. Regarding the former it has been estimated that by the late 1970s the share of GNP originating from the complex of corporate activities was about the same as that originating from direct manufacturing production: roughly one fourth of the GNP![4] In contrast, mainly consumer services (hotels, auto repairs, movie theaters, etc.) and retailing have shown relatively limited shifts, although together they have continued to play significant roles in an increasingly service oriented economy.

Our thesis is that these changes reflect in large measure responses to forces at work in the economy during the recent decades, of which at least four are of paramount importance: the increasing size of markets—from local to regional, national or even international; changes in transportation and technology—affecting in particular the manufacture of goods; the increased importance of public sector and non profit activities—especially in the areas of human capital formation; and the rise of the very large, multiproduct, often multinational, corporation—resulting in the multiplication of locationally distinct service-like corporate establishments: national headquarters, regional sales headquarters, divisional offices, R&D facilities, etc.

A review of key theoretical and empirical contributions by urbanologists indicates that there remain considerable differences in the way in which economists examine the system of cities and its recent transformation. These differences hinge partly on theoretical considerations, with some scholars stressing the importance of "central place" forces in the structuring of the urban system, while others emphasize the "asymmetrical" nature of numerous economic linkages between and among higher and lower rank order cities. But there are also disagreements as to the nature of recent regional shifts, with some economists emphasizing the autonomous nature of Sunbelt development, and others the complex linkages that continue to exist between the southern and northern economic regions. Our review of the literature suggests several general propositions that guide our investigation of structure and transformation within the U.S. system of cities:

> that size is likely to remain a major variable in determining the economic structure of metropolitan places, with the largest places likely to offer the most diversified economic bases;
>
> that the system of cities is likely to be characterized by the coexistence of cities that are "central place" in nature (i.e., cities that deliver a relatively wide range of goods and services to their surrounding hinterlands including lower rank order cities) and of cities that are "off-centered" (i.e., cities that deliver a relatively narrow and specialized range of goods and services to other cities within the economy);
>
> that specialization of places is determined in part by the cumulative effects of different stages of economic development on individual places;
>
> that there is evidence that the transformation has brought about both the rise of a new set of large metropolitan centers (mostly Sunbelt) and considerable adaptation among a number of older large places;
>
> that the recent transformation of the urban system must be understood in terms of the rise of complexes of corporate activities in key metropolitan centers and of the linkages that have developed between these complexes and other employment sectors in these and other urban centers;

that nonprofit and public sector institutions have often played a major role in the restructuring of the system of cities, but that their impact has not necessarily been felt most strongly in those cities where the complexes of corporate activities have developed most vigorously;

that, in a broad sense, the transformation process observed in cities is the result of changes in the intensity of both centrifugal forces (forces encouraging decentralization) and centripetal forces (forces encouraging urban agglomeration) at work in various economic sectors reflecting changes in the economics of factor inputs, changes in markets and so forth;

last, that the structure of the networks of corporate "control" and "development" functions must be explicated, if we are to understand the linkages that have developed among the cities.

Our empirical analysis proceeds by examining changes in the structure of the U.S. urban hierarchy, focusing on the recent transformation of the 140 largest Standard Metropolitan Statistical Areas (SMSAs). A typology of these 140 largest cities is developed based on their employment structure. The typology underlines functional differences among four major groups of metropolitan centers:

1. The *Diversified Service Centers* or *Nodal Centers*, which are centers specializing in the provision of headquarters functions, producer services, distributive services and to a varying extent nonprofit and government activities to national, regional, or subregional hinterlands. These centers may be classified into three major subgroups, largely on the basis of market area served and the level of sophistication of services rendered: the "national" nodal (e.g., New York or Chicago), "regional" nodal (e.g., Philadelphia, Houston, Boston, or Atlanta) and "subregional" nodal (e.g., Memphis, Charlotte, Omaha, or Des Moines) centers;

2. The *Specialized Service Centers*, which are centers specializing in the provision of a narrower range of intermediate service activities, and which fall into two categories: (a) "functional nodal" places, metropolitan economies which, although remaining strongly oriented to production activity, have strengthened their position as decision making centers in specific industrial areas (e.g., automobile in Detroit, office equipment in Rochester, semiconductors in San Jose, tires in Akron, etc.); or (b) centers specializing in government and nonprofit activities as in the case of "government-education" (e.g., Albany, Austin, or Madison) or "education-manufacturing" places (e.g., New Haven or Ann Arbor);

3. The *Production Centers* which are centers specializing in the production of manufacturing goods, military hardware (or services), or mineral resources. These comprise three subgroups: the "manufacturing" centers (e.g., Buffalo, Gary, Greenville-Spartanburg, or Davenport), the "industrial-military" centers (e.g., San Diego, San Antonio, or Newport News) and the "mining-industrial" centers (e.g., Bakersfield or Charleston, WVa);

4. The *Consumer-Oriented Centers* which are centers that are consumer serving in orientation, whether they be "resort-retirement" (e.g., Orlando, Las Vegas, or West Palm Beach) or "residential" places (e.g., Anaheim or Nassau-Suffolk).

Three initial findings set the stage for much of the analysis which follows.[5] The first relates to emerging patterns of metropolitan specialization. While there has been a considerable decentralization of manufacturing production and residential population both away from the older regions and away from the largest centers, activities of the corporate complex have decentralized little, and have grown disproportionately in a selected number of centers, mostly in the diversified and specialized service centers described above.

The second relates to the regional distribution of the various types of SMSAs. A major distinction between those areas classified as "Sunbelt" and those within the older "Snowbelt" regions is that it is within the latter that most of the typically slow growing functional nodal and manufacturing places are located, while most of the relatively fast growing industrial-military and resort-retirement places are located within the former. Other types of centers (such as nodal or government-education cities) demonstrate relatively less regional variations. Briefly, cities that tend to be central-place in orientation are relatively evenly distributed across the nation's geography, while other types of urban areas are more specialized in their location, reflecting both the unevenness of the processes of economic development through space and time and the unevenness of regional resources endowment. Thus the disproportionate presence of functional nodal and manufacturing centers in the northern regions of the country reflects the development of many of the nation's basic manufacturing industries in those regions prior to the most recent period of growth, that of industrial-military and resort-retirement centers in the southern regions, postwar trends in military expenditure, and new patterns of consumption with higher levels of discretionary income.

The third and perhaps most significant finding is that net growth measures fail to reveal the extent of the changes that have occurred in most SMSAs. For example, when transformation is measured by intra-SMSA shifts in industry of employment it is found that many of the large metropolitan centers, particularly the older nodal and functional nodal places, have been experiencing very radical transformations involving heavy losses of manufacturing jobs, but at least matching gains within key services. Clearly, overemphasis on growth without careful attention to the extent and nature of the developmental processes at work results in a failure to recognize what problems are being faced and to devise policy prescriptions that are appropriate.

These three initial findings are based on an analysis of aggregate employment measures developed for the 140 SMSAs under study. Despite their limitations, the measures point to complex structural and dynamic patterns, suggesting that more detailed analyses of the transformation undergone by key employment sectors of the economy are warranted. The analyses that follow rely heavily on data compiled from industry sources and special government reports.

Analysis of the transformation of the geography of manufacturing activities shows that there is an increasing spatial dichotomy between those centers where functions of management (headquarters), R&D, and high value added production takes place, and those where low value added production is sited. The former are increasingly gravitating toward the most centered places of the urban system (nodal or specialized service), and the latter, toward the more off-centered places (production and consumer-oriented), as well as the small SMSAs of the urban system (not included in our typology) and non-metropolitan areas.

Although national, regional and divisional headquarters and producer services have developed most vigorously in the diversified and specialized service centers, there remains considerable diversity in the locational patterns of various types of corporate non-production establishments and producer services. For example, while several measures show that certain producer services such as sophisticated banking services or advertising have become increasingly concentrated (or have remained highly concentrated) in the largest nodal centers, there is evidence that R&D functions are heavily concentrated in many specialized service centers. The analysis shows also that employment in the complex of corporate activities has grown somewhat faster in the regional nodal centers than in the larger national nodal places, in part because such centers have benefitted from both the tendency for the national headquarters of certain large corporations to relocate in these medium-sized cities and from the tendency for many large firms to establish full networks of regional sales headquarters in these key regional centers. Lastly, the analysis also points to the existence of cases such as that of the insurance industry in which strong decentralization tendencies are at work because much of the activity of the firms involve routine white collar work (e.g., data processing) which no longer needs to be carried out in the most central places of the urban system.

In terms of distributive services, the analysis shows that some services (e.g., air transportation) continue to be attracted most strongly to the largest central places whereas others (e.g., wholesaling) are, to some extent, being thrust outwards—with the medium size nodal centers becoming increasingly important as goods distribution centers.

Finally, in terms of public sector and nonprofit services, there appears to be considerable specialization—with a limited number of centers, often but not always those strongly characterized as central places, continuing to specialize heavily in these activities. Specifically, there is evidence of agglomeration of R&D facilities and technologically oriented firms near higher educational and medical institutions in specialized service centers in particular. At the same time, there is evidence that specialized nonprofit or governmental services, such as higher education, have expanded in some instances in metropolitan areas that were not strongly involved in these activities.

In general, our investigation of the dynamics of the transformation of the urban system suggests:

1. That there have been fundamental changes in the way in which the urban system is organized. While the largest central places of the industrial era

had long been characterized by their ability to deliver essential trade and finance services to surrounding hinterlands and lower rank order cities—a function largely inherited from the mercantile era—they were also the leading manufacturing centers for most of the nation's major industries. In the new era of services, the importance of production in central places (especially in diversified service centers) is decreasing sharply, with large and medium sized central places becoming increasingly specialized in the export of headquarters and producer services that permit firms to organize, manage and control production elsewhere (increasingly in production or consumer-oriented centers).

2. That there is no clear-cut distinction between central places and certain off-centered cities. Specialized service centers, in particular, are characterized by both "central place" and "off-centered" tendencies. Like nodal cities, specialized service centers export key services to other locations, yet over a much narrower range. But like most production or consumer-oriented cities, they also continue to operate as production centers (especially functional nodal and education-manufacturing cities), a role which is increasingly associated with off-centered places.

3. That there may be emerging, however, an increasing dichotomy between nodal and specialized service cities on the one hand and production and consumer oriented cities on the other, with the former serving as the locus of major economic decisions regarding new investments and availability of employment opportunities in various types and sizes of SMSAs; and the latter becoming increasingly dependent on the broad economic directions mapped out in the former and, thus, less in control of their own economic development process.

4. That many of the older and larger centers of the Snowbelt that played important roles as manufacturing centers during the industrial era have been relatively successful in rebuilding their economies away from an excessive dependence on traditional manufacturing activities through growth in the complex of corporate activities and in many instances in the government and nonprofit sectors and are thus retaining, as diversified or specialized service centers, a great deal of their economic importance or "dominance" over the urban system.

5. And that because of the strong structural differences that have emerged between centers that are, for the most part, succeeding in developing their export base through growth in key services areas (nodal and specializing service centers) and those that, to a large extent, are not (production and consumer-oriented cities), policy efforts in the area of urban economic development must recognize the necessity to tailor very different prescriptions for different types of urban places.

A Six-Class Typology of the Service Industries

Since so much of our analysis hinges on the industry classification that we have adopted, we present this scheme with no further delay.

THE TRADITIONAL FISHER-CLARK CLASSIFICATION

Conventional economic analysis of the service sector has long been dominated by the industry classification developed by Fisher and Clark,[6] consisting in grouping industries in three basic sectors:

Primary industries (agriculture, forestry, fishing and mining)
Secondary industries (manufacturing, construction and utilities)
Tertiary industries (trade, transport, communications, finance and services).

In large measure, this scheme continues to prevail in most of the literature on services and to underly the census reporting systems of most data-gathering bodies. The basic problem with such classification and the analytical framework which supports it is that they both assume, implicitly, either that the tertiary (service) sector plays a dependent, almost "parasitic" role to the secondary (manufacturing) sector—seen as the exclusive engine of growth—or that the ongoing shift of the economy towards the services is occurring almost regardless of shifts and changes at work within the manufacturing sector itself.

Evidence presented in this monograph (Chapter 2) and several recent studies vigorously contradicts both of these theses. To a very large extent, the services which have grown most rapidly in the postwar era are *intermediate outputs* in nature and are closely linked to the functioning of the manufacturing sector per se. Only a different classification scheme and a different analytical perspective can begin to address these issues adequately.

THE REVISED SINGLEMANN CLASSIFICATION

Following Harry Greenfeld's 1966 early study on *Manpower and the Growth of Producer Services*, a number of researchers have attempted to work within a different conceptual and analytical framework.[7] In this monograph, we follow some of the suggestions of their work. To analyze changes in the structure of both the national and metropolitan economies we use a classification scheme derived from one proposed by Joachim Singlemann,[8] which groups industries by general type of output.

Table 1.1 shows how the various 2-digit SIC industries are grouped to distinguish between services which are *primarily intermediate* as opposed to *primarily final* outputs and among service outputs provided under different institutional settings—private, public and nonprofit. Six major service groups are thus identified: four private sector service groups (the distributive services, the complex of corporate activities, the retail services, the mainly consumer services), along with the nonprofit services, and the public sector services.

Distributive services, which include transportation, communications, utilities (hereafter TCU) and wholesaling, are concerned with the distribution of goods and services from producers to *mostly* intermediate buyers—i.e., other producers, or retailers. They are thus to be distinguished from retail services which deliver goods (and a few selected services such as in restaurants and drinking places) to final consumers. The complex of corporate activities (or corporate complex), accounts for specialized producer services delivered by independent

Table 1.1 Classification of Sectors for Gross National
Product and Employment Analysis

Agriculture, Extractive and Transformative Industries

(1)	Agriculture	SIC 01 to 09
(2)	Extractive and Transformative	
	Mining	SIC 10 to 14
	Construction	SIC 15 to 17
	Manufacturing	SIC 20 to 39

Services

(3)	Distributive Services	
	Transportation, Communications and Utilities	SIC 40 to 49
	Wholesale	SIC 50 and 51
(4)	Complex cf Corporate Activities	
	Central Administrative Offices and Auxiliary Establishments	CAO&A of each 1 digit SIC grouping
	Producer Services	
	Finance, Insurance and Real Estate	SIC 60 to 67
	Business Services	SIC 73
	Legal Services	SIC 81
	Membership Orgs.	SIC 86
	Misc. Professional Svcs.	SIC 89
	Social Services	SIC 83[a]
(5)	Nonprofit Services	
	Health	SIC 80
	Education	SIC 82
(6)	Retail Services	SIC 52 to 59
(7)	Mainly Consumer Services	
	Hotel and Other Lodging Places	SIC 70
	Personal Services	SIC 72
	Auto Repair, Services and Garages	SIC 75
	Misc. Repair Services	SIC 76
	Motion Pictures	SIC 78
	Amusements and Recreation Services	SIC 79 and 84
	Private Households	SIC 88
(8)	Government and Government Enterprises	SIC 91 to 97

[a]After 1974.

Source: Adapted from J. Singlemann, From Agriculture to
Services, Beverly Hills, Ca.: Sage Publications,
1979. Based on Standard Industrial Classification
Manual, U.S. Office of Management and Budget,
Washington: U.S. Government Printing Office, 1976.

producer service firms to user firms and for service-like functions carried out within the central administrative offices of corporations. Producer services include finance, insurance, and real estate (hereafter FIRE) and other free standing corporate services (hereafter CS) such as accounting, law, advertising or consulting. Producer service-like functions of the central administrative offices of corporations (hereafter CAO&A) cover the legal, accounting, advertising, research and engineering as well as planning and general management services performed in-house by the staff of the corporation itself.

The grouping mainly consumer services (hereafter MCS) includes hotels, personal services, movie theaters, repair services and the like. Nonprofit services include mainly higher education and health services. As regards government and government enterprises, it should be noted that public education (e.g., grade schools or state colleges) and public health (e.g., municipal hospitals or publicly funded neighborhood clinics) are included in this sector and not among the nonprofit services, which is due to current reporting conventions that focus on sector of origin rather than function.

An important observation is that despite its improvement over the major groupings of the Standard Industrial Code, such a classification scheme remains flawed. Many services cater to both producers and final consumers. Thus, much of the output of the hotel or restaurant industry serves a consumer as well as a producer demand just as accountants or lawyers deliver services to both private individuals and firms. Of course, the same can be said of many government services and of part of the output of the nonprofit sector. In the cases of finance and insurance, whose dealings with consumers and producers are highly interdependent, the problem is even thornier.[9] In the end, improvements that can be made over conventional classification schemes are limited by the way census data are recorded and made available by government sources. Nevertheless, this revised scheme does represent considerable improvement over previous classifications.

Plan of the Study

This study uses the Bureau of the Census's concept of Standard Metropolitan Statistical Area (SMSA) as the basic urban territorial unit.[10] Our purpose is not to examine urban growth and transformation processes in terms of individual cities (e.g., to distinguish between central business districts and suburbs) but in terms of metropolitan economies, viewed as part of a national system of metropolitan centers.

Following this introductory chapter, this monograph is divided into nine chapters. The first three chapters set the ground for the study. Chapter 2 examines the principal forces that have driven the transformation of the U.S. economy towards an era of predominantly service sector jobs and white collar work. Chapter 3 sets forth some basic conceptual propositions regarding growth and development of the U.S. urban system. Chapter 4 presents our typology of the large and medium sized metropolitan places and reviews the main dimensions of growth and transformation in these economies during the past two decades. It provides a basis for much of the subsequent analysis.

The next five chapters examine the dimensions of transformation associated with the most important industry groups identified in this introductory chapter. Manufacturing (Chapter 5), the complex of corporate activities (Chapters 6 and 7), the distributive services (Chapter 8), and the public and nonprofit sectors (Chapter 9) are examined in turn for the light they shed on the transformations at work. Throughout these chapters, the emphasis is on how the changes undergone by each of the major sectors contribute to explaining structural differences among the various types of SMSAs identified in Chapter 4 and changes in their economic linkages.

These analyses are based mostly on measures developed from a variety of business sources (e.g., business directories) largely because of the inadequacy of conventional government data. While every attempt has been made to generate historical series from these less orthodox sources, a number of the data sets are available for recent years only (i.e., circa 1976). When this is the case, data are analyzed cross-sectionally (i.e., for type of place comparisons). Despite such limitations, important new insights are gained into the way in which the special locational tendencies of different economic activities have come to shape the new urban landscape.

In the final chapter (Chapter 10) we draw on the findings of the previous analyses in an effort to present an overall picture of the U.S. urban system as it exists and functions today. Our intent is to set forth some key propositions as regards developmental potentials and limitations in various types of metropolitan economies.

Notes

1. Richard V. Knight, "The Cleveland Economy in Transition: Implications for the Future," Working Paper, Cleveland: Cleveland State University, College of Urban Affairs, 1977.

2. "Whatever Happened to Akron," *Forbes*, November 22, 1982.

3. See Thomas M. Stanback, Jr. and Thierry J. Noyelle, *Cities in Transition*, Totowa, N.J.: Allanheld, Osmun & Co., 1982.

4. Thomas M. Stanback, Jr., et al., *Services/The New Economy,* Totowa, N.J.: Allanheld, Osmun, 1981.

5. Since the smallest metropolitan centers (126 SMSAs as of 1976) are excluded from our typology, they are not dealt with in most of the analyses that follow. Wherever possible, however, we do identify aggregate trends for all 126 small SMSAs combined with non-metropolitan areas. In general, there is evidence from this and other studies that the majority of these small centers tend to share the characteristics of large and medium size places classified in our typology as production or consumer-oriented centers. See, for example, Thomas M. Stanback, Jr. and Richard V. Knight, *The Metropolitan Economy*, New York: Columbia University, 1970.

6. A.G.B. Fisher, *The Clash of Progress and Security*, London: Macmillan, 1935; C. Clark, *The Conditions of Economic Progress*, London: Macmillan, 1940.

7. Op. cit., New York: Columbia University Press, 1966; see also Joachim Singlemann, *From Agriculture to Services*, Beverley Hills, Calif.: Sage Publications, 1979; Thomas M. Stanback, Jr., *Understanding the Service Economy*, Baltimore: The Johns Hopkins University Press, 1979; Thomas M. Stanback, Jr., et al., *Services: The New Economy,* op. cit.

8. Op. cit.

9. Harold Goldstein, "Recent Structural Changes in Employment in the United States," Working Paper, New York: Conservation of Human Resources, 1981.

10. SMSAs are defined in terms of aggregates of adjacent counties. Because SMSAs in New England are defined in terms of cities and townships, rather than counties, we use New England County Metropolitan areas (NECMAs) for metropolitan economies in that region. The definition of NECMAs follows criteria identical to those used to define SMSAs in the other states.

CHAPTER TWO

The Rise of Services and the Transformation of the U.S. Economy in the Postwar Era

In an important sense we rarely observe truly "national" economic trends. The overall economic system is geographically specialized and activities that rise to importance in some places may decline or remain unchanged in others. Moreover, the industrial or other categories by which we report statistics of economic behavior are aggregative and fail to disclose the often very different developments among component activities. In short, the national statistics from which we typically interpret the course of economic events are but aggregates, and the trends observed are but weighted averages of much more complex and differentiated developments that are occurring in cities and regions.

Yet examination of trends in the national data is an important first step prior to analyzing economic changes in urban economies. The data provide a general statement of major changes that are occurring within the system and raise questions regarding the extent to which individual urban economies or groups of places may have been affected. Our task, then, is to observe important changes as shown by the national data, to inquire into the principal forces at work and, finally, in the chapters to follow, to determine how these changes have impacted the economies of individual places.

A Look at the National Data

Perhaps the easiest way to capture the most important elements of recent change within the national economy is to examine three related structural shifts characteristic of the postwar era: (1) in manufacturing, (2) in services, and (3) in the importance of white collar and service worker employment.

MANUFACTURING

In purely employment terms, manufacturing stabilized and then moved into decline during the postwar years, with an absolute decrease from roughly 20 million jobs in 1970 to less than 19 million at the end of the decade. These developments resulted largely from the opening-up of the U.S. economy to foreign competition[1] and from investment in new equipment and plant, often embodying new technology and frequently leading to location of new plants and new industries in entirely new locales, both within the United States and abroad. The effect on the metropolitan system, as we shall see, has been profound.

It is important not to misread these data, however. If there has been a postwar decline in the role of manufacturing in providing jobs—the share of U.S. employment declined from 32 percent to 24 percent between 1947 and 1977 (Table 2.1)—there has not been a significant change in the importance of manufacturing in terms of the value of output. This major sector accounted for approximately the same share of GNP—roughly one-fourth—in 1977, as it did thirty years earlier.[2] Manufacturing continues to play a major role in the U.S. economy.

SERVICES

Services have grown in terms of both employment and output (Table 2.1). Today, firms and organizations engaged in services account for well over two-thirds of total employment and almost as large a share of national product.

But a lumping together of diverse service activities into a single service category is far from helpful if we are to understand what has been going on within the economy. Trends have differed sharply both among and within the various services when measured in terms of both employment and national product data.

In employment terms, the expansion of services has involved chiefly increases in the nonprofit services (education and health), government services and, not generally recognized, the producer services (finance, insurance, real estate, and other corporate services such as law, accounting, advertising). Closely associated with the growth of the latter, but not shown separately in Table 2.1, are producer service-like activities performed within the corporation (in-house).[3] Employment in such activities has grown extremely rapidly and is analyzed in some detail in Chapters 5 and 6.

In contrast, employment in the distributive services has declined as a share of the national total, as has the category "Mainly Consumer Services." In the case of distributive services, however, the decline is accounted for by gains in employee productivity. Measured in terms of share of gross national product, this group of services has gained, not declined, rising from 13 to well over 16 percent over the thirty-year period.

Last, the share of retailing in the U.S. economy measured either in employment or GNP terms has remained relatively stable throughout the entire period.

The case of consumer services is a curious one. In much of the popular discussion of the "rise of the service sector," attention has focused on the increasing importance of various consumer services (travel agents, recreational and resort activities, catering, beauty parlors, etc.).[4] Yet this group is the smallest among the six service categories and has shown the sharpest decline in share.

How are we to interpret this finding? Several points need to be made. The first is that the decline in share is due almost entirely to the very sharp and continuous decrease in employment of housekeepers during the entire postwar period, a decline which has offset significant gains in a number of other consumer services

Table 2.1   Percentage Distribution of Full-Time Equivalent Employment and Gross National Product (in 1972 dollars) by Industry, 1947, 1969 and 1977

	1947		1969		1977	
	Empl't	GNP	Empl't	GNP	Empl't	GNP
Agriculture, Extractive and Transformative	43.39	37.38	35.09	35.99	31.60	32.81
Agriculture	4.31	5.57	1.74	3.06	1.90	2.87
Extractive and Transformative[a]	39.08	31.81	33.35	32.93	29.70	29.94
Manufacturing	32.27	24.53	27.66	25.60	24.10	24.18
Services	56.61	62.68	64.91	64.03	68.40	66.09
Distributive Services	13.54	13.36	10.97	15.00	11.36	16.51
Retailing Services	12.57	11.06	13.00	9.78	14.18	9.89
Nonprofit Services	2.61	2.67	4.67	3.58	6.34	4.04
Complex of Corporate Activities[b]	6.06	15.50	10.03	18.26	11.96	20.12
Mainly Consumer Services	7.67	5.47	5.75	3.35	4.99	3.11
Government and Government Enterprises	14.16	14.62	20.48	14.07	19.57	12.43
	100.00	100.00	100.00	100.00	100.00	100.00

[a] Includes mining and construction (not shown).
[b] Because of data limitations, this grouping includes only the producer services (see Table 1.1). Employment and GNP originating from the Central Administrative Offices (CAO&A) are not disaggregated and are included in their respective categories: e.g., distributive services, retailing services, manufacturing and so forth.

Source: U.S. Department of Commerce, Bureau of Economic Analysis, The National Income and Product Accounts of the United States, 1929-74 Statistical Tables and Survey of Current Business, July 1978.

(e.g., hotels, car rentals). A second is that an important and growing category of consumer services sold in the marketplace, the services of restaurants and other eating places, is reported within the retailing classification.

Nevertheless, this finding that consumer services have played a relatively small role in the shift toward services must be accepted as essentially correct. Ours is not a society characterized by a pre-eminence of consumer services in the marketplace. The hallmark of modern capitalism is the ability to produce goods cheaply through capital intensive, high technology agriculture, mining and man-ufacturing. It is goods, not services, that constitute "best buys" in most pur-chase decisions. If there has been a trend toward buying more consumer services, it is in combination with goods, for goods and services are increasingly comple-mentary rather than substitutive (e.g., we require maintenance and repair serv-ices for our autos, TVs and appliances; motel and ski lift services in combination with the use of our automobile, skis, and ski attire on skiing weekends).[5]

What then can we conclude from Table 2.1? The answer would seem to be twofold: first, that the shift to services has been substantial and merits careful analysis in terms of its probable significance for industrial and employment change within metropolitan economies; second, that the rising importance of services is principally related to the role of producer services as intermediate in-puts in the roundabout and specialized processes of production and to the rising importance of government and nonprofit services in our increasingly complex and human capital intensive modern society.[6]

A final observation underlines the significance of the rise of services for urban development. Services by their very nature cannot be stockpiled, usually cannot be shipped, and typically must be produced to meet the special needs of the cus-tomer. Goods, in contrast, can for the most part be both stored and shipped, and can be designed and produced for market-wide, rather than individual demand. Thus, services production is likely to take place where accessibility to the cus-tomer is maximized—disproportionately in the metropolitan environment—while goods production can take place in plants often located away from metro-politan centers to take advantage of transportation, labor, energy, or other economies. This does not mean that the locational characteristics of all services production are alike: quite to the contrary, as we shall see in the subsequent anal-ysis. Nevertheless, there is a strong urban orientation, and the rise of services may be expected to significantly affect the urban system. Just how and where is the subject of much of the analysis to follow.

WHITE COLLAR AND SERVICE WORKER EMPLOYMENT

A corollary to the rising importance of services is the changing nature of work. Service sector jobs are classified predominantly within the white collar (profes-sionals, technicians, clerical personnel, sales persons) and service worker occu-pational categories.[7] Goods sector employment is heavily blue collar (opera-tives, craftsmen, laborers) though there are, of course, increasingly white collar and service worker jobs as well. Accordingly, a shift toward services involves not only changes in the industrial structure of employment, but in the occupa-tional structure as well.

The implication is that where cities lose goods production activities and gain services, they are likely to experience sharp changes in the demand for labor. Different groups of workers and different patterns of training are needed. Changes in the earnings distribution of workers are also likely to result. These important matters are not within the immediate scope of the present study, but are dealt with elsewhere.[8] Briefly, the implications for labor markets seem to be an increased need for professionals and technicians with special training and expertise in restricted segments of the job market, a reduced number of traditional blue-collar jobs and a greater demand for part-time and low skilled service workers to perform very routine tasks as clerks and service workers.

The Multifold Nature of the Postwar Transformation

In seeking a better understanding of the shifts observed above, it is helpful to think in terms of a multidimensional transformation involving at least the following: changes in *what* the economy produces, in *how* it produces, in *where* it produces, and in *how people work*. The last was touched on briefly above, but the first three require at least a brief discussion.

There have, in fact, been important changes in all dimensions and these changes have often been interactive (e.g., changes in what we produce affects both the way production is carried out and where it takes place). In terms of final products (*what is produced*), there has been a marked trend toward greater "production differentiation" in the marketplace as consumers, enjoying higher levels of income, are attracted to more stylized products and as producers seek new profits through targeting special groups of customers and through shortening product-model life spans. This has brought new challenges to firms and given rise to a changed emphasis on intermediate services both within and outside the firm. At the same time, new services, many closely related to product consumption (e.g., maintenance, finance, instruction) have come to the fore, while many of the more traditional consumer services seem to have played a secondary role.

It is the growth in government and nonprofit services that constitutes the most significant change in final demand within the arena of services. Curiously, these services may also be regarded as, at least in part, intermediate relative to the overall production process. Government-supported health and educational services are important ways by which society builds human capital (i.e., improves the stock of its workforce); and government clearly assists producers through providing information, security, and arrangements for litigation, by supplying much of the capital infrastructure (highways, sewer and various municipal services) for goods and service-oriented firms alike, and by intervening and assisting in domains as diversified as research and development or financing of foreign trade.

The transformation in the way we organize the productive process (*how we produce*) is directly associated with two closely related developments already noted: the changing technological and locational characteristics of production in manufacturing, and the rising importance of the producer services (both freestanding and in-house). Both of these developments have influenced importantly, but selectively, the economic role of metropolitan centers: the first by contributing to the decline of their manufacturing employment; the second by strengthening their role as hosts to corporate headquarters and producer services and as centers for major nonprofit and public sector institutions. Both are also closely associated with the rise of the modern industrial corporation discussed in the following section.

Changes in *where we produce* are thus closely related, involving changes in the siting of manufacturing plants and the increasing tendency for the complex of corporate activities to be located separately from production facilities, typically in larger metropolitan centers. Since study of these developments in where we produce is a central topic of the analysis of the present volume, it is useful to present here, for the Sunbelt and Snowbelt, a summary of changes that have occurred in the relative importance of different types of sectoral employment over the period extending from the late fifties to the mid-seventies. Table 2.2 presents for each of the major industry groupings and subgroupings defined in Table 1.1 and for Snowbelt and Sunbelt states,[9] respectively, shares of the U.S. employment in 1959, 1969, and 1976 as well as shares of job increases during the two periods, 1959–69 and 1969–76. Job increases (decreases) are computed on the basis of net job gains (losses) in each major industry subgrouping shown in the table (manufacturing, TCU, wholesale, CAO&A, FIRE, CS, retail, MCS, nonprofit and government) during each period.

The data show clearly that while the Sunbelt states have grown more rapidly in all industrial divisions, their pattern of growth has differed markedly from that in the Snowbelt. The 1969–76 period shows the most striking differences between the two regions, with the Sunbelt capturing 76 percent of all industry job increases and the Snowbelt a mere 24 percent. The Sunbelt accounts for all job increases in manufacturing (the Snowbelt experiencing a net job decline), 84 percent of job increases in distributive services, 85 percent in mainly consumer services and 68 percent in retailing. Growth in other sectors, however, though rapid, is relatively less important—57 percent of the job increases in government, 54 percent in the corporate complex and only 45 percent in the nonprofit services.

What we are observing in the case of the Sunbelt is a very rapidly growing area that is enjoying a preferred role in the location of new manufacturing activity at the same time that it is building its infrastructure of distributive, retail and consumer services. Its corporate complex, though important and increasing in size, is *relatively* less important in the development process. In addition, what cannot be discerned from the data but will be documented in Chapters 6 and 7 is that, qualitatively, these complexes of corporate activities are different: They have far fewer large corporate headquarters and less sophisticated producer services.

In contrast, the Snowbelt is an area caught up in a process of transformation under conditions of much slower growth. With well over half of total U.S. employment, but only 23 percent of all U.S. job increases in the second period, it shows net job losses in manufacturing and accounts for only 16 percent of all job gains in the distributive services. Yet there is considerable vitality in the corporate complex, in nonprofit services, and in government, with the Snowbelt's share of job increases in these sectors during the seventies well over twice as large as its share of total U.S. job increases.

In short, this simple tabulation provides considerable support to one of our major contentions: that the remarkably rapid growth of the Sunbelt during the past two decades has been accompanied by a fundamental transformation of the economic base of *both* the northern and southern regions. Just how this transformation has taken place is a matter for analysis in the chapters that follow.

Forces of Change

The changes revealed by the data in Tables 2.1 and 2.2 reflect in large measure responses to a number of forces at work within the economy of which at least four are of paramount importance: increasing size of the market, changes in transportation and technology, increased role of government and nonprofit institutions, and the rise of the large corporation.[10] The first three can be summarized, the fourth is discussed in somewhat greater detail.

INCREASING SIZE OF THE MARKET

By any measure, the U.S. market has grown enormously during the postwar years. During the three decades from 1950 to 1980, population rose from 152 million to 222 million, the civilian labor force from 62 million to 102 million, and disposable income from 362 to over 1,000 billion dollars (1972 prices).[11] There have also been major changes in the fundamental character of the market, involving a breakdown of regional barriers and the development of nationwide markets in which virtually all consumer goods are promoted and distributed on a coast-to-coast basis. Behind this development is a complex series of events, including three wars in which young men and their families were shuttled about from state to state, an increase in worker mobility (especially among corporate executives and professionals), increased opportunities for nationwide vacation travel, and the cumulative effect of both advertising and programming of television and other national media, which have acted to reduce the sense of local isolation.

Curiously, this has led not so much to the development of broad homogeneous markets as to the creation of sales potentials which permit the exploitation of a large number of specialized (but largely nationwide) markets in which products are specifically designed and advertised to cater to the interests of segments of the population: the homemaker, the teenager, the sports enthusiast, the hobbyist, the ethnic group, and so on.[12] The result has been a proliferation of products and services, an increased emphasis on product differentiation, branding, promotion—all combined with an intensified effort to introduce new products and to redesign old ones. These have given rise to new challenges for the seller which have, in turn, contributed to the increasing importance of the large corporation with its heavy focus on headquarters and other non-production activities as well as to the increasing importance of specialized producer service firms.

CHANGES IN TRANSPORTATION AND TECHNOLOGY

The importance of the changes which have occurred in transportation and technology can hardly be overstated. As regards transportation, what has been

Table 2.2 Distribution of Industry Employment and Job In-
          creases between Snowbelt and Sunbelt; Distribu-
          tion of U.S. Employment and Job Increases among
          Industries, 1959-1969 and 1969-1976

	All Indust	Mfg	Dist Serv	(TCU)	(Whl)
Snowbelt					
1959 Share of Emp.	61.3	68.5	59.9	(59.4)	(60.5)
1959-69 Share of JI	50.0	41.7	45.9	(46.3)	(45.5)
1969 Share of Emp.	58.3	63.7	57.1	(56.6)	(57.6)
1969-76 Share of JI	22.8	JD[a]	16.3	(10.6)	(26.4)
1976 Share of Emp.	54.0	58.5	53.0	(52.4)	(53.5)
Sunbelt					
1959 Share of Emp.	38.9	31.5	40.1	(40.5)	(39.4)
1959-69 Share of JI	50.0	58.3	54.1	(53.8)	(35.5)
1969 Share of Emp.	41.9	36.3	42.9	(43.4)	(42.4)
1969-76 Share of JI	75.9	100.0	83.7	(89.4)	(73.6)
1976 Share of Emp.	45.9	41.3	57.0	(47.4)	(46.4)
United States					
1959-69 JI in Industry as Share of all JI[b]	100.0	18.4	8.0	(4.2)	(3.8)
1969-76 JI in Industry as Share of all JI[c]	100.0	3.9	7.4	(2.5)	(4.9)

[a]Net job decrease (JD).
[b]1959-69 net job increase in the U.S. amounted to 18,563,539
jobs.
[c]1969-76 net job increase in the U.S. amounted to 10,949,362
jobs.

Column heads: Mfg: Manufacturing; Dist Serv: Distributive
               Services; TCU: Transportation, Communications
               and Utilities; Whl: Wholesaling; Corp Complex:
               Complex of Corporate Activities; CAO&A: Central
               Administrative Offices; FIRE: Finance,
               Insurance, Real Estate; CS: Corporate Services
               (producer services excluding FIRE); Ret:
               Retailing; NP: Nonprofit Services; Gov:
               Government.

Corp Complex	(CAO&A)	(FIRE)	(CS)	Ret	MCS	NP	Gov
66.3	(72.7)	(64.1)	(66.4)	58.6	54.3	65.3	55.7
57.2	(68.7)	(50.5)	(54.8)	50.4	43.9	60.1	49.1
62.5	(70.6)	(60.2)	(60.9)	56.4	51.7	62.7	53.5
46.3	(43.6)	(39.9)	(48.6)	32.4	14.8	55.3	53.5
58.6	(65.5)	(56.9)	(57.1)	52.3	47.2	60.4	50.6
33.7	(29.4)	(35.9)	(33.6)	41.4	45.7	34.7	45.7
42.8	(31.4)	(49.5)	(45.2)	49.5	56.2	38.8	51.0
37.5	(27.2)	(39.7)	(39.1)	43.6	48.3	37.3	47.5
53.7	(56.4)	(56.7)	(51.4)	67.6	85.2	44.7	57.3
41.4	(34.4)	(43.2)	(42.9)	47.6	52.9	39.5	49.4
19.1	(5.0)	(5.4)	(8.7)	14.9	4.1	9.7	22.2
25.7	(3.6)	(8.1)	(14.0)	19.1	3.3	13.8	26.7

Note: TCU and Whl, and CAO&A, FIRE and CS (shown in parentheses) are subsectors of larger industry groups, respectively Dist Serv and Corp Complex.

Source: County Business Patterns, 1959, 1969 and 1976; Employment and Earnings in State and Local Areas, 1959, 1969 and 1976.

witnessed is hardly less than an all pervasive change in the economics of location of many goods-producing activities. The putting in place of the interstate highway system alongside elaborate state road systems and the widespread shift from rail to trucks (except for specialized long distance cargo transport) has meant that metropolitan centrality no longer offers most producers favorable transport costs. At the same time, the movement toward saturation ownership of automobiles has altered the patterns of labor availability, making it possible to draw workers from extended areas when plants are located in towns and smaller metropolitan centers.

As regards technology, the postwar period has seen the advent of the computer and a wide array of developments in communication and other applications of electronics. We cannot attempt to assess the significance of applications of these new technologies except to note that we have clearly been thrust into an era in which the achievements of science are radically altering production methods, computational and communication capabilities, and the location of facilities. Quite clearly, the development of the semi-automated and, more recently, fully automated assembly line has radically altered the range of options available for the siting of plants. In addition, the capability of management to control large operations and to carry through detailed planning of complex projects has been pushed forward by magnitudes that are not yet fully comprehended.

INCREASED ROLE OF GOVERNMENT AND
NONPROFIT INSTITUTIONS

As was shown earlier, government and nonprofit activities have contributed major shares of employment expansion during the postwar decades taken as a whole. This rapid expansion, which has slowed somewhat in recent years, has occurred for a number of reasons.

At the federal level, government has been heavily committed to enlarging and modernizing the defense establishment (including extensive R&D activity), to increasing the scope of regulatory and administrative action, and to expanding the scope and size of its public services as well as grant-in-aid programs to states and localities (thereby encouraging them to appropriate additional funds, many of which were directed to increasing public sector and nonprofit services). At the state and local level, government has been responsive to a widespread demand for service expansion, especially for public education and social welfare, and for attention to the new requirements incident to suburbanization and other population shifts.

The growth of nonprofit institutions has also been of major significance, especially in the areas of health and education. In large measure, this process has occurred by means of the expansion of relatively new institutional arrangements involving both the public and private sectors (e.g., Blue Cross–Blue Shield and various major medical insurance plans, partial federal funding of hospital construction, or federal funding of higher education).

In general, the expansion of the government and nonprofit sector has reflected complex changes in the way the American economy has come to operate. The desire for a more equitable redistribution of the fruits of postwar growth as well as major changes in consumer demand have been important factors at play, but so has been the need for a more developed regulatory framework and a better trained and healthier labor force in an ever more technologically and institutionally complex society.[13] Hence, while the concern for the inflationary nature of some of these demands has led to efforts to reduce the role of government at all levels, especially at the federal level, it seems reasonable to assume that the government and nonprofit sectors will continue to play major roles in the economy.

A major question that must be raised as one explores the development of these sectors is the extent to which their growth has tended to favor certain places over others. Casual observation alone suggests that military installations or state bureaucracies have to various degrees prospered outside traditional population centers. It is not clear, however, to what extent the location of other public sector or nonprofit institutions—such as R&D or educational facilities—has followed a similar pattern or has tended to favor those cities where other high-level services have best developed.

THE RISE OF THE LARGE CORPORATION

At center stage of the transformation of the American economy stands the modern national or international corporation. While the existence of the large corporation as a major business institution dates back to the rise of the railroads, the extent of its control over a variety of markets and product lines, the scale of its operations, and the complexity of its organization have all increased dramatically since the 1930s.

Since many business economists and historians have observed the impact of the large corporation on today's economy in terms of either employment, sales, asset concentration, or profits, such analysis need not be repeated.[14] What is important to observe, however, is that the large corporation's capacity to break down regional barriers through nationwide promotion and distribution of products and services and its ability to marshall the ever more extensive financial and human resources needed to engage in aggressive product development, differentiation, and promotion required by nationwide markets have been made possible by changes in the standard "functional" organizational structure of the early decades of this century. These changes have resulted in the emergence of the more elaborate "regional-divisional" structure, which today characterizes the modern corporation.[15]

To a large extent, this shift in structure reflects attempts by large corporations to move many of the service functions performed traditionally at the *plant level* to the *level of the firm* as a way of achieving scale economies. This shift is also a reflection of increased managerial sophistication, of the possibilities opened by newer communication technologies (i.e., computerized data processing), of higher levels of rationalization in production methods, and of the increased importance of linkages between many service and non-service activities. The early "functional" structure (best suited to handle the managerial needs of the old-styled, single-product, single-market firm) typically called for the concentration of a relatively small corporate staff in a single location, the national headquar-

ters. But the rise of the ''regional-divisional'' structure has brought about a multiplication of locationally distinct divisional head offices, regional sales headquarters and single function, service-like establishments (research and
development establishments, account processing offices, etc.), in addition to the
corporation's major headquarters.

While there is no single model of the ''regional-divisional corporation,'' the
essential elements of the structure can be described simply as follows. At the top
of the organization stands the firm's headquarters. *Corporate (or national) headquarters* of the firm tend to be located in key cities of the urban system, though as
we show in Chapter 5, there are variations, depending on the business history of
the firm, the type of business that it carries out, and other factors as well. National headquarters carry out the strategic planning functions of the firm, decide
on major investment and merger policies, raise new financial resources (equity,
bonds, long-term borrowing from banks or private investors), oversee the auditing of the firm, often play a major role in advertising (although responsiblities
for such functions may, at times, be shared with lower level administrative
units), handle import/export activity of the firm, and decide on foreign investment. In the latter case, the firm may also choose to establish one or several
separate offices to oversee foreign activities, if it is far along the road of internationalization and derives a large portion of its earnings from foreign markets.
Such offices, however, report directly to headquarters, and their locations tend to
be restricted to a few cities (see Chapter 7).

Divisional head offices oversee more routine, day-to-day service functions related to the development and production of one or a set of related product lines
and are typically organized as profit centers of the firm. Divisions are usually
intra-firm organizational arrangements although, at times, they may be subsidiary corporations (usually if the division is a former independent business merged
into the firm and kept as a separate profit center). Tasks carried out by the divisional head offices include day-to-day accounting, personnel functions, employee relations, coordination of production schedules between the various
plants of the division, relations with supplier firms and guidance of the R&D
effort, which, in the large corporations, is usually conducted in establishments
separate from both the divisional head offices or the division's production facilities. In general, divisional head offices tend to be more dispersed throughout the
system of cities and are located in various urban centers in response to considerations such as proximity to key plants of the division or to supplier firms.

Divisional head offices are usually in close contact with the *regional sales
headquarters*, whose primary function is to oversee operations in the many
dealerships and sales and repair service offices located in the cities of major regional markets or districts. Depending on the degree of integration of the firm,
regional headquarters coordinate the sales of a few or many product lines from
the different divisions of the firm, partly as a way of continually exploring relationships of complementarity or redundancy among the different product lines of
the various divisions and of investigating new business opportunities. Where the
product delivered to final consumers involves substantial financing (e.g., automobile), they may also serve as a relay between the dealerships and the financial
arm of the corporation (e.g., acceptance corporation). In general, regional head-

quarters tend to be located in key market centers, while dealerships are scattered generously across the land.

Other service establishments of the corporation, such as foreign trade facilities, financial facilities or R&D establishments may locate in various types of urban centers, depending on the nature of the functions performed. These are investigated in some detail in Chapters 5 and 9.

In short, the importance of the rise of the modern corporation for urban development processes becomes readily apparent. Not only have service establishments of the large corporation tended to grow mostly in large metropolitan areas, but they have also had a major impact on the growth of attending producer service firms in these very same places. However, with a few important exceptions reviewed in the next chapter, the fundamental contribution of the rise of the central offices of the large corporation to the service transformation of metropolitan places has been generally overlooked.

Conclusion

The argument put forth in this chapter has been essentially twofold. First, we have argued that much of the importance of the rise of services in the U.S. economy has been in the growth of activities which are, in large part, intermediate inputs to other economic processes. Second, that the transformation of the economic geography of the U.S. economy associated with the growth of such services has been profound, and has been felt in both older and newer regions of the country.

It is our thesis that the rise of the large corporation, with its increasing emphasis on service-like activities carried out within its central offices, the opening of nationwide consumer markets, the rising importance of nonprofit and public sector services as well as postwar changes in transportation and technology have all been major factors in bringing about such a fundamental transformation. The significance of these and other developments discussed in this chapter is treated at length in the remainder of this book. In the next chapter, we set forth additional guidelines for the empirical investigation that follows by reviewing key theoretical and empirical contributions from the urban literature.

Notes

1. Between 1970 and 1980, the share of imports in the U.S. GNP grew from roughly 4 to 12 percent.

2. There have been major changes in the composition of this output, however, with service-like activities accounting for an increasing share of manufacturing output (see below). See also Thomas M. Stanback, Jr., et al., *Services/The New Economy*, op. cit., 1981.

3. Because of data limitations, employment and output of central administrative offices are not dissaggregated in Table 2-1 and are included in their respective category: distributive services, redistributing services, manufacturing and so forth.

4. For example, Victor Fuchs, *The Services Economy*, New York: National Bureau of Economic Research and Columbia University Press, 1968 and "The Services Industries and U.S. Economic Growth Since World War II," Working Paper 221, National Bureau of Economic Research, November 1977.

5. The complementary of goods and services is explored in some detail in Thomas M. Stanback, Jr., *Understanding the Service Economy*, Baltimore: The Johns Hopkins University Press, 1979.

6. The reader should note that the value of services of domestic dwellings (both explicit and imputed rent) is included in the real estate classification in producer services. This does not affect significantly the shift in GNP originating from producer services during the period 1947–77, however.

7. Here the term "service worker" is used to denote a specific occupational category rather than used in a generic sense. The occupation "service worker" is defined to include a wide range of jobs such as cooks, housekeepers, cleaning workers or health service workers.

8. Thomas M. Stanback, Jr. and Thierry J. Noyelle, *Cities in Transition*, op. cit. We return to some of these labor market issues in Chapter 10.

9. The Snowbelt includes states in the New England, Mideast, Great Lakes and Plains regions; the Sunbelt, those in the Southeast, Southwest, Rocky Mountains and Far West regions. Regional definitions are those of the U.S. Department of Commerce, Bureau of Economic Analysis.

10. These developments have been analyzed at greater length in Thomas M. Stanback, Jr., et al., *Services/The New Economy*, op. cit., 1981.

11. *Statistical Abstract of the United States*, 1980.

12. Ibid.

13. See, for instance, Moses Abramovitz, "Manpower, Capital and Technology," in *Human Resources and Economic Welfare. Essays in Honor of Eli Ginzberg*, edited by Ivar Berg, Columbia University Press, New York, 1972.

14. See, for example, Phillip I. Blumberg, *The Megacorporation in American Society*, Englewood Cliffs, N.J.: Prentice-Hall, 1975.

15. Alfred Chandler, *The Visible Hand: The Managerial Revolution in American Business*, Cambridge, Mass.: Harvard University Press, 1977.

CHAPTER THREE

The Development of the U.S. System of Cities: A Review of Key Theoretical and Empirical Contributions

This study is empirically rather than theoretically oriented. Yet theory must guide inquiry by suggesting key questions for investigation. We must, therefore, examine briefly some of the more important ideas regarding city growth and development that theorists have developed in order to set forth some key propositions to assist in the subsequent analysis. We need a way of looking at cities which will provide some understanding, first, of the principal determinants of urban structure (why and to what extent do cities differ in their industrial structure?; how and to what extent do they change their economic roles as they become larger?); and second, of the principal thrust of developmental change (what factors are likely to bring about significant alterations in the economies of individual cities, and along what lines may developmental responses be expected to occur?). Moreover, since our study builds in part upon related empirical investigations conducted by others in recent years, we must assess the importance of these contributions.

In the present chapter, our brief foray into urban theory falls into three parts: static theory of location (location theory and central place theory), dynamic theory of the individual city's growth and development, and theory treating the growth and development of the system of cities. Following this we examine some recent work that treats the role of corporate complexes (the closely linked system of large corporate headquarters and the various service firms upon which they rely) in city system development. In each of these four sections, we seek to call attention to those ideas that will be most useful for the subsequent analysis.

Static Theory of Location

The two principal branches of static theory that are useful here differ sharply in orientation and analytical approach.[1] The first, location theory, treats the problem of optimum siting of the producing firm given certain constraints such as transportation, materials and labor costs. The second, central place theory, treats the arrangement of firms within market areas and the resulting tendency for a systematic arrangement of towns or cities (central places) of various sizes to occur in space.

LOCATION THEORY

A major concern of location theory is to demonstrate how a firm may position itself in space in order to minimize transportation costs under varying conditions relating to location of raw materials and markets and to freight rates for transport of inputs and finished products. Although much of the analysis assumes that processing costs do not vary with location, such assumptions are readily modified to show how transport costs may be offset by locating in such a way as to affect reductions in processing costs.

Of special importance in treating processing costs is the concept of agglomeration economies. Such economies occur where the bringing together of firms (agglomeration) in a given industry within a restricted area results in savings for each firm (locationalization economies) for any of a number of reasons, including increased availability of trained labor, improved structure of transport rates, the attraction of supplying firms who operate under more favorable cost conditions than would be possible if their customer firms within the industry were widely scattered.[2]

Similar economies may also occur where the savings due to the agglomeration process are due to the presence of a larger number of firms within a metropolitan area even though they may be in different industries (urbanization economies). Here we are addressing the significance of *urban agglomeration* rather than *industry agglomeration*. A larger number of firms of various types located in relative proximity may act to reduce freight rates of common carriers; attract a variety of business service firms which provide business, finance, and other services with greater expertise and/or at rates more favorable than would be possible if firms being supplied had to perform such services within their own organizations; provide a large labor supply possessing a variety of skills. Thus, larger urban economies may offer favorable sites for the location of activities even though certain costs, typically rents and wage rates, may be somewhat higher than in smaller places and non-urban locales.

Central Place Theory

Central place theory treats the spatial arrangement of activities (firms, government, nonprofit organizations) which serve directly to the consuming public in surrounding market areas, or hinterlands.[3] Essentially, the theory relates to retail activities and, by extension, to wholesaling, rather than to manufactures, except, perhaps, a limited number of small manufacturing firms that are not resource bound and that deal directly with the hinterland consumer market. Such central place type goods and services may be thought of as being hierarchically ordered in terms of market size necessary to provide the demand needed to enable each activity to attain necessary economies of scale and operate with an acceptable return. The spatial limit, or "range," of the market, is the maximum distance the consumer will travel before cost of transport "chokes off" demand to the point that the activity cannot attain necessary scale.

The logic of this highly refined theory is that those activities that require small markets ("low level" activities) will locate in numerous small central places; those that require larger markets will locate in a smaller number of larger central places at greater distances from one another. An essential observation is that each higher order of central place will include not only those activities that require a hinterland market of its given size, but all lower order activities as well. Thus, central places will be progressively larger as we move from those that offer only the lowest order goods and services upward through the hierarchy to those that provide those goods and services characterized by the largest market threshold size, since each place will provide goods and services ranging from the lowest to the highest which its hierarchical position permits.

Moreover, the hierarchical ordering of places is a "nested" one. Medium level centers serve only lower order centers within their areas, and higher level centers only medium and lower. Lower order centers never serve higher order centers, nor do centers of any given level serve each other.

Although such a theory is limited in scope and highly artificial in certain of its assumptions, it makes a major contribution to our understanding of urban structure. It suggests that the performance of central place functions may be a major economic mission of cities and towns and that the logic of market threshold requirements will explain, at least in part, the differences in range of functions between large and small places as well as provide at least a partial explanation of the hierarchical structuring of the system of cities. The relatively few large places within the system are likely to house a wide array of central place activities ranging from those which require large hinterlands to those which are only local in scope. The many small places that dot the landscape will typically reach out to only limited market areas—at least in those activities in which they deal directly with the consuming public.

Urban Growth and Development Theory

Once the urban theorist turns to explaining growth and development, he must move beyond an analysis of simple adjustments that bring about a profit-maximizing equilibrium toward an explanation of how a series of complex changes can be set in motion, a process of "cumulative causation," that carries the city to ever new and altered levels of economic activity.

Fundamental to such an analysis is the concept that the city is an economy which exports to the outer world and imports in turn, and that this economy may be visualized as made up of two sectors: an export or basic sector composed of firms that are principally involved in producing exportable goods and services, and a non-basic supporting sector, composed of firms and organizations that provide for the needs of the populace and local firms. An important aspect of this basic/non-basic relationship is that increases in basic activities are presumed to bring about corresponding increases in non-basic activities with the result that there is a "multiplier" effect.

There is a considerable body of literature, much of it empirical, which treats so-called export base theory.[4] Traditionally, export base theorists have held that enlargement of the export sector (basic sector) results in a multifold expansion of the city's economy, since it results in a corresponding increase in the supporting (non-basic) sector. This points to the export base as the source of expansion, although some have argued that over time it is the non-basic sector which attracts new export industries and is the critical sector.[5]

The processes by which growth feeds on itself involve various changes that occur within the city's economy and that pave the way for further growth by creating conditions that cause new firms to set up shop and old firms to expand. Of special importance are the income effects of entry of new export firms and the possibility of import substitution as growth occurs. Income effects come about when the respending of export-generated income acts to generate new business in the local economy and leads to new jobs and income receipts and the possibility of still further rounds of income generation (i.e., the income multiplier). Import substitution possibilities increase with growth, due to the expansion of market potential, enabling servicing and supplying firms to attain size thresholds and set up shop. Import substitution may relate either to goods and services purchased from outside sources as inputs for export firms or to goods and services purchased by residents. Further, growth from whatever source tends to create agglomeration economies of the localization or urbanization variety and strengthens the conditions which set in motion still further growth by attracting new firms and encouraging expansion.

The various linkages and responses by which growth and development may be propelled are legion. Increasing size makes for larger and more varied labor resources, a greater range and more intense specialization of business and financial services, more diversified health and education services, and so on—all of which may create still further attractions for firms to enter.

But there are negative aspects as well. Most towns do not develop into cities. Some places decline and many cease to grow. Wilbur Thompson, whose model of urban growth visualizes a five-stage developmental process, sees a cessation of growth as an inability to move from one stage to another.[6] There is a failure of "momentum" due principally to the fact that one city "will rise from a group of rivals to become the mother city of the group. Whichever city gets the jump on the others and achieves early dominance, usually finds that success breeds success, as external economies of service industry agglomeration pave the way for progressive cumulative coups."[7]

Thompson is also well known for his suggestion of a number of years ago that large cities do not decline because an "urban size ratchet" prevents contraction.[8] He sets forth a number of possible factors that might act to protect large metropolitan places from decline including the likelihood that large cities are capable of generating a stream of inventions or innovations which bring fresh vitality to the economy, and that cities that have grown large tend to have developed a diversified industrial economy and a well-developed non-basic sector with the result that the failures of some industries are compensated by the successes of others and the environment favors the initiation of new enterprises.

Yet many large cities have, in fact, declined in recent years, and Thompson has had to modify his analysis to account for this problem. His argument is that U.S. urbanization was never a highly rational process with the result that "Our great industrial transformation has left us with a large number of overgrown cities—a ramification we have not faced up to."[9] The implication is that many among the largest cities must now undergo a painful process of shrinkage.

The second reason for decline relates to the spinoff process. Traditionally, the filtering down of economic functions through the nation's system of cities did not hurt the largest cities since these "continued innovating and more or less replaced what they lost. . . . There is some question today about whether the older and larger manufacturing centers are replacing industry as fast as they are losing it."[10] Thompson's hypothesis is that "today, economies of scale in production are less, relative to the scale of the market."[11]

At this point in his analysis, Thompson raises an important observation, to which we must return later on in this study:

> Ten years ago, we all talked optimistically about the new age of services. What happened to this new force that was supposed to come in and rebuild the cores of our aging metropolises?...The service age just did not come to the fore with the passing of manufacturing to rescue the big cities the way it was supposed to—not yet anyway![12]

Theory Treating the Growth and Development of the System of Cities

A major weakness of the urban growth and development theory sketched above is that much of it tends to be ahistorical, and to fail to relate the mechanisms by which growth and development take place to the changing industrial, institutional, and geographical requirements that have characterized the evolution of American capitalism. Clearly, the forces working to build cities 100 years ago are not the same as those which are most important today. Moreover, cities that grew to maturity in another era are likely to possess physical, institutional, and human resource characteristics which differ from cities that have come to maturity in the postwar era.

PRED'S THREE-STAGE HISTORICAL THEORY

Among urban scholars, Allan Pred has presented one of the most careful analyses of economic development of the system of cities in advanced economies within an historical context.[13] He treats three periods of city system development in the United States—the pre-telegraphic period (1790–1860), the early industrial period (1860–1914), the period of multilocation organization dominance (since World War II)—and proposes models of growth and change to underline the principal processes and driving forces at work during each era. One of Pred's major theses is that development is a cumulative process, one which enables certain cities to establish an advantageous position within the system at a relatively early date and thereafter to undergo growth and change in such a way as to maintain this advantageous position. Here Pred draws heavily on the dynamic theory of others, such as Thompson. A second concept is that the economies of cities are interdependent and that growth of one feeds growth of still others (increasingly so with the passage of time). Both of these tendencies—for individual city growth to feed on itself and for cities to be linked economically—has meant that for larger urban centers there has been a strong tendency toward relative stability of size rank within the U.S. economy as a whole and especially within regions. This stability of size and rank over extended time periods does not necessarily apply for smaller places, however. The fortunes of such places tend to be altered within a dynamic system by both economic opportunities and problems arising as a result of changing technology, markets, transportation, etc.

While Pred sees developmental processes as having been continuous and cumulative for the major metropolitan complexes, the principal driving forces at work during the three periods have been very different. During the pre-telegraphic period, it was their rising role as wholesale trading centers that fostered growth among the leading places; during the stage of early industrialization, the increasing growth and concentration of manufacturing in larger centers; and during the most recent period, it is the rise to preeminence of the very large corporation with its multiple administration, development and production establishments which has provided the principal thrust in the developmental process.

Pred's analysis and essential "modeling" of city system growth in each era can be sketched as follows:

The pre-telegraphic period.[14]   During this period, as in the later ones, local growth mechanisms, the development of spatial biases in innovation, and the circulation and availability of information are important in explaining how growth and development of individual urban centers takes place. But the local growth mechanisms are simpler and differently powered than those which are to obtain in later eras. During the pre-telegraphic period the focus is on increases in wholesaling-trading activities, which result in increases in dependent manufacturing activities, local respending of income on goods and services, and attendant new construction.

Pred observes that it is essential in examining growth during this period to understand

> that most long distance trade . . . was in some sense interurban. That is, at some point in their journey from ultimate origin to ultimate destination, agriculture products, raw materials and manufactured goods usually moved from one port city to another, or from an urban collection centre to an urban distribution centre.[15]

Thus, growth within the system is dependent on both the local growth processes and the trading relationships among centers.

Each increment in commodity and human spatial interaction contributes to what Pred calls "spatial biases in the circulation of specialized information"—information relating to market changes, prices, and opportunities originating in one center will have a greater probability of being acquired early in another center than elsewhere, since smaller places will have fewer and less frequent contacts. Similarly, any commercial, financial, or industrial innovation which is introduced in one major center will have a greater probability of being adopted in another larger center than in a smaller place. The essential point is that in this pre-telegraphic era, information is transported much more reliably among larger cities because of frequency and nature of both commercial and human intercourse, than between larger and smaller or among smaller places, thereby creating strong spatial biases of availability of essential information and innovative practices.

The period of urban industrial growth.[16]   The years 1860–1914 were dominated by the industrialization of the U.S. economy. Manufacturing rose from 32 percent of commodity output in 1860 to 53 percent in 1900. Moreover, with rising industrialization, production became increasingly concentrated in large cities: in 1860, the ten largest cities accounted for 24.1 percent of value added in manufacturing; in 1890, for 38.1 percent.[17] Accordingly, Pred finds industrialization to be the major force in the development of at least the larger U.S. metropolises during this era. He sees the perpetuation of major city growth, along with the tendency for manufacturing to concentrate in larger places, as the result of a number of dynamically interwoven factors:

1. There is a more complex and interactive growth process at work in which growth stimuli pass back and forth among cities. The spatially extensive input-output linkages of manufacturing enterprises are much more elaborate than those which obtained for the mercantile firm in the earlier period. The multiplication of well-articulated functions in the industrialization era result in multiplier effects of several sorts. Some involve relatively straightforward effects from employee expenditure and new construction of the sort described in the model of the earlier era. Others involve backward or forward linkages with the entire national system. Backward linkages involve increasing demand for materials and supplies, which set off growth stimuli in other manufacturing centers. Forward linkages involve improved supply availability under price and delivery conditions favorable to expanded activity elsewhere. The combined effect not only tends to make for increased industrialization overall but also for the attainment of new local and regional market size thresholds, permitting additional activies to be viable. Once production facilities are constructed in accordance with these new thresholds, still further multipliers come into effect and additional thresholds are attained. In addition, there is a secondary multiplier process derived from the addition of non-industrial jobs (e.g., construction, transportation, public utilities, consumer goods and services).

2. In treating the industrialization process, Pred emphasizes once again the role of increased specialization in information and innovation. The complex expansion processes described above generate specialized information and the origination of more efficient managerial and financial practices. Technological improvements and inventions are stimulated. "Once *some* inventions or ideas are implemented . . . the web of interpersonal communications is again extended and densened, the chances for invention and

innovation are further enhanced, and the circular process continues . . . until diverted or hindered."[18]

3. The period of industrialization corresponds to the period in which the U.S. railroad network was, to a large extent, put in place with freight rates declining by 70–75 percent or more.[19] The process was one which contributed in a major way to both the overall industrialization process and the concentration of manufacturing in major centers. From the outset, the larger centers were given favorable rates because of higher volumes of traffic. This in turn attracted additional factories and the enlargement of existing facilities, thereby justifying still further reductions and the provision of more complete facilities and input-output linkages. In addition, the continuous improvement of rate structures made it feasible for firms to reach out to wider and wider markets, thereby justifying larger scale production to the advantage of major producers in large centers and to the disadvantage of smaller producers elsewhere.

4. In addition to the above, Pred notes the role of increased merger activity, especially during the period 1897–1905. These mergers brought about larger firms and the adoption of new strategies, including the arbitrary closing down of capacity in a number of smaller cities.

5. Pred also points out that the expanded industrial activity often gave rise to labor requirements that could only be readily met by the population system of a large city. This was particularly true where very large establishments require substantial numbers of skilled laborers.

6. Finally, capital availability and costs worked to the advantage of high-ranking cities. Bankers in the most rapidly growing large urban industrial cities offered lower interest rates and greater opportunities for obtaining substantial financing. To this, Pred adds: "Moreover, once manufacturing became spatially concentrated in large cities, it was not likely to shift, because management was much more prone to augment existing facilities than to relocate and repeat large initial capital expenditures."[20]

The period of multilocational corporate growth.[21]   Pred sees the postwar era as one in which the large industrial corporations have played a major role in influencing the interurban transmission of growth. General evidence of the importance of these large organizations is found in the fact that between 1960 and 1973 the number of domestic and foreign jobs controlled by the 500 largest U.S. industrial organizations grew by 68 percent, while total jobs grew 36 percent.[22] The record indicates that a clear majority of private sector employment is directly associated with domestically headquartered "multilocational" corporations.

The principal argument is that city system interdependence is increased by growth of the large corporation as a result of intraorganizational linkages. Large corporations typically have a larger share of resources given over to administrative and office activities. Expansion within a multilocational organization at a subordinate unit or the opening of a new subordinate unit is likely to bring about expansion of the headquarters unit (or other high or intermediate-level administrative unit). Merger activity in particular is likely to result in increased intercity interdependencies, involving the locating of headquarters increasingly in large metropolitan complexes. Pred maintains, however, that the transmission of intraorganizational growth between cities is not restricted to growth of administrative units, but may also involve the flow of goods, services and specialized information among two or more units of a large organization without necessarily affecting the organization's headquarters.

Interdependence may also involve interorganizational relationships. A number of factors have contributed: transportation advances have lowered the relative costs of shipping goods; jet plane and telecommunications have facilitated the movement of specialized information and encouraged the growth of specialized financial, insurance and other services; and new industrial technology has altered production processes, changed location requirements and created more elaborate input-output relationships. In addition, the pressure to adjust complex production organizations quickly has brought about the need for increased coordination within the firm and frequently necessitated the utilization of specialized outside services.

Pred observes that though large complex corporations are hierarchical in organization, such organization is not symmetrically arranged in the manner suggested by central place theory. Headquarters may be located in any of a number of places with other administrative units in still other places, many but not all being large. The result is a complex linking of cities.

Pred's general argument is summed up as follows:[23]

. If multilocational organizations have been acquiring control over an ever greater share of the economy in economically advanced countries, if the headquarters of such organizations are predominantly found in large metropolitan complexes (rather than only in the highest-ranking metropolis), and if intraorganizationally and interorganizationally based city-system interdependencies are as complex as just described, then it follows that *regardless of where major new investment or activity expansion occurs, it is very likely to result in some intraorganizationally* (and interorganizationally) *based multiplier effects at a nearby or distant large metropolitan complex.*

In presenting this model of multilocational organizations and city-system growth, Pred calls attention to three points. (1) Insofar as multilocational business and government dominate advanced economies, their explicit and implicit locational decisions are directly or indirectly responsible for the creation and perpetuation of most employment opportunities. (2) Explicit and implicit locational decisions are typically reached after a limited search and are influenced by a desire to reduce uncertainty. Accordingly such decisions tend to favor already established centers. (3) There is some evidence that location decisions are greatly influenced by existing spatial biases in the availability of information (i.e., existing organizational contact patterns) and that these decisions, in turn, contribute to subsequent spatial biases.

It is important to recognize that the model for city growth during the postwar years provides for a number of growth processes of the sort presented for the industrialization era. Pred notes that "although technology, economic institutions and the forms of business operation have undergone enormous changes . . . the process of city system growth and development . . . remains dominated by the constantly repeated interplay between existing local and interurban linkages, spatial biases in the interurban circulation of specialized information, and new and expanded local and interurban economic linkages."[24]

But there are special features as well. In calling attention to these special features of the new model, Pred notes Edgar Dunn's observation (discussed below) that each new and enlarged interurban goods and service linkage requires certain matching flows of routine or non-routine specialized information. He cites two types of feedback loops which act to perpetuate employment and population growth at metropolitan complexes of high national or regional rank. The first is largely managerial, the second relates to planning and innovation. Each has strong locational implications. Pred holds that each of these feedback loops makes for spatial biases favoring established centers since such centers are favored both in terms of information availability and the likelihood of adoption of innovations.

To conclude, one of the strongest themes that emerges from Pred's conceptual model of the most advanced period of urbanization is the notion of assymetry of interurban linkages. Contrary to the tenets (largely based on a central-place model of the urban system) of growth pole theory, Pred repeatedly argues that a growth impulse in a major metropolitan center does not necessarily result in a regularly (evenly) distributed multiplier effect in centers of lower-rank order, because of the very asymmetry which characterizes intraorganizational linkages of large multilocational organizations and because of decision making biases which tend to favor established places. Empirically, Pred illustrates this asymmetry through his probes of "job control" by major multilocational organizations,[25] which, while crude, are important in suggesting ways in which decision-making in private sector firms is diffused throughout the system of cities. In the final chapter of this book we examine some of the issues raised by Pred in the light of our own findings.

DUNN'S NETWORK THEORY

A number of Pred's ideas underscore the work of Edgar Dunn.[26] Dunn visualizes all economic activities in terms of network relationships, in which two or more transformation processes are linked by one or more transfer processes.[27] Transformation processes (or activities) are broadly conceived as those which change the form or function of some physical, biological, or informational entity and range widely from physical processes (e.g., plowing, cutting, pressing, heating) to information processing and decision-making. Transfer processes relate to activities which move goods, services, or information from producer to user, but include also those activities which relate to "the operation of accumulators of storage buffers (inventories) necessary to the generation of matched and controlled flows over both space and time." Thus, transfer functions include retail and wholesale as well as transportation and communication activities.

Tree networks and circuit networks.[28]   Networks are of two types: tree networks and circuit networks. Tree network systems are functional systems which have the general characteristic that they have a common transformation objective, typically, the production of one or a group of products. They are readily exemplified by any typical multiprocess industrial establishment in which processes are linked. A tree network system may, of course, be much larger in scale as in the case of integrated primary metals, or petrochemical complexes, and it is not unusual for such networks to be under a single corporate management. Tree networks are linked by transfers that are high volume in character and make heavy use of special purpose transfer processes and channels. Nevertheless, common purpose transfer activities such as railways and trucking concerns may also serve activities within a variety of large industrial complexes that rely heavily on single purpose transfer systems. For example, firms may use their own transfer facilities for individual operations within plants and between plants at different stages of production but find it economical to make use of common carriers as well.

Circuit networks are found where a number of different transformation processes make use of common transfer facilities. In such networks, transfers associated with any given transformation activity are likely to be intermittent and low volume in character. The beauty salon and the auto repair shop are part of the same network system because they share the same transfer channels to reach the same consumer.

Networks of both types intersect in innumerable ways. The national economy may be regarded as constituted of myriad interlocking tree and circuit network systems. Urban economies are agglomerations of economic activity which result when network linkages are sufficiently numerous and of such a nature as to bring about relatively high employment and population densities in restricted areas. Although city or metropolitan regional level network systems are linked in numerous ways to the outside economy and are not neatly bounded, there is typically a significant level of system closure which results in part from the dual role played by households as consumers and as factor inputs (see below).

Networks relating to central place functions and to goods production.[29] By thinking of all economic activities in terms of their network relationships, Dunn is able to distinguish readily between those systems treated in central place theory and those treated in industrial location theory and to shed light on the way each type is involved in the structuring of the system of cities.

Regarding central place activities, Dunn writes:[30]

> Consider the usual trade, service or small scale manufacturing activities oriented directly to final demand. Some of these activities (e.g., retail food, personal services, automobile repairs, etc.) are fairly ubiquitous on a fine geographical grain— they share local transfer networks. Other activities are more specialized (e.g., retail specialty, eating and drinking, professional services, hotels, custom cabinetwork, architects, soft drink manufacturing, newspaper publishing, etc.). They tend to be ubiquitous on a coarser geographical grain because either their transfer relationship with each household is more intermittent or the transfer level is lower relative to the technological scale at which the nodal service can be efficiently maintained. In either case, they serve a larger set of hinterland population and share a larger scale transfer network. At a still larger scale may come such things as heart surgery, tall

girl shops, specialized services, legitimate theater, etc. Some of these network circuits serve as intermediate links once removed, that is, they serve the activity complexes serving final demand. Thus, transportation, wholesaling and communication
activities generally operate on a larger scale, and within each activity (e.g., as between trucking and railways) there may exist further differences in natural scale.
The scale is larger for these network circuits because each one may interact with
several lower order network circuits.

The major strengths and limitations of central place theory are readily observed
when we reflect on the kinds of network relationships that are treated and the
kinds that are not. The theory provides an explanation of the spatial
organizational tendencies of a very large group of activities which are essentially
people-serving—and accordingly suggests criteria for analyzing such activities
within the national system of urban places. Moreover, the observation that there
are economies of scale thresholds that place lower limits on the size of the city in
which an activity may locate if it is to serve a market of sufficient size is fundamental to understanding locational tendencies of a wide variety of business and
government services as well as those flowing directly to final consumers.

On the other hand, the theory does not treat locational tendencies based on a
variety of factors which figure importantly in industrial location theory, e.g., the
importance for certain weight-losing processes of locating close to resources, the
importance of entrepot locations as centers for certain types of processing and
distribution activities, the agglomerative tendencies among certain multistaged
manufactures and their suppliers. Indeed, the weakness of central place theory as
a basis for explaining interurban relationships is readily illustrated by noting the
fact that it makes no provision for any commerce among cities of the same size
category—all cities are ''nested'' and all trade is unidirectional: from larger to
smaller place within its hierarchical sub-system.

Since the limited assumptions and linkages inherent in central place theory do
not adequately explain the size and distribution of urban systems, Dunn turns to
other types of linkage networks and suggests that where material and energy
transformations and transfers are involved, linkages may be of a number of types
and may result in urban agglomeration tendencies related to opportunities for
special transformation economies, special transfer economies or both. While we
cannot examine in detail the various ways in which such non-central place agglomerations may develop, several somewhat overlapping observations may be
made:

1. Intermediate processes which result in production of finished goods des-
   tined for transfer to households are quite often subject to very considerable
   transformation economies of scale. This is not visualized in central place
   theory and clearly introduces a new factor making for urban agglomeration. While in theory such processes would be located in the higher eche-
   lons of a central place system, in practice they are likely to be found in
   places that are ''off centered'' when viewed in terms of the hinterland-
   serving criteria of central place theory, because firms are seeking to realize
   economies not treated within the framework of central place theory (e.g.,
   the need to be in close proximity to raw materials or to be tied into a complex, spatially specialized, industrial network system).

2. Production of goods typically involves a number of intermediate processes. Moreover, firms frequently produce outputs for a wide variety of users. Producers will tend to cluster with user firms to effect communications or other economies and the resulting clustering will in itself tend to bring about modified *transfer* channels which in turn increase efficiency and contribute further to clustering. The result is agglomeration through the development of metropolitan and regional industrial complexes. Dunn notes:[31]

> the importance of transformation economies related to transfer scale economies results in the fact that they break the hierarchical symmetrical pattern and build up off-center activity concentrations, reshaping patterns of urban transfer circuits in the process.

3. Moreover, these agglomerations of intermediate activities tend to build up concentrations of physical and human capital providing additional attractions for further agglomeration.
4. Intermediate activities may be drawn toward the location of physical resources. This is true not only for those establishments engaged in initial processes but also for subsequent processing of materials which are substantially weight- or bulk-losing. Even where there is not a direct link to resources, intermediate processes may be drawn to urban sites which are in relative proximity to resources because of economies related to sharing urban transfer networks and access to concentrations of physical and human capital.
5. Intermediate processes may be drawn to locations that offer special transfer economies related to access to transportation systems. Here, of course, we observe the special attractions for manufacturers and resource processers of ports and other entrepot locations.
6. What we regard as cities or metropolitan areas are not neatly identified network systems. Although open and intricately linked with the remainder of the national and world economy, they are characterized by a significant degree of closure which is largely the result of linkages to households. On the one hand, as consumers, on the other as labor inputs, households are linked to a variety of producers of goods and services. It is these linkages involving households that bring about in large measure the density of human settlement which characterizes cities.

Control and developmental networks.[32] In addition to the networks involved with the production and distribution of goods discussed above, the economic system comprises two other general categories of networks, each of which involves transformations and transfers relating to information. The first relates to control functions within the economy (what Dunn calls the ''dual''), the second to activities involved in development—''social learning.''

Control networks include not only managerial and communications systems but also banking and monetary institutions, legal and judicial processes and market institutions (e.g., brokers).

Although these may be regarded as essentially "shadow" networks, networks involved in the transformation and transfer of information necessary for the functioning of the physical processing and distributing network system, they do not completely duplicate the physical processing network system (although they may in part), because both their transformation and transfer scale economies are frequently different. For example, managerial (transformation) functions are often subject to significant economies of scale (e.g., a single headquarters office can handle a large share of the managerial functions of a number of production plants) and the associated information communications (transfer) systems (e.g., telephone, teletype) will be also subject to very different scale economies.

The result is that the topology of the control information systems is likely to be different from that of the related goods production and distribution system, with its plants, warehouses and so on, although the location of the control system is likely to be influenced by the location of the latter. The special significance for the development of the urban system is that control information systems tend to be efficient—and to agglomerate—at higher levels of the urban system than production systems and that, since they often minister to the requirements of production-distribution systems which, from a central place point of view, are "off-center," they are frequently off-center as well.

Developmental networks must be distinguished from control networks.[33] Dunn emphasizes that we are continuously involved in processes of "social learning." The essentially developmental changes within the system involve information transformation and transfers which are quite different from those related to the monitoring and instructing needed to keep the system operating in conformity with existing targets and social values. Within this new category are included entrepreneurial functions, R&D, education, and the innovative aspects of governments.

While it is true that in some measure such functions can be performed within the institutional arrangement designed for control or production (e.g., entrepreneurial functions can be performed by managers, research can take place within the plant, etc.), in a highly specialized society these functions become more articulated and are organized into separate transformation-transfer networks. The essential point is that the two sets of processes are different and subject to different organizational and cost characteristics. Among control network activities there is an emphasis on the transfer of more or less standardized signals; among social learning activity networks, the emphasis is on transformation (rather than transfer) of information. Attention focuses on new ideas, new behavioral designs.

This makes for different locational characteristics. Processes of social learning are less standardized and more dependent on face-to-face communication. Dunn concludes that[34]

Many of these creative activities, particularly the entrepreneurial functions, seek locations in the dominant centre and major sub-centres of the urban mega-system. The research, design and political functions are characterized by more intermittent transfers and can frequently be asymmetrical with respect to the topology of a central place hierarchy. In any case, the tendency is to create agglomerated communities of scholars, financiers, politicians, etc.

Technological change and development. Thus far in our discussion of Dunn's work we have dealt largely with the structure of the national urban system—the way in which it is organized topologically and in terms of size and number of urban places as a result of the relational networks which exist in order to carry out production, control and developmental processes. Although the discussion has been put forward in essentially static terms, it is already clear that the urban system cannot be visualized statically since a large number of relational networks exist to provide primarily for the growth and developmental processes which are continuously underway.

In dealing with developmental activity, Dunn's focus is on technology which he defines broadly as enhancing "all those applications of knowledge that serve practical social purposes." Technological changes are seen as falling into two general categories: (1) technological changes in physical processes, and (2) technological changes in information processes.

Technological changes in physical processes may involve either production or transport. Both have been of tremendous importance. Both have altered input-output relationships of existing processes and even initiated entirely new patterns of agglomeration.

The dramatic changes in technology which characterize our recent history have also impacted both managerial (control) networks and entrepreneurial (developmental) networks. As regards managerial networks, the new technology alters functional span of control and makes possible control of complex operations which previously could be only monitored imperfectly and with delay:[35]

> The list of possible examples seems endless and it is clear that such changes in spatial and functional spans of enterprise control must combine to make substantial modifications in urban system networks. Some activities tend to become more agglomerated and centralized. There are increased opportunities for enterprises to merge under common managerial direction the top level management function of more and more establishments (sometimes engaged in quite diverse physical and information process). In addition, traditional functions at the apex of control hierarchy (like financial management and those functions that monitor operating environments and regulate external transactions) are more easily set up in metropolitan locations substantially removed from component establishments. . . .
>
> The same information-processing developments act to facilitate the decentralization of other activities. Many production establishments may now be spun off to more remote locations in search of more economical access to resources, workers, and markets.

Regarding entrepreneurial developmental adaptations, Dunn makes the cogent point that these processes are being redefined by changes in the span of control which have, themselves, been "wrought by developing information technology":[36]

> Many enterprises now have the power (either internally or through consulting services) to model or monitor larger fields of their operating environments so that they can more readily identify, and even anticipate, emerging disturbances. The more creative and inventive concept-and-design generating activities are greatly

simplified. . . . As long as the industrial structure of the urban system was dominated by physical throughput systems, most entrepreneurial adaptations were relative and ex post in nature. Problems were recognized and dealt with *after* they had
taxed the limits of managerial adjustments. As the development of the new technology has coincided with an increase in the rate of environmental feedback,
entrepreneurship has tended to become more anticipatory and pre-adaptive in
nature.

An important result of this growing significance of anticipatory functions has
been to increase the importance of enterprise headquarters activities and to render
them locationally more independent of the processes of physical production. In
addition, there has been a tendency for "creative, inventive design work necessary to devise developmental, adoption responses. . . to be spun off into basic
and applied science laboratories."

Finally, technology has also impacted households in a variety of ways which
involve a wider range of choice and a greater volume of consumer goods and
services consumer, new patterns of shopping or recreational activities, a rising
significance of education, and an increase in the importance of non-work-related
activities.

In concluding his analysis of technology in both physical and information
processing, Dunn takes note of a variety of ways in which the new technology
has increased the scope of government and the way in which it is carried out as
regards locational aspects. He observes that many developmental aspects tend to
gravitate to the nation's capital, while others are likely to generate agglomerations of highly specialized activities (e.g., naval bases, research establishments,
space centers) elsewhere.

Contributions to the Analysis of Metropolitan Complexes of Corporate Activities

Our presentation has focussed thus far on theoretical contributions to the study of
the U.S. system of cities. At this juncture, however, it is helpful to shift the emphasis and to recall that many of the recent debates among urban economists
have been cast against developments which have culminated in the late 1960s
and early 1970s and which have brought about rapid employment and population
growth in Sunbelt centers and stagnation or even decline in Snowbelt places. The
terms "growth," "stagnation," or "decline" must be used with caution, however, since meanings vary depending on who uses them and on what phenomenon one chooses to emphasize.

To simplify, these debates have run along two, somewhat opposite, lines. One
school of thought has essentially defended the thesis that the recent shift of economic activity to the South must be regarded as essentially a regional power
shift. The other has tried to follow a more elaborate analytical line of argument
and to show that the recent and dramatic growth of complexes of corporate
activities—the real centers of decision-making in our advanced capitalistic
economy—has tended to favor older, northern places even though overall employment and population growth has been found largely in so-called Snowbelt
areas. We review some of the principal themes put forth by these two schools of

thought as they set the stage for much of the argument which follows in the remainder of this book.

THE RISE OF THE "SUNBELT" AND THE DECLINE OF
THE "NORTHERN" ECONOMY

Interestingly enough, the thesis favoring the shift of economic power to the Sunbelt came to prominence, in good part, through the work of a political scientist-journalist, Kirkpatrick Sale, whose best seller *Power Shift: The Rise of the Southern Rim and its Challenge to the Eastern Establishment*[37] influenced much of the thinking adopted by a large number of urban economists.

Sale's thesis is that the postwar era has been characterized by three powerful trends:[38]

1. a massive population expansion:

> From 1945 to 1975, the Southern Rim underwent the most massive population expansion in history, from about 40 million people to nearly 80 million people in just three decades.

2. a wide-spread transformation of the Southern economy brought about by the sophisticated new technology developed since World War II:

> In broad terms there has been a shift from the traditional heavy manufacturing long associated with the Industrial Belt of the North East to the new technological industries that have grown up in the Southern Rim—aerospace, defense, electronics— and from the dependency upon railroad transportation to the growth of air and highway transportation, both relatively more important in the Southern Rim.

3. a large-scale shift of employment patterns:

> The single most important development has been the gradual decrease in blue collar industrial workers–these the backbone of the Industrial Belt–and the sharp increase in service and government workers–these the ones most important in the newly populated states with expanding governments and in the tourist-and-retirement areas like Florida, Texas, Arizona and Southern California.

Sales concludes that the Southern Rim having succeeded in establishing its strength on six basic industrial "pillars"—agribusiness, defense, advanced technology, oil and natural gas production, real estate and construction, and tourism and leisure—has quite simply "shifted the balance of power in America away from the North East."[39]

Sales' somewhat journalistic and dramatic presentation was followed by the work of more academically oriented writers, with several major collections of articles published in the mid 1970s defending the same general themes.[40]

It is interesting that these writers, though influenced by very different theoretical orientations, end up with essentially the same general argument. In the words of David Perry and Alfred Watkins:[41]

> The rapid ascent of Sunbelt cities represents a dramatic break with past conditions. Not only have the Northeastern cities lost their position as the preeminent national urban centers, but their role at the top has been usurped by a region which has over-

come the deeply embedded subordination built up during two epochs (mercantile and industrial—our clarification) of carefully crafted institutional and economic barriers. The Northeastern cities, once the recipient of the benefits of these barriers, found themselves trapped by their elimination. While they were saddled with an old, slowly growing industrial foundation, the sunbelt cities, because they had previously been blocked from adopting these same activities, were in more flexible position to shift with the changing needs of the economy. In a sense, they represented the economy with a *tabula rasa*, uncluttered with the outmoded infrastructure and habits characteristic of past eras. Moreover, the Sunbelt has seemingly erected a new set of barriers in the form of inequitable Federal disbursements which, in the Northeast, are viewed as inhibiting any possible revitalization of the region. Thus the tables have been turned and the previously dominant cities of the Northeast are witnessing an erosion, not only of their preeminent position in the urban system, but of their vital, life sustaining economic functions as well. While the Northeastern cities are losing population and jobs at an alarming rate, the Sunbelt is picking up the slack and leading the economy into new rounds of capital accumulation.

While the argument put forth by this school of thought has a certain validity, what is usually missing is a solid analytical insight into the nature of the linkages that have developed between the two economic regions during the postwar era. This lack of insight is due to a failure to appreciate the kinds of institutional arrangements and service activities which have come to link the two regional economies.

THE "RISE OF THE SUNBELT" REVISITED: THE GROWING
IMPORTANCE OF METROPOLITAN COMPLEXES OF
CORPORATE ACTIVITIES

The idea of fundamental linkages between Sunbelt and northern metropolitan economies was put forth most strongly in the mid 1970s by the authors of a study of the *Corporate Headquarters Complex in New York City*[42] who suggested that, beyond the manufacturing and population decline underway in the New York economy, one had to see the strengthening of linkages between New York's complex of advanced corporate services (finance, insurance, legal counsel, accounting, advertising, and so forth) and corporations headquartered elsewhere. Although cautious in their statement, since they wrote in the aftermath of a 10 year period during which the headquarters of close to 40 of the *Fortune* 500 firms had left the city for its suburbs or other regional centers, they concluded:

> The agglomeration of corporate service activities in a small number of world cities is no accident. There is no prospect that the American economy could dispense with the complex presently located in New York. The challenge that New York faces is to keep its preeminence rather than yield to another center. At present it boasts assets that cannot be matched by any other metropolis in the world.[43]

It should be emphasized here that the authors of the study were careful not to confuse New York's strength as a center of corporate decision-making with the sheer number of industrial corporations headquartered in the city, but saw it resting in "New York's unique agglomeration of advanced corporate services." Had they done otherwise, they surely would have ended with a much gloomier assessment of the situation at hand.[44]

It is fair to report that the study mentioned above owed much to Cohen's ground-breaking work on "The Internationalization of Capital and U.S. Cities."[45] Cohen's principal focus was to analyze why and how advanced corporate services had grown to become so important throughout the postwar era:

> The Modern Corporation is much more directly affected by its changing external environment than were its predecessors. It has had to develop ways to respond to changes in its environment, changes caused by itself, its competitors, government agencies and major foreign political and economic events. Because it has been impossible for the corporatåion to cope with all these factors solely by using its internal staff, it has built up extensive ties to the advanced corporate services. Through specialization and concentration of skills, major firms in the advanced services have developed symbiotic relationships with the largest corporations. Because such specialization also involves concentration and economies of scale of a geographic nature, it has resulted in the agglomeration of advanced services and corporate headquarters in but a few of the largest cities in the nation.[46]

Indeed Cohen's second important focus was to show how spatially restricted the developments of these agglomerations of advanced services had become, finding some—but limited—decentralization away from the traditional centers of finance and corporate sources.

In the end, Cohen was the most articulate in arguing that the transformation of the system of cities ought to be analyzed from the perspective of the rise of metropolitan complexes of corporate activities—although, because of the somewhat different focus of his own work, he fell short of carrying out fully such analysis:

> Although some authors, including Pred and Westaway, have attempted to analyze the hierarchy of cities based upon the location of corporate headquarters or the control of corporate production activities by head offices in certain urban places, the analysis of urban hierarchy should be based upon the complex of institutions in the business community. Thus, one should focus upon which centers are foci of corporate strategy, planning, control and interaction with governmental bodies.[47]

The study presented in this book is an attempt to take Cohen's suggestion to heart and to carry out a full assessment of the transformation of the U.S. system of cities from the perspective of the importance of metropolitan complexes of corporate activities. We believe that in so doing we should be in a position to put the Snowbelt-Sunbelt debate in a different light and to present new evidence of changes in the key linkages that structure the system of cities.

Conclusion: Highlights from the Review

The preceding summary of some key concepts and empirical findings directs our attention to a number of the more critical aspects of urban economic structure and development and serves to guide the analysis in the chapters to follow. At least eight general propositions emerge:

1. *Size and economic specialization.* Size is a major variable in examining metropolitan economic structure. Size permits the attainment of market thresholds sufficient for external economies to come into being through the

functioning of specialized establishments. Moreover, size supports a broader diversity of specialized activities. Thus there is likely to be both a higher level of specialization and a greater diversity of available specializations in the large city environment than in the small.

2. *The diversity of agglomeration patterns.* Urban economies will differ because their roles within the economic system differ. To a considerable extent the national economic system is specialized spatially. Accordingly, some metropolitan economies are uniquely structured to serve the special needs of given manufacturing or extractive industries, while others may be specialized in terms of their roles in providing a more general range of services of the central place sort.

Theory suggests, then, that metropolitan economies differ in terms of their industrial mix—the relative importance of various goods and service-producing activities—and that analysis of structure and change in terms of industrial makeup is likely to be a fruitful approach in gaining a better understanding of the processes of urban development. Theory also suggests that it is important to identify both "central place" and "off-centered" types of urban economies and to investigate the economic relationships that link them.

3. *The cumulative effect of economic development and specialization.* The city's economy is likely to be affected by the stage of capitalistic development in which it has experienced its major growth.

The specialization of physical capital, institutional arrangements, and human resources are likely to reflect the functional specialization of the era of a city's major development. Large cities, because they have attained great size through development over extended periods, are likely to reflect several historical roles, each of which may continue to be of significance. Thus, larger, older cities may currently play important roles as mercantile centers, industrial centers, and modern centers of corporate, government, and nonprofit activities.

By the same logic, smaller places are likely to have passed through a shorter period of active development and growth. If this period occurred and was brought to a close in an earlier era of agricultural or industrial growth, their industrial structure will tend to reflect this fact. If active growth and development has occurred recently or is currently underway, their industrial composition is likely to reflect some presently favored export activities as well as newer technologies.

The implications for regional differences in urban systems are clear. Regions developed in an earlier era are likely to have a disproportionate number of places specialized in older industries and shaped by earlier technologies. Regions recently developed or currently developing will be characterized by towns and cities that do not carry to the same degree the mark of past economic eras in industrial structure or technological artifacts (though they may trace their earliest beginnings to relatively early times). Accordingly, their problems, their prospects and their paths of optimum development are likely to be quite different.

4. *The cumulative effect of economic development, the effect of size and the ability of places to transform.* Because large places have well developed and relatively sophisticated physical, economic, and social infrastructures, theory would seem to suggest that size makes possible greater capacity to adjust to economic change. This remains a highly controversial argument, however. As we have seen, many urban theoreticians have been arguing that the older and larger places are the most entrenched in the old way of doing things and thus the least likely to transform. As a result, they contend, major periods of economic transformation are usually characterized by the rapid rise of a new set of large urban centers and the sharp decline of older ones. Others argue just the opposite. We think that the issue is perhaps more empirical than theoretical in nature and that it may be impossible to generalize from one period of transition to another. Evidence presented in this monograph indicates that the impact of the current transformation lies somewhere in between: in both the rise of a new set of large metropolitan centers (mostly Sunbelt) and considerable adjustment and adaptation among a substantial number of older large centers (mostly Snowbelt).

5. *The implications of the rise of the complexes of corporate activities.* The rise of the modern corporation has been a major factor contributing to the changing spatial organization of the economy. There has been a shift in emphasis within the corporation from production to control and development and a concomitant divorce of the location of administrative and developmental activities from those related to production. The growth of the administrative and developmental apparatus of the modern corporation and its demand for specialized services has become a major factor in the development of agglomeration of advanced corporate services in certain metropolitan areas. The agglomeration processes at work are at the heart of growth and development in a number of places and their analyses must be at the center of any study of the restructuring of the U.S. system of cities.

At the same time, because these complexes are intrinsically related to other major sectors of activities, their analysis must be carried out with due regard to what is taking place in these other economic sectors. In short, one must be able to handle both the newer and the older sectors of the economy and the way these are being transformed.

6. *The rise of nonprofit, public sector, and associated activities.* The rise of employment and output in nonprofit, public sector, and associated activities has been an important feature of urban development during the postwar era. Their growth has been related partly to the private sector need for more sophisticated networks of control and developmental institutions (R&D, foreign trade, improved financial and marketing statistics), partly to society's increasing demand for high level manpower, and partly to other factors as well (e.g., military needs).

In Chapter 2 it was suggested that such services have not necessarily developed where the complexes of corporate activities have expanded.

Dunn, for his part, has stressed the spatial distinction between control and developmental networks—with nonprofit and public sector institutions playing a major role in the latter. The issue of where these services locate and how they are related spatially to each other and to other activities is a critical one in examining the way in which metropolitan economies are developing in a service oriented era.

7. *Centripetal and centrifugal forces.* In an important sense there are two general types of locational forces that are at work changing the spatial organization of the American economy: centripetal and centrifugal. Centripetal forces prevail wherever the factors encouraging agglomeration are strong. They are of major importance in those centers favored by the development of the corporate complex, but they are significant also in the off-centered development of complexes relating to resort-recreation, government, or even of the new high technology centers. Historically, the development of the old manufacturing centers of the industrial area also reflected such forces.

Centrifugal forces are observed principally in production activities—the relocation of plants not only in suburban but in rural and offshore areas. But they are also at work wherever an activity—either goods- or service-producing—can operate efficiently at lower cost away from the dense activity networks of the metropolitan area. As Dunn has noted, certain activities of corporations (e.g., back office data processing) are characterized by different network requirements than others and favor off-center locations. Moreover, it is clear that the impact of changes in transportation and technology act to modify network relationships throughout the system in important ways. In a rapidly changing economy the issue of what forces are at work drawing activities into and pushing them away from metropolitan areas and how sensitively such forces operate in different places is clearly of major concern if we are to understand how best to work toward optimum developmental policy.

8. *The changing nature of intermetropolitan linkages.* Both theoretical and empirical studies reviewed in this chapter suggest major changes in the nature of intermetropolitan linkages. At a conceptual level, both Pred and Dunn associate this change with the rising importance of "control" and "development" functions in the economy. Pred, in particular, is the most explicit in suggesting that the nature of control and developmental networks is such that they do not necessarily yield the kinds of linkages between higher-order and lower-order cities characterized by a regularity of the sort predicted by central place theory. These are fundamental observations which must be kept in mind as one tries to explore the nature of intermetropolitan linkages in today's system of cities.

Notes

1. The best single reference covering the material treated in this section is Alfred J. Watkins, *The Practice of Urban Economics*, Beverley Hills, Calif.: Sage Publications, Inc., 1980, Chapters 2,3. Watkins' book contains a useful bibliography.

2. The concept of external economies was first put forward by Alfred Marshall in order to distinguish between economies brought about by increases in size of firms and of industries. Marshall dealt at some length with economies of agglomeration, stressing economies due to favorable effects on skill and availability of labor, access to markets, shared technical knowledge, supplier availability and a number of other factors. (Alfred Marshall, *Principles of Economics*, 9th ed., London: Macmillan & Co., 1961, Vol. 1, Text, Book 4, Chapters 9–11). Among the first to make clear the significance of external economies in modern cities were Edgar Hoover and Raymond Vernon in their study of the New York Metropolitan Region (Edgar M. Hoover and Raymond Vernon, *Anatomy of a Metropolis*, Cambridge, Mass.: Harvard University Press, 1959).

3. Brian J.L. Berry and William L. Garrison, "The Functional Basis of the Central Place Hierarchy," *Economic Geography*, Vol. 34, 1958; and Brian J.L. Berry, *Geography of Market Centers and Retail Distribution*, Englewood Cliffs, N.J.: Prentice-Hall, 1967.

4. See for example, *The Practice of Urban Economics*, op. cit., Chapter 4, especially footnote 1.

5. Cf. Wilbur R. Thompson, *A Preface to Urban Economics*, Washington, D.C.: Resources for the Future, Inc., 1965, pp. 28–30.

6. Ibid., Chapter 1.

7. Ibid., p. 17.

8. Ibid., p. 22–24.

9. Wilbur R. Thompson, "Economic Process and Employment Problems in Declining Metropolitan Areas," in George Sternlieb and James W. Hughes, *Post Industrial America: Metropolitan Decline and Inter-Regional Job Shifts*, New Brunswick, N.J.: Center for Urban Policy Research, 1975, p. 189.

10. Ibid., p. 189.

11. Ibid.

12. Ibid., pp. 191–92.

13. Allan Pred, *City Systems in Advanced Economies*, New York, N.Y.: Halsted Press, 1977.

14. Ibid., pp. 38–84.

15. Ibid., p. 66.

16. Ibid., pp. 84–97.

17. Ibid., p. 85.

18. Ibid., p. 92.

19. Ibid., p. 94.

20. Ibid., p. 97.

21. Ibid., pp. 98–182.

22. Ibid., p. 99.

23. Ibid., p. 116.

24. Ibid., p. 174.

25. Ibid., Chap 5; also Allan Pred, *Major Job Providing Organizations and Systems of Cities*, Commission on College Geography, Resource Paper No. 27, Washington, D.C., Association of American Geographers, 1974.

26. Edgar S. Dunn, "A Flow Network Image of Urban Structures," *Regional Studies*, 1971, and *The Development of the U.S. Urban System*, Baltimore: The Johns Hopkins University Press, 1980.

27. Op. cit., "A Flow Network . . . ," p. 240.

28. Ibid., pp. 240–44.

29. Ibid., pp. 244–53.

30. Ibid., pp. 245–46.

31. Ibid., p. 250.

32. Ibid., pp. 253–58.

33. Ibid., p. 256.

34. Edgar S. Dunn, Jr., op. cit., *The Development of the U.S. Urban System*, pp. 37–43.

35. Ibid., p. 40.

36. Ibid.

37. Random House, 1975.

38. Ibid., pp. 18–19.

39. Ibid., p. 6.

40. Among the most important, see George Sternlieb and James W. Hughes, *Post Industrial America: Metropolitan Decline and Inter-Regional Job Shifts*, Center for Urban Policy Research, New Brunswick, N.J.: 1975; David C. Perry and Alfred J. Watkins, *The Rise of the Sunbelt Cities*, Sage Publications, Beverly Hills, Calif.: 1977.

41. David Perry and Alfred Watkins, editor, op. cit., p. 41.

42. Conservation of Human Resources, op. cit., New York: 1977.

43. Ibid., p. 76.

44. Indeed, such a gloomier conclusion was the one arrived at by Quante who, writing roughly at the same time, focused his analysis almost exclusively on the issue of headquarters. See Wolfgang Quante, *The Exodus of Corporate Headquarters from New York City*, Praeger, New York: 1976.

45. Robert Cohen, op. cit., Ph.D. dissertation, New York: New School for Social Research, 1979.

46. Ibid., p. 451.

47. Ibid., p. 472. References in the quote are to Allan Pred's *City Systems in Advanced Economies* and John Westaway, "The Spatial Hierarchy of Business Organizations and its Implications for the British Urban System," *Regional Studies*, 8, 1974.

CHAPTER FOUR

A Typology of Large and Medium Size Metropolitan Areas and Some Observations Regarding Patterns of Change

In the present chapter, our concern is with the industrial structure of large and medium size metropolitan economies (SMSAs), the extent to which such structure has changed during recent decades, and patterns of growth and development which have characterized various types of metropolitan economies.

The concept of industrial structure employed here derives from the discussion of urban agglomeration in the previous chapter. Metropolitan economies are made up of private sector firms and of government and nonprofit organizations which carry on a variety of activities, some of which produce goods or services exported to a hinterland or to distant points, some of which provide for the needs of local consumers or local businesses and other organizations. Theory leads us to expect that the mix of activities will vary among places, although some activities (low-level central-place type activities) are more or less ubiquitous. Cities that have achieved large size over the years can support certain activities that smaller places cannot. Moreover, some metropolitan areas are built around specific industrial, urban, or resource-based agglomerations, while others are specialized as port cities, trading centers, resorts, and so on.

Thus, theory—and general observation as well—tell us that metropolitan economies differ in terms of the relative importance of various activities, or stated in more formal terms, in their industrial composition or structure. What is needed is a method of analyzing these individual metropolitan structures to arrive at a useful typology of SMSAs as a first step in studying the nature of postwar urban development. We need to examine the extent to which developmental patterns have varied among various types of places and to assess the likelihood that some groups enjoy developmental opportunities which others do not. This chapter, which is based entirely on employment data, carries us some distance toward these objectives.[1] Examination of institutional materials in the chapters to follow will supplement the analysis and provide the reader with a clearer picture of the urban system as it stands today.

An Approach to the Measurement of Industrial Specialization

Our approach is first to determine for each SMSA the relative level of specialization in each of a number of key industrial groupings as measured by the share of employment in that industrial category. We then classify SMSAs into types on the basis of similarities in patterns of industrial specialization. Relative levels of specialization are determined by comparison of the share (percentage) of SMSA employment accounted for by an industry group with the share (percentage) of total U.S. employment accounted for by that same industry group. The measure used is known as a "location quotient" and expresses the share of employment in a given industry in a specified SMSA as a percentage of the share of employment in the same industry within the total U.S. economy. Thus, if wholesaling accounts for 8.7 percent of employment and manufacturing for 17.6 percent in the Memphis SMSA, while wholesaling accounts for 5.5 percent and manufacturing for 22.8 percent of U.S. employment, the Memphis location quotients for wholesaling and manufacturing are 158.2 and 77.2, respectively.[2] Memphis is considered to be relatively specialized in wholesaling; not in manufacturing.

The location quotient has traditionally been used to distinguish export activity, with the extent to which the measure exceeds 100 indicating the degree to which the product or service is presumed to be exported. We make no attempt to build up estimates of total metropolitan exports, however. Rather, we seek simply to determine those industrial groupings in which individual SMSAs are specialized in the sense that such groupings account for relatively large allocations of resources.

It is important to recognize what the location quotient does and does not measure. Clearly, it measures employment rather than total resources employed, and it measures employment without regard to number of hours worked, levels of skill, or rates of pay. We learn nothing regarding utilization of capital or other factors of production, nor do we gain insight into the level of expertise or training of the workers employed.

Nevertheless, the practice of computing location quotients separately for each industry does adjust to a large extent for interindustry differences. The fact that the share of total employment accounted for by retailing may be somewhat overstated in comparison to wholesaling because of the prevalence of part-time work in the former does not of itself give rise to error. The characteristic is a general one, largely recognized by comparing retailing percentages in each place with the U.S. average percentage for retailing. It is only when practices vary from place to place that error is likely to creep in.

Finally, the measure is the best available. There are no systematic industry-by-industry estimates for individual SMSA value added or for capital employed. Some estimates of income are published but not for all SMSAs, not for an extended period, and not in terms of industrial groupings. Employment, after all, is the single most important factor of production from a social point of view and should provide a fairly reliable basis for estimating patterns of industrial specialization. In the chapters that follow, additional sources of information will be examined in order to assess the validity of our first-order analysis and to shed further light on some key aspects of metropolitan structure and development.

Industrial and Size Characteristics of SMSAs

A DETAILED FUNCTIONAL TYPOLOGY OF THE
140 LARGEST SMSAs

In order to arrive at a typology, we analyzed patterns of location quotients in SMSAs in 1976. Location quotients were computed for each of the 11 industrial groupings shown in Table 4.1 in each of the 140 large and medium size SMSAs (1976 population above 250,000). Cluster analysis was utilized to break out those groups of places which were most similar, bringing about an arrangement of places in which (in statistical terminology) overall variance was minimized. The technique employed is described in Appendix A.

The analysis resulted in nine categories or types:

Classification	*No. of SMSAs*
Nodal	39
Functional nodal	24
Government-education	15
Education-manufacturing	5
Residential	3
Resort-retirement	9
Manufacturing	25
Industrial-military	13
Mining-industrial	7

Most SMSAs fitted readily into one of these types, but there were a few borderline cases. These are identified and the basis for final classification is explained in Appendix A. The SMSAs are listed in Table 4.2 according to the nine classifications indicated above and criteria of population size discussed shortly hereafter. For simplicity, major type and size groupings are brought under four major headings described on pages 62–63.

Perhaps the best way to begin to set forth the principal characteristics of each group is to indicate the extent to which the SMSAs classified within that group appear to be specialized in each of the industries. This is done in Table 4.1, which indicates for each industry and type of SMSA the percentage of places with location quotients above 100.

We observe immediately that *nodal* places (e.g., New York, Chicago, Philadelphia, Boston, Houston, Atlanta, Charlotte, or Omaha) are specialized in providing a variety of intermediate services (i.e., distributive and corporate complex services). Most of these SMSAs have relatively large shares of employment in a number of such services: 90 percent of nodal SMSAs have location quotients of more than 100 in TCU, 95 percent in wholesaling, 93 percent in FIRE, 85 percent in corporate services. Although not every nodal SMSA is overrepresented in all four of these industry groupings, most are overrepresented

Table 4.1 Percentage of SMSAs with Above-Average Location Quotients (100 plus) in Major Industry Groups by Type of Place, 1976

Type of Place	Mfg	TCU	Whl	CAO&A	FIRE	CS	Ret	MCS	NP	Gov	Min
Nodal (39)[a]	18	90[b]	95	64	93	85	31	44	52	23	-
Functional Nodal (24)	87	25	55	87	33	21	17	-	62	4	-
Government-Education (15)	14	13	20	26	47	53	40	7	34	100	-
Education-Manufacturing (5)	80	20	20	20	20	40	60	-	80	40	-
Residential (3)	33	-	67	33	67	100	100	67	67	67	-
Resort-Retirement (9)	-	67	33	-	67	78	100	100	33	33	-
Manufacturing (25)	100	20	16	12	12	4	32	4	48	4	-
Industrial-Military (13)	23	23	23	-	15	23	85	46	23	100	-
Mining-Industrial (7)	14	58	58	14	14	29	71	43	43	43	100

[a] Numbers in parentheses indicate number of SMSAs in each category.
[b] Underlining is for emphasis.

Column heads: Same as Table 2.2; Min: Mining.

Source: County Business Patterns, 1976; Employment and Earnings in State and Local Areas, 1976; and Appendix A.

in several.[3] In addition, more than half of the nodal SMSAs are specialized in CAO&A activities and nonprofit services.

Functional nodal places (e.g., Detroit, Pittsburgh, San Jose, Rochester, Akron, or Wilmington) are principally older manufacturing centers in which major corporations carry out headquarters and other non-production activities. The most interesting observation—which calls for further analysis below—is that although these places are specialized in corporate administrative and developmental activities they are underrepresented in financial services, corporate services and most of the distributive services (percentages of SMSAs with 100 plus location quotients in FIRE, corporate services, and TCU are only 33, 21, and 25, respectively). The fact that more than 60 percent have 100 plus location quotients in nonprofit services does indicate a significant presence of medical and/or educational centers in a number of SMSAs of this type.

The *government-education* group is made up of SMSAs which are for the most part centers of government combined in most cases with university related employment. In addition to Washington, D.C., the group includes ten state capitals (e.g., Albany, Harrisburg, or Austin). It is clear from the data that such places are likely to show a significant presence of producer services. Roughly half of these SMSAs have 100-plus location quotients in FIRE and corporate services.

The five *education-manufacturing* SMSAs are places which in a sense have led a double life. They are predominantly old industrial centers which are also the sites of university complexes (e.g., New Haven, South Bend, or Ann Arbor). These characteristics are revealed by above average location quotients in nonprofit services and/or government (the latter due principally to state supported educational services) in all SMSAs.

The three *residential* SMSAs are all major exurban complexes which have grown in recent years to such an extent that they have become identified as metropolitan areas. Two, Nassau-Suffolk and Long Branch-Asbury Park, are extensions of the greater New York City area; the other, Anaheim, is a part of the agglomeration extending southward from Los Angeles. These places have strongly consumer-oriented economies (all have above average levels of retail and mostly consumer service employment) but show substantial employment in distributive, FIRE and corporate services as well.

The *resort-retirement* group is made up of places with familiar names such as Ft. Lauderdale, Orlando, West Palm Beach and Las Vegas. Not unexpectedly, all of these SMSAs have above average employment in retailing and MCS. What is more interesting is that TCU, FIRE, and corporate services also score quite high: 67 percent or more show 100-plus location quotients. No doubt, this is due in part to the fact that these services, which are generally regarded as playing an intermediate role in the production process, are also partly consumer services: resort centers have heavy airline patronage; brokerage services flourish where the well-to-do gather, and so on. But the amenities of pleasant climate and attractive surroundings also make some of these places appealing sites for a variety of financial and business services and corporate "back office" units that are free to operate away from major financial-commercial service complexes such as New York or Chicago (see our subsequent discussion of Orlando and Fort Lauderdale).

Table 4.2 140 Largest SMSAs Classified by Type and Size under Four Major Groupings, 1976

DIVERSIFIED SERVICE CENTERS

National Nodal
Rank	City	Size
1	New York	1
2	Los Angeles	1
3	Chicago	1
7	San Francisco	1
32	Indianapolis	2
33	New Orleans	2
34	Portland	2
35	Columbus	2

Regional Nodal
Rank	City	Size
4	Philadelphia	1
6	Boston	1
10	Dallas	1
11	Houston	1
12	St. Louis	1
14	Baltimore	1
15	Minneapolis	1
17	Cleveland	1
18	Atlanta	2
21	Miami	2
22	Denver	2
23	Seattle	2
26	Cincinnati	2
28	Kansas City	2
30	Phoenix	2

Subregional Nodal
Rank	City	Size
41	Memphis	3
45	Salt Lake City	3
46	Birmingham	3
52	Nashville	3
53	Oklahoma City	3
56	Jacksonville	3
58	Syracuse	3
65	Richmond	3
66	Charlotte	3
69	Omaha	3
91	Mobile	4
101	Little Rock	4
106	Shreveport	4
110	Des Moines	4
114	Spokane	4
20	Jackson MS	4

SPECIALIZED SERVICE CENTERS

Functional Nodal
Rank	City	Size
5	Detroit	1
13	Pittsburgh	1
16	Newark	1
24	Milwaukee	2
31	San Jose	2
36	Hartford	2
38	Rochester	3
40	Louisville	3
44	Dayton	3
47	Bridgeport	3
50	Toledo	3
51	Greensboro	3
57	Akron	3
62	Allentown	3
63	Tulsa	3
67	New Brunswick	3
70	Jersey City	4
75	Wilmington	4
78	Paterson	4
86	Knoxville	4
96	Wichita	4
100	Fort Wayne	4
103	Peoria	4
137	Kalamazoo	4

Government-Education
Rank	City	Size
8	Washington, D.C.	1
39	Sacramento	3
48	Albany	3
77	Raleigh-Durham	4
81	Fresno	4
82	Austin	4
84	Lansing	4
85	Oxnard-Ventura	4
88	Harrisburg	4
89	Baton Rouge	4
99	Columbia, SC	4
111	Utica	4
112	Trenton	4
113	Madison	4
117	Stockton	4

Education-Manufacturing
Rank	City	Size
54	New Haven	3
64	Springfield	3
90	Tacoma	4
130	South Bend	4
140	Ann Arbor	4

PRODUCTION CENTERS

Manufacturing

27 Buffalo	2	
42 Providence	3	
59 Worcester	3	
60 Gary	3	
61 N.E. Pennsylvania	3	
71 Grand Rapids	3	
72 Youngstown	3	
73 Greenville	3	
74 Flint	3	
80 New Bedford	4	
92 Canton	4	
93 Johnson City	4	
94 Chattanooga	4	
98 Davenport	4	
104 Beaumont	4	
107 York	4	
109 Lancaster	4	
115 Binghamton	4	
116 Reading	4	
119 Huntington	4	
124 Evansville	4	
125 Appleton	4	
131 Erie	4	
134 Rockford	4	
136 Lorain	4	
123 Huntsville	4	
126 Augusta	4	
127 Vallejo	4	
128 Colorado Springs	4	
132 Pensacola	4	
133 Salinas	4	

Industrial-Military

20 San Diego	2
37 San Antonio	3
49 Norfolk	3
87 El Paso	4
97 Charleston SC	4
102 Newport News	4
121 Lexington	4

Mining-Industrial

83 Tucson	4
105 Bakersfield	4
118 Corpus Christi	4
129 Lakeland	4
135 Johnstown PA	4
138 Duluth	4
139 Charleston WV	4

CONSUMER-ORIENTED CENTERS

Residential

9 Nassau	1
19 Anaheim	2
76 Long Branch	3

Resort-Retirement

25 Tampa	2
29 Riverside	2
43 Ft. Lauderdale	3
55 Honolulu	3
68 Orlando	3
79 West Palm Beach	4
95 Albuquerque	4
108 Las Vegas	4
122 Santa Barbara	4

Note: Number preceding city indicates 1976 population rank; number following city, 1976 population size group (see text).

Source: U.S. Bureau of the Census, Current Population Report, Series P-25 and Appendix A.

Manufacturing SMSAs (e.g., Buffalo, Gary, Flint, Greenville or Erie) stand in sharp contrast to the preceding groups—even to the functional nodal places, where manufacturing employment is high. Although all of these SMSAs are characterized by manufacturing location quotients greater than 100—in most instances, much greater—very few are significantly overrepresented in employment in any of the services. Only retailing and nonprofit services have above averages shares of employment in as many as 30 percent of the SMSAs within this large group of SMSAs.

Industrial-military SMSAs (e.g., San Diego, San Antonio, or Newport News) are hosts to important military and other defense type installations. The tentative evidence offered by Table 4.1 is that such places have not proven to be attractive sites for intermediate services. Only consumer oriented services have shown any tendency to thrive: above average location quotients in retailing are found in 85 percent of these SMSAs; in mostly consumer services, 46 percent.

The seven *mining-industrial* places all show location quotients which indicate heavy concentration in mining or resource oriented employment. More than half of the shares in the distributive services categories (TCU and wholesaling) are above average. The complexes of corporate activities, on the other hand, appear to be of relatively little importance: only one place, Charleston, W. Va., boasts significant CAO&A employment, and three others, above average employment in FIRE (Lakeland) or corporate services (Tucson and Duluth). On the other hand, all but two show relatively heavy retail employment indicating significant roles as retail trading centers.

THE ROLE OF SIZE IN THE TYPOLOGY OF CITIES

Both central place theory and theories of urban growth and development lead us to expect that the industrial structure of metropolitan economies will vary with size. Moreover, they lead us to expect that the number of places that succeed in gaining great size will be relatively small, the number of medium sized places will be somewhat larger and so on. Evidence of the latter—i.e., that the system of metropolitan places is hierarchically structured—is readily summarized in the following frequency distribution:

SMSA size group	1976 population range	No. of SMSAs
Size 1	over 2 million	17
Size 2	1 to 2 million	19
Size 3	0.5 to 1 million	39
Size 4	0.25 to 0.5 million	65

A fifth size category (below 0.25 million population) includes 126 SMSAs and, in the analysis which follows, is combined with all non-metropolitan areas. Analysis of location quotients computed for each of these size groups demonstrates conclusively that industrial composition is influenced by size of SMSA.

This is particularly true for the distributive services and the corporate complex, which are very important in the industrial structure of very large places and relatively unimportant in the smallest (to repeat, the last group includes smaller urban and non-urban places): average 1976 location quotients range from 112.5 in size 1 places to 83.3 in size 5 places for distributive services and from 136.4 to 59.2 for the corporate complex. Manufacturing location quotients also show considerable variation among size groups: roughly 90 in the top two size groups, 113 in the smallest size group. The magnitude of the location quotient for manufacturing does not rise systematically as we move from the largest to the smallest size group, however, and in certain other industrial categories the effect of size is even less clear. The conclusion to be drawn is that size of place is an important variable but that it is not the only factor at work. We need to examine the role of size within the typology of metropolitan places.

In Table 4.3 the SMSAs in the major type of place categories are grouped according to the above size classification, the principal exception being the nodal places.[4] Analysis of both the employment data and materials presented in the following chapters suggest a slightly different, but size-related, typology for nodal centers. New York, Chicago, San Francisco, and Los Angeles—all size 1—stand apart in that the scope of their markets and influence far exceed regional boundaries. These we classify as "national nodal" places. The next largest 19 SMSAs are the major centers within large, but, nevertheless, somewhat more restricted market areas. This group, the "regional nodal" centers, includes 8 very large (size 1) and 11 large (size 2) SMSAs. The size 1 regional SMSAs range from two to slightly less than five million population and are located for the most part in the older areas (in terms of economic development), but include the two major Texas centers, Houston and Dallas. The size 2 regional SMSAs range from one to two million. Finally, the 16 smallest, nodal places (size 3 and size 4) are important service centers in more limited hinterlands. These are designated as "subregional nodals."

Table 4.3 also presents under each type of place heading for 1976, average location quotients for major industry groups in each of the various size classes shown. In presenting these measures it is important once again to stress that the location quotients measure relative specialization only in terms of shares of employment. We cannot make judgments regarding the level of specialization in qualitative terms without examining additional evidence. Thus, when we note that the location quotient for the four national nodals for corporate services is 141, we learn only that the share of this employment in these activities is 41 percent above the national average. We can say nothing regarding the level of expertise of these firms, although general observation suggests that the most specialized legal, advertising, accounting, management consulting, engineering firms are likely to be found in these major cities. Concrete evidence regarding size and level of specialization in a number of activities is presented in subsequent chapters.

Only a few highlights regarding size of place characteristics are offered here. They relate only to the larger groups (nodal, functional nodal, government-education and manufacturing groups) which include enough SMSAs to permit significant size of place comparisons.

Table 4.3 Location Quotients of Employment in Major Industry Groupings and Subgroupings by Type and Size of SMSA, 1976

	SMSA Size	# of SMSAs	Mfg	Dist Serv	(TCU)	(Whl)
Diversified Service Centers						
National Nodal	1	4	90.1	125.2	131.4	119.5
Regional Nodal	1	8	95.2	111.2	110.5	111.8
	2	11	79.8	129.8	131.9	128.0
Subregional Nodal	‛3	10	75.7	128.1	124.6	131.2
	4	6	66.6	129.9	120.3	138.6
Specialized Service Centers						
Functional Nodal	1	3	112.6	94.0	96.0	92.2
	2	3	134.5	85.9	78.3	92.8
	3	12	132.5	96.1	94.8	97.4
	4	6	126.3	96.5	76.1	151.1
Government-Education	1	1	16.7	68.7	86.0	52.9
	3	2	52.6	82.2	75.2	88.6
	4	12	69.8	83.9	79.8	87.6
Education-Manufacturing	1-4	5	117.6	80.8	82.7	79.1
Consumer-Oriented Centers						
Residential	1-4	3	90.7	87.7	75.3	99.1
Resort-Retirement	1-4	9	47.8	95.4	104.9	86.8
Production Centers						
Manufacturing	2	1	121.2	93.3	88.0	98.1
	3	8	151.8	84.7	79.6	89.3
	4	16	148.9	91.8	90.7	92.8
Industrial-Military	2	1	67.0	77.9	89.5	67.4
	3	2	45.6	100.8	94.1	107.0
	4	9	83.9	75.3	82.7	68.5
Mining-Industrial	4	7	57.0	98.6	101.5	96.0
Size 5 SMSAs and Non-metropolitan areas			113.1	83.4	81.4	85.1
Share of U.S. Employment in Major Industry Groups			22.9	10.4	5.0	5.4

Column heads: Same as Table 2.2.

Note: Location quotients are unweighted modified averages for major size-type groups of SMSAs. Location quotients for the mining sector are not shown. They are well below 100, except for the group of "Mining-Industrial" places with a quotient of 749.9.

Corp Compl	(CAO&A)	(FIRE)	(CS)	Ret	MSC	NP	Gov
149.7	159.5	154.4	141.2	84.2	110.1	104.4	80.9
122.6	148.7	112.6	120.2	97.6	94.6	117.4	79.2
119.7	116.3	124.7	116.6	103.4	122.0	95.8	88.7
114.6	104.6	123.8	110.8	98.5	106.5	93.8	101.6
125.8	56.3	148.1	135.9	99.7	106.4	105.8	99.8
135.4	254.0	111.2	105.9	89.4	84.5	106.1	79.0
111.9	87.9	125.2	110.3	96.4	82.8	112.1	69.2
105.7	200.2	79.3	88.5	93.2	80.6	97.5	77.3
96.6	141.6	87.4	85.4	104.4	88.0	103.4	74.6
138.2	81.9	102.0	194.9	90.5	99.4	96.3	194.0
90.1	80.9	76.7	105.9	99.5	83.5	106.9	182.1
92.3	56.7	97.5	103.0	97.9	86.1	98.1	156.3
85.1	60.8	86.9	93.9	104.8	77.6	140.4	99.3
102.9	81.8	101.0	113.6	120.1	109.9	114.5	97.8
98.1	44.8	109.1	111.2	133.9	229.4	98.8	102.2
89.5	67.3	79.9	107.7	102.4	90.0	106.4	95.6
74.6	57.3	78.4	78.7	96.5	74.3	104.9	71.5
68.4	56.8	69.2	72.6	100.9	85.8	93.4	76.6
96.1	45.8	96.8	171.1	116.2	145.6	91.4	134.9
89.0	48.9	100.6	95.9	112.6	120.1	96.6	142.9
67.0	31.5	71.2	78.2	110.0	107.0	83.2	153.4
81.7	72.9	79.3	87.7	116.3	112.7	98.2	108.9
59.7	36.6	65.4	63.4	105.6	91.1	90.0	118.6
14.7	2.7	5.7	6.3	16.0	4.3	6.5	19.5

Source: County Business Patterns, 1976; Employment and
Earnings in State and Local Areas, 1976.

Nodal places. The national nodals clearly stand as a well-defined subgroup. Not only are they by far the largest metropolitan systems in the nation, but location quotients indicate the largest shares in corporate complex activities taken as a whole and the largest or nearly the largest shares in CAO&A, FIRE and corporate services. At the same time they rank at or near the top in TCU and wholesaling shares. They also show large location quotients in mainly consumer services, though not in retailing, indicating that their strength lies in activities such as hotels and theaters. The location quotient for manufacturing is 90, well above that for the size 2 regional nodals and for the subregional nodals, indicating a significant (though declining) manufacturing presence.

In comparing regional and subregional nodals, the principal difference in location quotients appears to lie in CAO&A activities, manufacturing and wholesaling. Regional nodal places are much better developed than subregional nodal places in terms of their roles as hosts to CAO&A activities, although location quotients are not higher for FIRE and corporate services. They are also somewhat higher than the subregionals in employment shares in manufacturing, reflecting the fact that they are to a greater extent located in areas strongly touched by earlier industrialization. In wholesaling, location quotients are high, but not as high as among the subregional nodals, which are clearly the most specialized of all places in this type of distributive activity.

Functional nodal places of all size classes are characterized by high location quotients in manufacturing and CAO&A, below average quotients in distriubtion, mainly consumer services and government. Size of place differences are found only in FIRE and corporate services, the large SMSAs (size 1 and 2) showing significantly higher location quotients than the medium size (sizes 3 and 4).

Among the *government-education* places, the most important comparison is between the single large place, Washington, D.C., and the remaining fourteen SMSAs. Washington shows a much higher location quotient in corporate services (195), FIRE(102), and, of course, government (194, the highest in the nation). It is also higher in mainly consumer services (99 versus 84 and 86 in the smaller groups) and much lower in manufacturing (17), though all size groups are far below the average in this industrial category.

The most interesting observation regarding *manufacturing* places is that there are relatively few significant size of place differences. Manufacturing location quotients are high in all size classes; distributive service, corporate complex, mostly consumer services, and government quotients are low; retailing quotients are roughly normal in each.

A MORE GENERAL GROUPING OF TYPES OF SMSAs

Although the analysis of the industrial composition of employment justifies the type and size category scheme set forth above, it is helpful for much of the analysis in subsequent chapters to regroup these categories under four major headings: *diversified service centers* or *nodal centers, specialized service centers, consumer-oriented centers*, and *production centers*. Such groups recognize common functional characteristics and provide a basis for more convenient analysis of employment and developmental problems and opportunities than would be possible with the less wieldy type and size category arrangement.

The *diversified service centers* or *nodal centers* continue to stand apart. These places are to an important extent, central places (serving hinterlands). They are providers of both corporate complex activities and distributive services and are frequently centers of government and nonprofit activities as well.

The group of *specialized service centers* comprises the functional nodal, government-education, and education-manufacturing places. As such, it is a mixed group of places. Functional nodal and education-manufacturing centers seem to have retained an important role as centers of manufacturing production whereas government-education centers are (and have always been) weak in this respect. They all have in common, however, that they are specialized in certain service areas even though these differ from type to type and even though such specialization remains relatively narrow.

Thus functional nodal centers have strong complexes of corporate activities especially because of their strength in the CAO&A sector (central offices of corporations). Government places are strong providers of public sector services. Education centers are strong centers of nonprofit activity. As we show in Chapter 9 the three types of centers are all strong centers of higher education and research—a phenomenon which the data presented thus far are ill equipped to measure.

The *consumer oriented centers* include residential and resort-retirement SMSAs. Here the common thread is the provision of services to individuals. What must be recognized, however, is that consumer orientation of these places has brought about the development of an infrastructure of amenities which appears to have been conducive to the growth of an export base of business and financial services in at least some of the largest centers.

Finally, the *production centers* (manufacturing, industrial-military, and mining-industrial) are essentially goods oriented in export base terms, and are weak centers for services other than those serving local populations.

Distribution of SMSAs Among Regions

The regions which together make up the U.S. economy differ sharply in terms of both resource endowment and economic developmental experience. Accordingly, we may expect to find differences in numbers, types, and sizes of metropolitan economies located within those regions.

In Table 4.4 all large and medium size SMSAs are classified by size and type, and distributed among the eight Department of Commerce regions and the two broad geographical classifications, "Snowbelt" and "Sunbelt."

The tallies of SMSAs within this cross-classification demonstrate strikingly how differently specialized the urban systems of the various regions are, particularly when the regions are arranged collectively as "Snowbelt" and "Sunbelt."

The major differences between the two areas would appear to find their origin in their very different history of economic development. The Snowbelt includes the old manufacturing areas of the Mideast, Great Lakes and New England regions, developed during the period of industrialization, as well as the long estab-

Table 4.4   140 Largest SMSAs by Type, Size and Region, 1976

		Snowbelt				
	Size	New England	Mid-East	Great Lakes	Plains	Total "Snow-belt"
Diversified Service Centers						
National Nodal	1	-	1	1	-	2
Regional Nodal	1,2	1	2	4	3	10
Subregional Nodal	3,4	-	1	-	2	3
Specialized Service Centers						
Functional Nodal	1,2	1	2	2	-	5
	3,4	1	6	6	1	14
Government-Education	1	-	1	-	-	1
	3,4	-	4	2	-	6
Education-Manufacturing	3,4	2	0	2	-	4
Consumer-Oriented Centers						
Residential	1,2	-	1	-	-	1
	4	-	1	-	-	1
Resort-Retirement	2	-	-	-	-	0
	3,4	-	-	-	-	0
Production Centers						
Manufacturing	2	-	1	-	-	1
	3,4	3	6	10	-	19
Industrial-Military	2	-	-	-	-	0
	3,4	-	-	-	-	0
Mining-Industrial	4	-	1	-	1	2
Total	1,2	2	8	7	3	20
	3,4	6	19	20	4	49
	Total	8	27	27	7	69

Source: U.S. Bureau of the Census, Current Population Reports, Series P-25.

| | Sunbelt | | | | |
Southeast	Southwest	Rocky Mountain	Far West	Total "Sunbelt"	Total U. S.
-	-	-	2	2	4
3	3	1	2	9	19
10	1	1	1	13	16
-	-	-	1	1	6
3	1	-	-	4	18
-	-	-	-	-	1
3	1	-	4	8	14
-	-	-	1	1	5
-	-	-	1	1	2
-	-	-	0	0	1
1	-	-	1	2	2
3	1	0	3	7	7
-	-	-	-	-	-
4	1	-	-	5	14
-	-	-	1	1	1
7	2	1	2	12	12
2	2	0	1	5	7
4	3	1	8	16	36
32	9	2	12	55	104
36	12	3	20	71	140

lished agricultural areas of the Plains region. The Sunbelt comprises largely states which were traditionally agricultural and which have enjoyed their most rapid development during the postwar years under the multiple influence of expanding government space and military programs, location of manufacturing plants under a new set of criteria that no longer require metropolitan sites or the skilled and unionized labor of the old industrialized centers, and an increasing importance of resort and retirement activities as an export base for selected metropolitan economies. Thus we find that 19 of the 24 functional nodal places and 20 of the 25 manufacturing places are located in the Snowbelt states, but none of the 13 industrial-military or 9 resort-retirement places.

The contrast in type of place composition includes also a significant difference in the number of subregional nodal places: 3 in the Snowbelt states compared to 13 in the Sunbelt. The explanation of this difference is found principally in the roles played by these smaller nodal places in different areas. Agricultural and widely diffused industrial or resource exploiting activities seem to require distributive, producer, and selected consumer services from medium size and small nodal places located in reasonable proximity. On the other hand, many among the manufacturing oriented metropolitan economies that developed during the era of industrialization appear to be structured to supply substantial shares of their own requirements of such central place type services. These places now have significant corporate complexes of sufficient importance to be classified as functional nodal places.

Evidence of the validity of this explanation is found in specific regions of both the Snowbelt and Sunbelt. In the Plains region, which is largely agricultural, five of the seven SMSAs are nodal; and in the Southeast, where agriculture is of considerable importance and manufacturing has tended to be located in small towns and rural areas, there are thirteen nodal SMSAs, ten of which are subregional.[5]

Thus we find that Snowbelt and Sunbelt areas of the economy differ sharply in their type of place composition. To the extent that these types of places have their own characteristic patterns of growth and change such a difference between the two areas in terms of SMSA composition provides a basis for a better understanding of what has been going on as regards growth and development and what is likely to take place in the years ahead.

Growth and Transformation by Type of Place

GROWTH

Taken as a whole, the growth performance of Snowbelt and Sunbelt SMSAs during the period 1959 to 1976 differed sharply (Table 4.5). Among the 69 Snowbelt SMSAs, only 7 ranked within the top two growth quintiles; among the 71 Sunbelt places, 49. Where comparisons could be made among SMSAs of the same type and size—among nodal and government-education—the Snowbelt places tended to grow more slowly, although there were exceptions. Comparisons for the functional nodal, manufacturing, education-manufacturing, mining-industrial and residential groups are inconclusive, however, because the number of places in the Snowbelt and the Sunbelt differs widely or is too small for comparison. Comparisons for resort-retirement and industrial-military groups are, of course, impossible since there are no Snowbelt SMSAs so classified.

Clearly, a major factor contributing to growth disparities between the two regions is that the Snowbelt is heavily loaded with places—especially manufacturing and functional nodal—which are structurally committed to older types of manufacturing that are stable or declining.

In any event, analysis of growth is but a preliminary step in determining what kind of developmental processes have been at work and what kinds of adjustments are likely to evolve. We need to examine also the extent to which metropolitan economies have been transforming—the degree to which patterns of development differ.

EVIDENCE OF TRANSFORMATION

The distinction between growth and development is an important one. Strictly speaking, growth is a scalar concept: an organization or system becomes bigger without changing disproportionately any of its constituent elements. Development involves change: the organization or system changes the way it functions or the proportion of resources utilized. In practice, of course, growth does not take place without some developmental change—frequently with very substantial developmental change. In economic systems this is particularly true. Both the mix of outputs and of inputs change. On the output side, tastes change and new products and services are introduced. On the input side, factor substitution occurs with change in prices of inputs and in technologies.

But there is still more that must be noted. Change may occur in economic systems with little or no growth or even with decline. Systems may adapt to altered circumstances by sloughing off certain activities and adding others or, when overall growth is occurring, by experiencing different rates of growth in certain sectors with the result that the most favored sectors become increasingly important, the least favored sectors increasingly less so.

An approach to development that recognizes differential changes is of special interest here for it best describes the kind of adjustments at work in connection with the larger transformation of the economy toward a greater role of services that was discussed in Chapter 2. Accordingly, we seek to measure the extent of "transformation" in metropolitan economies and to observe the kinds of shift that are occurring in periods when gains or losses are occurring in the relative importance of certain industrial groups.

Our first measure of extent of transformation is a simple one, based once again on the employment data for individual SMSAs in 1959 and 1976. We simply subtract the share of employment in each industry group in a given SMSA in 1959 from the share in that industry in 1976 and sum separately all increases and all decreases in shares. These sums will be equal, of course, but of opposite signs. Without signs they are taken as a single estimate of the extent of transfor-

Table 4.5 140 Largest SMSAs by Type, Size and Quintile of Growth, 1959-1976

			Snowbelt				
	Size	Total	I (highest)	II	III	IV	V (lowest)
Diversified Service Centers							
National Nodal	1	2	-	-	-	-	2
Regional Nodal	1,2	10	-	-	3	2	5
Subregional Nodal	3,4	3	-	-	2	1	-
Specialized Service Centers							
Functional Nodal	1,2	5	-	-	-	3	2
	3,4	14	-	1	3	7	3
Government-Education	1	1	-	1	-	-	-
	3,4	6	-	2	-	2	2
Education-Manufacturing	3,4	4	1	-	-	-	3
Consumer-Oriented Centers							
Residential	1,2	1	-	1	-	-	-
	4	1	1	-	-	-	-
Resort-Retirement	2	0	-	-	-	-	-
	3,4	0	-	-	-	-	-
Production Centers							
Manufacturing	1,2	1	-	-	-	-	1
	3,4	19	-	-	5	6	8
Industrial-Military	2	0	-	-	-	-	-
	3,4	0	-	-	-	-	-
Mining-Industrial	4	2	-	-	-	1	1
Total	1,2	20	-	2	3	5	10
	3,4	49	2	3	10	17	17
	Total	69	2	5	13	22	27

Note: SMSAs were arranged by rate of growth during the 1959-1976 period and assigned quintile ranks. The table indicates the number of SMSAs in each type-size category with growth quintiles shown at the top of each column.

| | Sunbelt | | | | | |
Total	I (highest)	II	III	IV	V (lowest)	Total U. S.
2	-	-	1	1	-	4
9	6	1	2	-	-	19
13	1	8	1	3	-	16
1	1	-	-	-	-	6
4	-	1	3	-	-	18
0	-	-	-	-	-	1
8	5	2	1	-	-	14
1	-	-	1	-	-	5
1	1	-	-	-	-	2
0	-	-	-	-	-	1
2	1	1	-	-	-	2
7	5	2	-	-	-	7
0	-	-	-	-	-	1
5	1	-	2	2	-	24
1	-	1	-	-	-	1
12	4	6	2	-	-	12
5	1	1	2	-	1	7
16	9	3	3	1	-	36
55	17	20	12	5	1	104
71	26	23	15	6	1	140

Source: County Business Patterns, 1959 and 1976.

mation (i.e., an *index of transformation*) and may be computed without regard to growth or decline. The computation is illustrated below:

	Portstown SMSA			
	1959	*1976*	*Change*	
Industry	*(%)*	*(%)*	+	−
A	25	30	5	
B	25	27	2	
C	35	33		2
D	15	10		5
	100	100	+7	−7

Table 4.6 presents measures of growth and transformation for each type of SMSA in matrix form. The procedure followed was to array separately 1959–1976 growth rates and 1959–1976 transformation indexes for the 140 large and middle size SMSAs and to establish quintiles of each of these arrays. SMSAs falling in the top two quintiles of an array were labeled H (high); in the third quintile, M (medium); and in the lower ranking two quintiles, L (low). Thus each SMSA was assigned a double ranking with the use of symbols H, M, L. For example, New York, which ranked in the fourth quintile for growth and in the second quintile for transformation, was assigned the rating L, H and is shown in the matrix for national nodal places as one of the two SMSAs counted in the lower left hand box.

The ranges of growth rates and transformation indexes that are represented by the symbols H, M, L are also presented in Table 4.6. They indicate clearly how varied has been the growth and transformation experience among SMSAs. Slow growth rates (L) ranged from -4.0 to 51.0 percent; high rates (H) from 74.3 to 102.9 percent. Slow transformation (L) from 2.9 to 11.0 percent; high transformation (H) from 13.2 to 23.9 percent.

It is clear from the evidence in Table 4.6 that to look at growth rates alone is to view change one-dimensionally. About two-thirds of the slow growing places have been undergoing very considerable alteration in industrial composition involving, as we shall see below, significant reductions in manufacturing employment in most instances, alongside gains in various private and public sector services. Such changes are likely to involve wrenching adjustments with loss of jobs and of job opportunities for some and gains for others. Moreover, the matrix for all SMSAs tells us that there have been major shifts even with many rapidly growing places, although we may expect a growth environment to cushion the shock of such change.

Table 4.6 shows us where some of the major transformations are taking place: (a) in two of the slow growing national nodal centers (actually the two Snowbelt giants, New York and Chicago); (b) in six of the slow growing (all Snowbelt) and one of the moderate growth (Sunbelt) regional nodal places; (c) in nine of the slow growth (all Snowbelt) and four of the moderate growth (two Snowbelt and two Sunbelt) functional nodal places as well as in one of the high growth functional nodal centers (Snowbelt); and (d) in 12 of the slow growth (all Snowbelt) and 2 of the moderate growth (both Snowbelt) manufacturing places as well as in the single high growth manufacturing SMSA (Sunbelt).

There were also a few instances of rapid transformation among high growth places, principally among resort-retirement, government, and residential SMSAs and occurring almost entirely in the Sunbelt. These may be regarded as very significant transformations since under high *average* growth conditions those industrial categories which increase their shares sharply must grow very fast indeed.

In gaining a new perspective on economic change by examining growth and transformation measures jointly, we also raise new questions. Which industries are gaining and which industries losing when transformation occurs? Is the metropolitan economy rebuilding itself in such a way that it will function more competitively in the years ahead or is it experiencing transformation by default, with low productivity, often local sector type activities taking over as previously strong and productive industries are eliminated by the national and international competitive struggle? Finally, what is occurring in the low transformation, high growth places? Has sustained growth on all fronts placed the metropolitan economy in a position where adjustment must now take place and growth decline as some sectors attain a scale where expansion is no longer required?

Patterns of Employment Change

In the present section we examine patterns of employment change among the various types of SMSAs by making use of three different analyses. The first examines rates of change in employment in major industry groups. The second examines the importance of growth in these industries by measuring shares of total job increase accounted for by each. The third takes a quite different tack, looking for linkages among industrial categories as employment change occurs. In this last analysis it is correlation among growth rates of employment in the several industries that is measured.

RATES OF CHANGE IN EMPLOYMENT

Transformation in the industrial composition of a metropolitan economy occurs when the various industries grow (and/or decline) at different rates. Table 4.7 reveals clearly that both periods were characterized by sharp differentials among industries, differentials which reflect, in part, the national trends discussed in Chapter 2. These differentials are noted not only among average rates of change of industries for the 140 SMSAs taken as a whole, but with few exceptions among average rates for each of the various types of SMSAs as well.

If the averages of industry rates of change within each type of places are ranked, analysis is facilitated. There is a strong similarity in rankings of industrial employment growth rates among types of SMSAs and a tendency for rankings to change little for most industries from the first to the second periods in

Table 4.6 Cross-Tabulation of Measures of Growth and Transformation by Type of SMSA, 1959-1976

| | Growth | Transformation | | |
		H	M	L
Diversified Service Centers				
National Nodal	H	-	-	-
(4)[a]	M	-	-	1
	L	2	-	1
Regional Nodal	H	-	2	5
(19)	M	1	3	1
	L	6	-	1
Subregional Nodal	H	-	1	8
(16)	M	-	2	1
	L	1	2	1
Specialized Service Centers				
Functional Nodal	H	1	-	2
(24)	M	4	2	-
	L	9	5	1
Government-Education	H	2	3	5
(15)	M	-	-	1
	L	3	-	1
Education-Manufacturing	H	-	-	1
(5)	M	-	1	-
	L	3	-	-

Note: SMSAs have been assigned quintile rankings for both growth and transformation (see text) and cross-classified. "H" indicates top two quintiles; "M", middle quintile; "L", bottom two quintiles in both growth and transformation arrays. Each cell specifies the number of SMSAs in specific type group with characteristics of growth and transformation indicated by row and column heads. Ranges for growth are as follows: "H" includes places with 1959-1976 rates of growth from 74.3 percent to 102.9 percent; "M" from

	Growth	Transformation		
		H	M	L
Consumer-Oriented Centers				
<u>Residential</u>	H	2	-	1
(3)	M	-	-	-
	L	-	-	-
Resort-Retirement	H	4	1	4
(9)	M	-	-	-
	L	-	-	-
Production Centers				
<u>Manufacturing</u>	H	1	-	-
(25)	M	2	-	5
	L	12	1	4
Industrial-Military	H	1	2	8
(13)	M	1	-	1
	L	-	-	-
Mining-Industrial	H	-	2	-
(7)	M	-	-	2
	L	1	1	1
<u>Total</u>	H	11	11	34 (56)
(140)	M	8	8	12 (28)
	L	37	9	10 (56)
		(56)	(28)	(56)

51.9 percent to 73.9 percent; "L" from -4.0 percent to 51.0 percent. Ranges for transformation are as follows: "H" includes places with 1959-1976 shift in share ranging from 13.2 percent to 23.9 percent; "M" from 11.1 percent to 13.1 percent; "L" from 2.9 percent to 11.0 percent.

[a]Number of SMSAs in each type group.

Source: <u>County Business Patterns</u>, 1959 and 1976.

spite of the general decline in rates of growth. Average rankings (7 types of SMSAs shown in Table 4.7) for the two periods were as follows:

	1959-69	*1969-76*
Manufacturing	8.4	10.0
TCU	8.1	8.6
Wholesale	9.0	7.1
CAO	1.9	2.7
FIRE	5.3	4.1
Corporate Services	2.1	1.1
Retailing	6.3	5.5
Mainly Consumer Services	7.4	7.9
Nonprofit Services	2.1	3.0
Government	4.4	5.3

Nevertheless, there were certain changes among industries in terms of relative growth performance and in rankings that deserve mention. Manufacturing growth rates fell more sharply than average employment growth rates everywhere, and for the national regional nodal, functional nodal, and manufacturing SMSA groups there were actual declines in manufacturing employment during the second period. On the other hand, wholesaling, FIRE, corporate services, and retailing employment growth rates showed relative improvement in almost every comparison (i.e., rankings were nearer the top of this list) and in a number of cases (principally in FIRE and retailing) showed increases in actual rates of employment growth (indicated by asterisks in Table 4.7) from the sixties to the seventies.

But the above in no way contradicts an important second observation: different types of SMSA grew at very different rates and in very different ways. The evidence is only partially visible in Table 4.7: although we can determine growth rates from the data shown we can not determine just how important employment increases in a given industry were in contributing to the overall growth process or the extent to which differential rates of growth (or decline) were bringing about a transformation of the metropolitan economies concerned. What is missing, of course, is information regarding the relative importance of each industry group within a given type of place against which the rate of employment change is applied. Clearly a given rate of employment increase in FIRE in national and regional nodal places, which are characterized by very large finance sectors, would be expected to make a more important contribution to the overall growth process than a similar rate of increase in FIRE in manufacturing places, which typically have relatively small finance sectors.

SHARES OF JOB INCREASE

Table 4.8 illustrates this point by displaying for the nation and for each of the various types of place the average share of job increases accounted for by each major industrial category. In interpreting these data it must be recognized that they deal with job increases alone (not job decreases) and in each instance reflect the combined influence of the rate of job increase in the given industry and the relative size of the given industry group at the beginning of the period.

The data shed light on which industries are making the most significant contributions to job expansion both in the economy as a whole and in the various types of SMSAs. We observe immediately that the largest contributions to employment expansion in the economy have been in the public sector (28.1 percent), health services (13.1 percent), and the complex of corporate activities (27.1 percent). Retailing was also a major contributor (20.1 percent), but mainly consumer services accounted for only 3.1 percent. The distributive services were much less important, accounting for less than 7.0 percent of all job increases. The combined nonservice groups (largely manufacturing) showed a net decline in employment.

When we compare shares of job increases *among* types of places it is clear that there have been significant differences in patterns of employment change. In terms of major groups of cities, nodal centers continued to make advances in FIRE, corporate services and education. In addition, the largest among them (national and regional nodal centers) further strengthened their position in terms of CAO&A and health, while the subregional nodal gained an above average share of TCU and wholesale employment.

Most specialized service centers did well in terms of corporate services, health and education,[6] and government. Functional nodal centers, it should be noted, performed well not only in the corporate service area but in the entire range of sectors of the complex of corporate activities—with well over one-third of total job increases accounted by this major sector—and in wholesaling as well.

In terms of consumer-oriented and production centers, the overwhelming tendency was for above average shares of job increases in the retailing and mostly consumer service sectors accompanied by very limited diversification into other service areas with the exception of wholesaling. Only in the case of the three residential centers was there consistent indications of a building of strength in distributive services, activities of the corporate complex and the nonprofit sector. A final observation about consumer-oriented and production centers: with the exception of the manufacturing centers, most—along with the size 5 SMSAs and nonmetropolitan areas of the country—were adding jobs, mostly manufacturing jobs, in the nonservice sector during both periods.

CORRELATIONS IN EMPLOYMENT CHANGE AMONG INDUSTRIES

There is still another way to analyze the employment data in order to shed light on the nature of growth and development. In this approach we correlate, within major groups of SMSAs, rates of employment change in each given industry with rates of employment change in each of the other industries.[7] The end result of the analysis is the preparation of a matrix of correlation coefficients by type of SMSA (Table 4.9).

This use of simple correlation analysis provides evidence for most of the categories of SMSAs as to how consistently employment change in each industry is associated with employment change in each of the other industries.[8] The correla-

Table 4.7 Average Annual Rates of Employment Change in Major
Industry Groupings (with industry rank shown in
parentheses) by Type of SMSA, 1959-1969 and 1969-
1976

	All Ind	Mfg	TCU	Whl
	(%) (normalized against all ind. average)			

1959-1969

Diversified Service Centers				
National/Regional	3.68	.67 (9)	.78 (8)	.65(10)
Subregional	3.32	.79 (8)	.94 (6)	.67 (9)
Specialized Service Centers				
Functional Nodal	3.20	.55 (10)	.83 (9)	.89 (8)
Government-Education	4.21	.69 (10)	.84 (8)	.77 (9)
Consumer-Oriented Centers				
Resid.-Resort-Retir.	6.58	1.13 (4)	.87(10)	.89 (9)
Production Centers				
Manufacturing	2.73	.53 (10)	.68 (9)	.98 (8)
Industrial-Military	4.41	.94 (7)	.94 (6)	.69(10)
140 Largest SMSAs	3.66	.72 (10)	.84 (8)	.78 (9)

1969-1976

Diversified Service Centers				
National/Regional	1.83	(-1.71)[b](10)	.52 (9)	.86 (8)
Subregional	3.20	.13 (10)	.83 (7)	.78*(8)
Specialized Service Centers				
Functional Nodal	1.32	(-1.82) (10)	.05 (9)	1.87 (6)
Government-Education	3.31	.27 (10)	.33 (.9)	.89 (7)
Consumer-Oriented Centers				
Resid.-Resort-Retir.	5.03	.31 (10)	.79 (9)	.95 (8)
Production Centers				
Manufacturing	1.28	(-1.02) (10)	.38 (9)	1.25 (7)
Industrial-Military	3.77	.62 (10)	.72 (8)	1.05*(6)
140 Largest SMSAs	2.37	(-0.50) (10)	.56 (9)	1.08 (7)

Note: Actual average annual rates of change (in %) are shown
for all industry combined. Rates of change for major
industries are normalized against the all industry
rates of change for each type of SMSA. Industry ranks
are shown in parentheses. Rates are not computed for
mining places (group is too small). National and
regional nodal places are combined in one group, as are
residential and resort-retirement places.

CAO&A	FIRE	CS	Ret	MCS	NP	Gov

2.74 (1)1.05 (5) 2.01 (3) .95 (6) .82 (7) 2.14 (2) 1.23 (4)
2.17 (2)1.03 (5) 2.44 (1) .87 (7) .66 (10) 1.91 (3) 1.22 (4)

2.85 (1)1.04 (7) 2.14 (3) 1.05 (6) 1.06 (5) 2.27 (2) 1.48 (4)
1.12 (6)1.18 (3) 2.02 (1) 1.03 (5) .87 (7) 2.00 (2) 1.10 (4)

2.49 (1)1.11 (5) 1.56 (3) .95 (7) .90 (8) 1.68 (2) 1.11 (5)

4.71 (1)1.08 (7) 2.14 (3) 1.18 (5) 1.09 (6) 2.54 (2) 1.53 (4)
1.41 (3)1.15 (4) 2.05 (1) .89 (8) .86 (9) 1.89 (2) 1.15 (5)

2.49 (1)1.09 (5) 2.07 (2)^a .99 (6) .91 (7) 2.07 (2)^{a}1.28 (4)

2.36 (3)1.93 (4) 3.05 (1) 1.37 (6) .88 (7) 2.80 (2) 1.77 (5)
1.56 (3)1.33*(4) 2.42 (1) 1.15*(6) .69 (9) 2.03*(2) 1.18 (5)

4.53 (1)3.16*(4) 4.36 (2) 1.80 (7) .86 (8) 4.10ʹ(3) 2.35 (5)
2.21*(2)1.39 (4) 2.24 (1) 1.39 (4) .42 (8) 1.90 (3) 1.23 (6)

1.87 (2)1.52*(4) 1.97 (1) 1.31*(5) 1.05 (6) 1.60 (3) 1.02 (7)

1.56 (6)2.05 (4) 4.44 (1) 1.91 (5) .98 (8) 4.08 (2) 2.40 (3)
2.57*(1)1.31 (4) 2.13 (2) 1.30*(5) .70 (9) 1.70 (3) .82 (7)

2.40 (3)1.75*(4) 2.78 (1) 1.39 (6) .77 (8) 2.44 (2) 1.51 (5)

Column heads: Same as Table 2.2.
*Actual annual average rate of change was higher in 1969-76
 than in 1959-69.
^{a}CS and NP rank equally during the 1959-69 period.
^{b}Negative rates are not normalized and are shown in
 parentheses.
Source: County Business Patterns, 1976, 1969 and 1959; Employ-
        ment and Earnings in State and Local Areas, 1976, 1969
        and 1959.

Table 4.8 Shares of Job Increases in the Nonservice and Service Industries by Type of SMSA, 1969-1976 and 1959-1969

	Non Serv	TCU	Whl	CAO&A	FIRE	CS
Diversified Service Centers						
National/Regional	JD	2.6	4.0	6.3	10.8	18.1
	(19.6)	(5.7)	(4.6)	(6.8)	(6.6)	(10.4)
Subregional	7.0	5.8	5.8	3.2	9.2	15.0
	(21.1)	(6.0)	(5.4)	(3.7)	(6.9)	(10.6)
Specialized Service Centers						
Functional Nodal	JD	0.5	6.6	9.7	10.5	14.8
	(25.3)	(3.8)	(4.4)	(8.0)	(4.3)	(7.8)
Government-Education	JD	1.4	4.6	2.3	7.1	14.0
	(15.7)	(3.5)	(3.9)	(1.8)	(5.7)	(9.1)
Education-Manufacturing	JD	JD	2.5	2.4	6.4	14.0
	(14.0)	(3.9)	(3.4)	(3.7)	(5.1)	(9.2)
Consumer-Oriented Centers						
Residential	4.6	3.2	8.7	3.3	9.8	13.8
	(25.9)	(2.9)	(5.3)	(3.3)	(5.1)	(6.8)
Resort-Retirement	6.0	4.3	3.7	1.9	8.0	10.7
	(18.7)	(4.9)	(4.1)	(1.4)	(5.9)	(7.6)
Production Centers						
Manufacturing	JD	3.7	5.7	1.3	5.4	13.8
	(31.2)	(2.8)	(3.8)	(4.6)	(3.8)	(6.4)
Industrial-Military	16.4	2.3	4.4	1.4	5.4	9.1
	(19.8)	(4.2)	(3.0)	(1.5)	(4.6)	(7.6)
Mining-Industrial	5.6	3.1	5.9	3.8	6.6	10.9
	(18.1)	(4.8)	(3.1)	(0.2)	(4.8)	(8.5)
Size 5 SMSAs and Non-metropolitan Areas						
	13.0	2.7	6.3	0.8	4.8	8.7
	(29.6)	(2.1)	(2.7)	(1.8)	(3.9)	(5.9)
United States	JD	1.9	5.0	3.8	8.6	14.7
	(21.8)	(4.2)	(3.8)	(5.0)	(5.4)	(8.7)

Note: First line shows share for 1969-76 period; second line, share (in parentheses) for 1959-69 period. "JD" indicates Job Decrease. Each line adds to 100 percent.

Source: County Business Patterns, 1976, 1969 and 1959; Employment and Earnings in State and Local Areas, 1976, 1969 and 1959.

Ret	MCS	Hlt	Educ	Gov	rates of change JI	JD	NET
16.1	3.2	13.9	2.0	22.8	15.7	-3.4	12.3
(14.5)	(4.0)	(7.1)	(2.6)	(18.0)	(41.1)	(--)	(41.1)
18.1	3.3	9.8	1.4	21.4	25.3	--	25.3
(13.7)	(3.4)	(6.8)	(2.0)	(20.4)	(42.2)	(--)	(42.2)
17.7	1.8	14.7	1.4	22.5	13.8	-4.5	9.3
(15.0)	(3.8)	(7.2)	(2.5)	(18.0)	(35.7)	(--)	(35.7)
18.1	1.5	10.0	1.1	39.3	23.5	-3.9	19.6
(15.0)	(4.1)	(6.0)	(3.2)	(32.0)	(46.4)	(--)	(46.4)
23.9	JD	19.0	1.9	29.8	10.7	-6.1	4.6
(18.0)	(4.3)	(8.6)	(5.0)	(24.4)	(34.0)	(--)	(34.0)
19.5	3.7	11.9	2.1	19.4	29.4	--	29.4
(19.1)	(5.3)	(5.7)	(1.8)	(18.9)	(99.0)	(--)	(99.0)
26.5	11.4	8.5	0.6	18.5	41.2	--	41.2
(19.4)	(9.5)	(6.3)	(1.7)	(20.2)	(72.0)	(--)	(72.0)
21.9	2.2	16.0	1.6	28.4	12.1	-1.1	11.0
(16.5)	(3.4)	(8.1)	(2.2)	(16.9)	(32.8)	(--)	(32.8)
23.3	3.3	8.8	0.9	24.7	27.6	--	27.6
(14.9)	(4.8)	(5.4)	(1.8)	(31.1)	(51.8)	(--)	(51.8)
23.7	4.0	9.2	0.2	27.0	24.0	--	24.0
(16.2)	(4.3)	(8.9)	(1.5)	(29.1)	(31.5)	(--)	(31.5)
20.1	3.1	10.5	0.5	29.5	19.0	--	19.0
(14.9)	(4.1)	(7.3)	(2.0)	(25.8)	(46.4)	(--)	(46.4)
20.1	3.1	13.1	1.4	28.1	15.1	-1.3	13.8
(14.9)	(4.1)	(7.2)	(2.5)	(22.2)	(37.1)	(--)	(37.1)

Column heads: Same as Table 2.2. Nonprofit is broken down
between health (Hlt) and education (Educ).
The nonservice grouping (Non Serv) includes
employment in agriculture, extractive and
transformative industries (see Table 1.1).

Table 4.9 Coefficients of Correlation among Rates of Employment Change in Major Industry Groupings for Major Types of SMSA, 1969-1976

DIVERSIFIED SERVICE CENTERS
National Nodal and Regional Nodal (23 Places)

TCU	Whl	CAO	FIRE	CS	Ret	MCS	Hlth	Educ	Gov	
.75	.60	-	.74	.63	.67	.50	.36*	-	.68	Mfg
	.70	.51	.84	.81	.82	.81	.49	-	.60	TCU
		.79	.80	.87	.91	.85	.45	-	.83	Whl
			.72	.70	.71	.81	.47	-	.60	CAO
				.82	.83	.83	.67	-	.76	FIRE
					.92	.88	.51	-	.77	CS
						.89	.50	-	.76	Ret
							.55	-	.67	MCS
								-	.53	Hlth
									-	Educ

Subregional Nodal (16 Places)

TCU	Whl	CAO	FIRE	CS	Ret	MCS	Hlth	Educ	Gov	
-	.82	-	-	.52	.66	-	-	-	-	Mfg
	-	-	-	-	-	-	-	-	-	TCU
		.40*	-	.54	.64	.55	-	-	-	Whl
			-	.48	.41*	-	-	-	-	CAO
				-	-	-	-	-	-	FIRE
					.62	.44*	-	-	-	CS
						-	-	-	-	Ret
							-	-	-	MCS
								-	.46*	Hlth
									-	Educ

SPECIALIZED SERVICE CENTERS

Functional Nodal (24 Places)

	TCU	Whl	CAO	FIRE	CS	Ret	MCS	Hlth	Educ	Gov	
	-	.34*	-	-	.86	.76	.53	-	.42	-	Mfg
		.71	-	.44	-	-	-	-	.46	-	TCU
			-	.52	.37*	.60	-	-	.54	-	Whl
				-	-	-	-	-	-	-	CAO
					-	.41	.44	-	.35*	-	FIRE
						.75	.44	-	-	-	CS
							.61	-	.35*	-	Ret
								.39	-	-	MCS
									-	-	Hlth
										-	Educ

Government-Education (15 Places)

	TCU	Whl	CAO	FIRE	CS	Ret	MCS	Hlth	Educ	Gov	
	.52	.52	.52	.76	.48*	.79	.69	.53	-	-	Mfg
		.46	.54	.32	.25	.67	.51	.71	-	.60	TCU
			.41	-	.47*	.74	.66	. -	-	.40*	Whl
				-	-	.57	-	.63	-	-	CAO
					.53	.69	.78	-	-	-	FIRE
						.65	.59	.41*	.51	-	CS
							.75	.59	-	.52	Ret
								-	-	.42*	MCS
									-	-	Hlth
										-	Educ

(continued on next page)

Table 4.9 (continued)

PRODUCTION CENTERS
Manufacturing (25 Places)

TCU	Whl	CAO	FIRE	CS	Ret	MCS	Hlth	Educ	Gov	
-	.65	-	.43	-	.53	.37*	-	-	-	Mfg
	-	-	-	-	-	-	-	-	-	TCU
		-	-	-	-	.55	-	-	.37*	Whl
			-	-	-	-	-	-	-	CAO
				.25	.48	-	-	-	.32*	FIRE
					.24	-	-	.40*	-	CS
						-	-	-	.43	Ret
							-	-	-	MCS
								-	-	Hlth
									-	Educ

Industrial-Military (13 Places)

TCU	Whl	CAO	FIRE	CS	Ret	MCS	Hlth	Educ	Gov	
-	-	-	-	-	.49*	-	-	-	-	Mfg
	-	-	.46*	.50*	-	-	-	-	-	TCU
		-	.67	.48*	-	-	-	-	-	Whl
			-	-	-	-	.68	-	-	CAO
				.66	-	.64	-	-	-	FIRE
					-	.54	-	-	.66	CS
						-	-	-	-	Ret
							-	-	-	MCS
								-	-	Hlth
									-	Educ

Residential and Resort-Retirement (12 Places)

TCU	Whl	CAO	FIRE	CS	Ret	MCS	Hlth	Educ	Gov	
-	-	-	-	-	.68	-	-	-	-	Mfg
	-	-	-	.64	-	.61	.59	-	.73	TCU
		-	-	.47*	-	-	.49*	-	-	Whl
			-	-	-	-	-	-	-	CAO
				.60	.65	-	-	-	.62	FIRE
					-	-	.65	-	.78	CS
						-	-	-	-	Ret
							-	-	-	MCS
								-	-	Hlth
									-	Educ

Note: Only coefficients of correlation of .20 or more with a
        statistical reliability of .90 or better are shown.
        Where reliability is between .90 and .95 the coeffi-
        cient value is identified with an asterisk. There are
        11 industry groups resulting in a total of 55 correla-
        tion coefficients in each matrix. National nodal and
        regional nodal SMSAs are combined, as are residential
        and resort-retirement places. Education-manufacturing
        and mining-industrial places are omitted. They are too
        dissimilar from other groups to be combined and too
        small a group for separate analysis.

Column and row heads: Same as Table 2.2.   Nonprofit is broken
                        down between health and education.

Source: County Business Patterns, 1976 and 1969; Employment
          and Earnings in State and Local Areas, 1976 and 1969.

tion coefficient, itself, does not measure the strength of the relationship (e.g., whether or not a one percent change in "x" is associated with, say, one percent change in "y"). Essentially, what the matrix of correlation coefficients provides is *prima facie* evidence as to whether of not there are linkages among industries that are generalized throughout a given group of SMSAs. Thus, the correlation coefficient measure will be high where employment in two industries increase or decline together in more or less the same way in most of the SMSAs within a given group. Where several industries are linked by relatively high correlations we find evidence that there exists a more elaborate set of linkages, indicating an underlying complex of functional relationships whether of not there are linkages among industries that are generalized throughout a given group of SMSAs. Thus, the correlation coefficient measure will be high where employment in two industries increase or decline together in more or less the same way in most of the SMSAs within a given group. Where several industries are linked by relatively high correlations we find evidence that there exists a more elaborate set of linkages, indicating an underlying complex of functional relationships.

We must recognize, of course, that such linkages do not, in themselves, spark growth, although their presence does suggest what the pattern of growth may look like if forces of growth are strengthened. Nor do the correlation coefficients tell us anything about the reason for these linkages. Manufacturing (typically an export-base category) is likely to be linked with retailing largely through an income multiplier relationship. Corporate services may be linked with CAO&A and with FIRE as a result of a corporate complex interaction. Wholesaling may be linked with manufacturing because industrial suppliers sell to manufacturers or because it is linked to retailing as a supplier and retailing is, in turn, linked to manufacturing by this income multiplier relationship—and so on.

Table 4.9 presents seven matrices, each with correlation coefficients for the period 1969–76.[9] Matrices for the 1959–69 are shown separately in Appendix B, but it is important to observe here that during the first period correlations tended to be stronger than during the second. This is shown in Table 4.10.

This tendency for more significant correlations to occur during the first period is probably due largely to the fact that the forces of growth were much stronger then. Where growth is stronger employment in all sectors tends to rise (thereby increasing correlation tendencies) even though underlying technical input-output relationships and other linkages are not necessarily stronger. Although we cannot disentangle the effects of stronger aggregate growth from other factors that increase linkages it seems fair to conclude that in those instances where the number of correlations increase or hold virtually constant during the second period (as was the case in the national nodal/regional nodal and the government-education/ education manufacturing groups) there is evidence of strengthening linkages.

The above tally also permits a general comparison of tendencies toward agglomeration among the broad groups of metropolitan economies. Taken as whole the *nodal* SMSAs show the strongest linkages although there are sharp differences between the national/regional nodal and the subregionals. The *specialized service centers* fall in second place, followed by the *consumer-oriented* and the *production centers*. This comparison provides at least initial evidence of the extent to which the various groups have developed growth and development link-

Table 4.10 **Number of Significant Correlations among Rates of Employment Change in Major Industry Groupings for Major Types of SMSA, 1959-1969 and 1969-1976**

	1959-69	1969-76
Nodal Centers		
National Nodal/Regional Nodal	42, (6)	43, (1)
Subregional Nodal	12, (7)	8, (4)
Specialized Service Centers		
Functional Nodal	44, (1)	16, (4)
Government-Education/Education-Mfg.	23, (3)	34, (6)
Consumer-Oriented Centers		
Residential/Resort-Retirement	26, (5)	10, (2)
Production Centers		
Manufacturing	19, (7)	8, (4)
Industrial-Military	7, (9)	6, (4)

Note: Correlation of .20 or above is considered significant. Numbers not in parentheses indicate correlations significant at .95 or above level of probability; numbers in parentheses, correlation probability between .90 and .95. There is a grand total of 55 correlation coefficients in each matrix.

Source: Table 4.9 and Table B.1.

ages among goods and service (especially service) activities which provide a basis for development in the years ahead.

We shall not attempt to carry out a detailed analysis of the matrices, but two comparisons of some of the largest subgroups are clearly very interesting: the national-regional nodal centers with the subregional nodal centers and the functional nodal centers with the manufacturing places. For the large nodal places (national-regional), we observe high correlations among almost all industries except education. In contrast the linkages among industries for the subregional nodal places are limited, the highest being among wholesaling, manufacturing, corporate services, retailing and mainly consumer services. Our interpretation is that the matrix evidence for the largest nodal places strongly supports Pred's analysis of the way in which the large metropolises of the country have grown by

Table 4.11 Location Quotients of Major Industry Groupings by Type of SMSA, 1976 and 1959

	# of SMSAs	Mfg	Dist Serv	TCU	Whl
Diversified Service Centers					
National/Regional	23	86.9	122.5	124.4	120.9
		(94.7)	(122.3)	(120.3)	(124.2)
Subregional	16	72.3	128.8	123.0	134.0
		(72.5)	(127.4)	(110.0)	(144.1)
Specialized Service Centers					
Functional Nodal	24	128.7	94.7	88.2	109.6
		(135.3)	(88.0)	(87.9)	(88.1)
Government-Education	15	64.0	82.7	79.6	85.4
		(72.2)	(84.6)	(87.0)	(82.2)
Education-Manufacturing	5	117.6	80.8	82.7	79.1
		(133.8)	(79.0)	(83.3)	(74.9)
Consumer-Oriented Centers					
Residential	3	90.7	87.8	75.3	99.1
		(89.9)	(71.3)	(85.0)	(58.1)
Resort-Retirement	9	47.8	95.4	104.9	86.8
		(44.3)	(100.8)	(104.1)	(97.7)
Production Centers					
Manufacturing	25	148.7	89.6	87.0	91.9
		(141.1)	(82.5)	(81.3)	(83.6)
Industrial-Military	12	67.8	79.8	85.2	75.0
		(66.6)	(81.9)	(87.7)	(76.4)
Mining-Industrial	7	57.0	98.6	101.5	96.0
		(68.6)	(97.0)	(99.2)	(95.0)
Size 5 SMSAs and Non-metropolitan Areas					
		113.1	83.4	81.4	85.1
		(92.8)	(84.1)	(87.8)	(80.6)
Share of U.S. Employment in Major Industry Groups					
		22.9	10.4	5.0	5.4
		(31.5)	(12.0)	(5.8)	(6.0)

Column heads: Same as Table 2.2.

Note: First line shows location quotient in 1976; second line (in parentheses), in 1959. Location quotients are unweighted modified averages for major type groups of SMSAs.

Corp Compl	CAO&A	FIRE	CS	Ret	MCS	NP	Gov
125.9	135.1	125.7	122.1	98.0	110.4	104.8	84.0
(119.8)	(109.8)	(123.2)	(119.9)	(99.6)	(113.3)	(105.8)	(84.2)
118.8	86.5	132.9	120.2	99.0	106.5	98.3	100.9
(116.6)	(85.8)	(139.8)	(97.9)	(105.7)	(120.5)	(114.9)	(107.2)
107.9	178.2	91.1	92.6	95.9	83.2	101.9	75.8
(96.8)	(156.8)	(83.5)	(86.5)	(91.6)	(79.3)	(96.6)	(71.7)
95.1	61.6	95.0	109.5	97.2	86.6	99.2	162.3
(93.2)	(87.0)	(91.7)	(98.5)	(97.8)	(95.6)	(100.9)	(176.0)
85.1	60.8	86.9	93.9	104.8	77.6	140.4	99.3
(79.2)	(44.5)	(83.8)	(88.4)	(91.2)	(72.1)	(145.5)	(88.8)
102.9	81.8	101.0	113.6	120.1	109.9	114.5	97.8
(80.8)	(36.4)	(78.8)	(103.5)	(126.3)	(102.2)	(99.7)	(116.0)
98.1	44.8	109.1	111.2	133.9	229.4	98.8	102.2
(93.7)	(24.9)	(101.1)	(114.4)	(126.3)	(198.3)	(99.3)	(126.8)
71.2	61.4	72.6	76.0	99.6	82.3	97.6	75.7
(70.0)	(48.6)	(74.7)	(73.1)	(94.7)	(81.0)	(94.3)	(71.9)
73.1	27.3	78.2	88.9	111.0	112.4	86.1	150.1
(67.7)	(38.1)	(76.3)	(68.9)	(110.2)	(119.2)	(74.5)	(181.5)
81.7	72.9	79.3	87.7	116.3	112.7	98.2	108.9
(86.1)	(124.7)	(75.2)	(83.9)	(117.5)	(117.1)	(118.0)	(104.7)
59.7	36.6	65.4	63.4	105.6	91.1	90.0	118.6
(60.3)	(48.1)	(66.1)	(58.1)	(109.1)	(89.6)	(93.5)	(125.1)
14.7	2.7	5.7	6.3	16.0	4.3	6.5	19.5
(10.2)	(1.6)	(5.0)	(3.6)	(15.2)	(4.5)	(3.5)	(16.2)

Source: County Business Patterns, 1976 and 1959; Employment and Earnings in State and Local Areas, 1976 and 1959.

way of a complex set of feedback loops, becoming over time the prominent centers of a wide variety of distributive, corporate complex, and nonprofit activities. Even their manufacturing sectors, largely the result of earlier development, remain linked to other activities. The national or regional nodal centers are, *par excellence*, complexly interrelated metropolitan economies.

In contrast, the smaller subregional nodal place is less fully developed and is likely to be less similar to its counterparts. As we have shown, the common characteristic of these places is that they are central places whose principal function is to serve their immediate hinterland, and distributive services are relatively well developed. But hinterlands differ: some are agricultural, some industrial, and so on; and there are a number of regionally or subregionally specialized "off-centered" activities in these widely dispersed places. Accordingly, we would expect, and indeed we find, a more restricted set of *common* linkages.

When we turn to the comparison between functional nodal and manufacturing places, the general finding for the functional nodal places is that there are significant linkages among manufacturing, wholesaling, FIRE, corporate services, retailing and mainly consumer services; among manufacturing places, however, there are fewer significant relationships and the coefficients are typically smaller. The principal linkages are among manufacturing, wholesaling, and retailing. Such evidence confirms that manufacturing centers as a group have poorly developed networks among the services.

Comparison of Industrial Composition of Employment, 1976 and 1959

Although the previous analysis has been useful in demonstrating how growth patterns differ, comparison of the industrial composition of employment at the beginning and end of the periods studied provides the most effective means of summarizing the industrial changes in employment that have occurred in metropolitan economies over time.

Tables 4.11 and 4.12 provide a summary picture of the changes that have occurred in the industrial composition of employment in each of the various types of metropolitan economies within the U.S. economy between 1959 and 1976. Average shares of employment in major industrial categories are presented both in terms of percentage (Table 4.11) and in normalized form (i.e., as location quotients, with the share for the U.S. economy in each category in the two years taken as 100) (Table 4.12). In the latter table normalization adjusts for system wide changes in the importance of the various industries and indicates the degree of relative specialization that obtained in each of the two years, at least insofar as specialization can be measured in employment terms.

Before examining the measures it is important to note the magnitude of employment shares within the U.S. economy (at the bottom of the table) against which normalization computations have been made and to observe how these shares have changed over time. Here we are observing the generalized tendencies throughout the system, already noted, for manufacturing, TCU, and wholesaling to have grown more slowly than total employment thereby decreasing the share of employment accounted for by these industrial categories, while the remaining industries have tended to grow more rapidly increasing their shares.[10] It is clear then that cities were being transformed to a considerable extent by these nationwide shifts at the same time that changes were occurring in terms of relative specialization (indicated by changes in location quotients). Indeed, it is clear that if our classification scheme had been based purely on the 1959 data we would not have classified SMSAs in quite the same manner since certain services which have grown rapidly would not have appeared important enough to warrant the emphasis given later.

Nevertheless, the location quotients make clear that, in most instances, tendencies toward specialization observed among various types of SMSAs in 1976 were already stamped upon their economies seventeen years earlier. Thus, the national and regional nodal places, already showed in 1959 very high location quotients of employment in the corporate complex services; government-education places were already heavily specialized in public sector services; education-manufacturing centers were already characterized by high location quotients in manufacturing and the nonprofit services; and the manufacturing centers already showed heavy specialization in manufacturing.

At the same time, these measures indicate significant shift in industrial specialization during the period, among which some of the most interesting were (a) the decline of manufacturing in many of the nodal and specialized service centers and the tendency for the smallest urban places and the nonurban areas of the country to become increasingly specialized in this activity; (b) the tendency for regional nodal places and functional nodal centers to have increased their specialization in activities of the corporate complex and for certain distributive services to have become more widespread, especially wholesaling among functional nodal and TCU and wholesaling among subregional nodal centers; (c) the tendency for many of the production and consumer oriented centers to become somewhat overspecialized in retail and mainly consumer services.

Conclusion

In the previous chapter a review of key urban economic theories and of recent empirical work suggested that investigation should be directed toward analysis of (a) size and economic specialization within the system of cities, (b) the nature of agglomeration in the individual metropolitan economy, (c) the cumulative effect of metropolitan economic development, (d) the ability of places to transform, (e) the locational implications of the rise of the corporate complex, (f) the locational implications of the rise of the nonprofit and public sectors, (g) centripetal and centrifugal tendencies within the system of cities, (h) the changing nature of intermetropolitan linkages.

The present chapter has sought to probe several of these areas, especially the first six, through analysis of employment data for the largest 140 SMSAs. By analyzing location quotients in major industry groupings for the year 1976 we classified all of these SMSAs within a functional type-size scheme. This scheme was then used to examine patterns of growth and transformation for the period 1959–1969 and 1969–1976 and to call attention to evidences of the strength of agglomeration linkages and of the types of linkages that have played key roles in various types of SMSAs.

Table 4.12 Employment Shares of Major Industry Groupings by Type of SMSA, 1976 and 1959

	# of SMSAs	Mfg	Dist Serv	TCU	Whl
Diversified Service Centers					
National/Regional	23	19.9	12.7	6.2	6.5
		(29.8)	(14.7)	(7.0)	(7.5)
Subregional	16	16.6	13.4	6.2	7.2
		(22.8)	(15.3)	(6.4)	(8.6)
Specialized Service Centers					
Functional Nodal	24	29.4	9.8	4.4	5.9
		(42.6)	(10.6)	(5.1)	(5.3)
Government-Education	15	14.7	8.6	4.0	4.6
		(22.7)	(10.2)	(5.0)	(4.9)
Education-Manufacturing	5	26.9	8.4	4.1	4.3
		(42.1)	(9.5)	(4.8)	(4.5)
Consumer-Oriented Centers					
Residential	3	20.8	9.1	3.8	5.4
		(28.3)	(8.6)	(4.9)	(3.5)
Resort-Retirement	9	10.9	9.9	5.2	4.7
		(14.0)	(12.1)	(6.0)	(5.9)
Production Centers					
Manufacturing	25	34.1	9.3	4.4	5.0
		(44.4)	(9.9)	(4.7)	(5.0)
Industrial-Military	12	15.5	8.3	4.3	4.1
		(21.0)	(9.8)	(5.1)	(4.6)
Mining-Industrial	7	13.1	10.3	5.1	5.2
		(21.6)	(11.6)	(5.8)	(5.7)
Size 5 SMSAs and Non-metropolitan Areas					
		30.0	8.7	4.1	4.6
		(29.2)	(10.1)	(5.1)	(4.8)
Share of U.S. Employment					
in Major Industry Groups		22.9	10.4	5.0	5.4
		(31.5)	(12.0)	(5.8)	(6.0)

Column heads: Same as Table 2.2.

Note: First line shows share in 1976; second line (in parentheses), in 1959. Shares are unweighted modified averages for major type groups of SMSAs.

Source: Same as Table 4.11.

Corp Compl	CAO&A	FIRE	CS	Ret	MCS	NP	Gov
18.5	3.6	7.2	7.7	15.7	4.7	6.8	16.4
(12.2)	(1.8)	(6.2)	(4.3)	(15.1)	(5.1)	(3.7)	(13.6)
17.5	2.3	7.6	7.6	15.8	4.6	6.4	19.7
(11.9)	(1.4)	(7.0)	(3.5)	(16.1)	(5.4)	(4.0)	(17.4)
15.9	4.8	5.2	5.8	15.3	3.6	6.6	14.8
(9.9)	(2.5)	(4.2)	(3.1)	(13.9)	(3.6)	(3.4)	(11.6)
14.0	1.7	5.4	6.9	15.6	3.7	6.4	31.6
(9.5)	(1.4)	(4.6)	(3.5)	(14.9)	(4.3)	(3.5)	(28.5)
12.5	1.6	5.0	5.9	16.8	3.3	9.1	19.4
(8.1)	(0.7)	(4.2)	(3.2)	(13.9)	(3.2)	(5.1)	(14.4)
15.1	2.2	5.8	7.2	19.2	4.7	7.4	19.1
(8.2)	(0.6)	(3.9)	(3.7)	(19.2)	(4.6)	(3.5)	(18.8)
14.4	1.2	6.2	7.0	21.4	9.9	6.4	19.9
(9.6)	(0.4)	(5.1)	(4.1)	(19.2)	(8.9)	(3.5)	(20.5)
10.5	1.7	4.1	4.8	15.9	3.5	6.3	14.8
(7.1)	(0.8)	(3.7)	(2.6)	(14.4)	(3.6)	(3.3)	(11.6)
10.7	0.7	4.5	5.6	17.8	4.8	5.6	29.3
(6.9)	(0.6)	(3.8)	(2.5)	(16.8)	(5.4)	(2.6)	(29.4)
12.0	2.0	4.5	5.5	18.6	4.8	6.4	21.2
(8.8)	(2.0)	(3.8)	(3.0)	(17.9)	(5.3)	(4.1)	(17.0)
8.8	1.0	3.7	4.0	16.9	3.9	5.9	23.1
(6.2)	(0.8)	(3.3)	(2.1)	(16.6)	(4.0)	(3.3)	(20.3)
14.7	2.7	5.7	6.3	16.0	4.3	6.5	19.5
(10.2)	(1.6)	(5.0)	(3.6)	(15.2)	(4.5)	(3.5)	(16.2)

The importance of the rise of the corporate complex is clearly in evidence within certain types of place as is the role of size and, by implication, the cumulative effect of historical development in large places. Some evidence of centrifugal forces appears in the tendencies for export type service functions to develop vigorously in recent years in medium sized nodal and specialized service centers whereas in earlier years such activities were for the most part confined to the largest centers within the urban system. In the case of nonprofit and public sector activities, the evidence is less clear, very likely because of the highly mixed nature of the employment measures used here in the analysis of these sectors (see Chapter 1).

Although these analyses have been revealing they are by no means definitive. What is required is further probing of a sort which provides qualitative detail which permits investigation of additional aspects of structure and growth. It is to this analysis that we now turn.

Notes

1. Employment by industry data were developed for each of the SMSAs, according to the industry classification scheme presented in Chapter 1, for 1959, 1969 and 1976 using the 1976 definition of SMSAs. The data come from U.S. Department of Commerce, *County Business Patterns* (CBP) 2-digit SIC employment figures, except for employment in the government sector (not included in CBP) which comes from U.S. Department of Labor, *Employment and Earnings*.

2. $(8.7 \div 5.5) \times 100 = 158.2$; $(17.6 \div 22.8) \times 100 = 77.2$.

3. Actually, all 39 have location quotients of 100 plus in two or more, 38 in three or more, 24 in all four.

4. The education-manufacturing, residential, resort-retirement, and mining categories, each with 9 or less SMSAs are not broken down by size.

5. The analysis suffers from lack of information regarding the number and spatial distribution of small nodal places, which are not under study here. However, an earlier study based on 1960 data indicated that such places were relatively numerous in the Plains and the Southeast. Cf. Thomas M. Stanback, Jr. and Richard V. Knight, *The Metropolitan Economy*, op. cit.

6. In several government centers, education is often public-sector based (state universities and colleges).

7. In several cases SMSA groups have been combined where single groups were too small for statistically reliable analysis. Thus, national nodal SMSAs were combined with regional nodal SMSAs and residential with resort-retirement SMSAs. Subregional nodal, functional nodal, government-education and manufacturing SMSAs were treated as separate groups. The education-manufacturing and mining groups were omitted because they were considered to be too dissimilar from other groups to be combined and were too small for a separate analysis.

8. In technical language, the coefficient of simple correlation (R) is a measurement of the extent to which the variance among rates of change in variable "x" is accounted for by a fitted regression equation which expresses changes in "x" as a linear function of changes in "y." The regression equation is of the form x = a + by where x equals annual rate of change in the first variable; y equals annual rate of change in second variable, "a" is the intercept value, "b" is the coefficient indicating the estimated relation between changes in value of x in terms of a given change in y.

9. Only coefficients of correlation of .20 or above and a statistical reliability of .90 or better are shown. Where reliability is between .90 and .95 the coefficient value is identified with an asterisk. There are 11 industry groups, resulting in a total of 55 correlation coefficients in each matrix.

10. With the exception of the small mostly consumer service sector (MCS).

CHAPTER FIVE

The Transforming Geography of Manufacturing

While the main emphasis of this study is on the growing importance of services in shaping the urban landscape, the role of manufacturing cannot be overlooked. Manufacturing production remains a leading employment sector in the economy of many cities, despite major job losses in a large number of centers. Perhaps more important, the transition to producer services experienced so vigorously by many metropolitan areas is closely related to the transformation of manufacturing itself.

This chapter outlines key shifts and changes in the spatial organization of manufacturing. It examines how changes in the cost of major factor inputs, such as land, transportation, technology and labor, have influenced the tendency towards large scale relocation of production establishments away from the old industrial centers, and how special linkages between production and service activities carried out by large manufacturing organizations have further determined the directions followed by this relocation process.

To analyze the transformation of the geography of manufacturing in the postwar era, two types of activities must be distinguished from the outset: *production activity*, which takes place in plants where goods are manufactured and where both "production" and "non-production" workers are employed, and *service-like activity* of the manufacturing firm, which is increasingly being carried out in establishments separate from production plants. The latter are the establishments captured in census classifications under the label "Central Administrative Offices and Auxiliary Establishments" (CAO&A) and comprise the national headquarters, regional sales headquarters, divisional head offices, R&D facilities and other auxiliary establishments of the firm (see Chapter 2).

Ideally, one would like to be able to differentiate among various types of production or service-like establishments on the basis of the kind of production or service that they carry out, the kind of workers they employ (white collar or blue collar, skilled or unskilled) and the kind of capital they utilize. Unfortunately, this is not possible since conventional government data are often incomplete in identifying key differences at such a level of detail. In this chapter we do, however, make use of data from industry sources in addition to employment and value added data collected by government agencies, in order to augment as far as possible our information base.

Employment Trends in the Manufacturing Sectors: Production Establishments vs. Central Administrative Offices

The locational tendencies of manufacturing employment during the 1959–76 period are presented in Table 5.1 for the system of cities defined in Chapter 4, with location quotients of employment in production establishments and in Central Administrative offices shown separately.[1]

The first observation is that the period 1959–76 is accompanied by sharp declines (measured in relative terms) in the role of production employment in the economic base of almost all large and medium sized, diversified, and specialized service centers, and by significant relative increases in consumer-oriented centers, production centers as well as size 5 SMSAs and non-metropolitan areas.

On a type of place basis, note that while functional nodal centers exhibit large relative losses, production employment clearly continues to play a major role in their economic base. By comparison, the losses recorded in national and regional nodal centers suggest that these places are continuing to lose the prominent position they once occupied in the nation's production networks.

The observation that production employment has increased in relative terms in many of the consumer-oriented production and smaller urban centers (although increases have taken place on sharply differing initial bases) is consistent with our earlier finding (Chapter 4). The continued importance of production employment in manufacturing centers underlines the largely unaltered specialization tendencies of such centers.

The second major observation is that employment in the central administrative offices of industrial corporations demonstrate a behavior roughly opposite to that of production. The broad tendency is towards heavy and most often increasing spatial concentration of such employment in nodal and functional nodal centers, with the greatest degree of specialization shown by the largest centers, and weak and most often declining concentration in most other centers (with some exceptions that are addressed in more detail in the following two chapters).[2] These gains, though they do not loom large when measured as shares of total employment, are significant because of their relationship to increases in other sectors of the corporate complexes.

In the sections that follow, the emphasis is on spelling out more carefully the behavior of production employment. Employment in CAO&A establishments is also dealt with, but is subject to more detailed analysis in Chapter 6.

The Dispersion of Manufacturing Production: The Evidence

The locational tendencies of production employment just identified reflect the outcome of the large scale process of dispersion away from the largest and oldest industrial centers that has characterized manufacturing production through much of the postwar era. Over the years, this process has proceeded in several phases, albeit with considerable overlapping among phases. Chronologically these can be identified as the phase of "suburbanization," "regionalization," "decentralization," and "internationalization."[3]

Table 5.1 Location Quotients of Employment in Manufacturing Production and Central Administrative Offices and Auxiliary Establishments by Type and Size of SMSA, 1976 and 1959

	SMSA Size	# of SMSAs	Manufacturing Production		CAO & A	
			1976	1959	1976	1959
Diversified Service Centers						
National Nodal	1	4	90.1	95.1	159.5	145.2
Regional Nodal	1	8	95.2	107.9	148.7	119.1
	2	11	79.8	85.0	116.3	90.2
Subregional Nodal	3	10	75.7	75.3	104.6	102.0
	4	6	66.7	67.9	56.3	58.7
Specialized Service Centers						
Functional Nodal	1	3	112.6	123.0	254.0	294.0
	2	3	134.5	134.0	87.9	145.6
	3	12	132.5	138.4	200.2	151.2
	4	6	126.3	135.7	141.6	106.9
Government-Education	1	1	16.7	16.6	81.9	49.7
	3	2	52.6	77.6	80.9	99.5
	4	12	69.8	75.9	56.7	88.0
Education-Manufacturing	1 to 4	5	117.6	133.8	60.8	44.5
Consumer-Oriented Centers						
Residential	1 to 4	3	90.7	89.9	81.8	36.4
Resort-Retirement	1 to 4	9	47.8	44.3	44.8	24.9
Production Centers						
Manufacturing	2	1	121.2	132.3	67.3	88.4
	3	8	151.8	149.0	57.3	57.0
	4	16	148.9	137.7	56.8	41.9
Industrial-Military	2	1	67.0	94.4	45.8	16.2
	3	2	45.6	41.3	48.9	44.1
	4	9	83.9	69.1	31.5	39.2
Mining-Industrial	4	7	57.0	68.6	72.9	124.7
Size 5 SMSAs and Non-metropolitan Areas			113.1	92.8	36.6	48.1
Share of U.S. Employment in Manufacturing and CAO&A			22.9	31.5	2.7	1.6

Note: Location quotients are unweighted modified averages for major type-size groups of SMSAs.

Source: County Business Patterns, 1976 and 1959.

THE "SUBURBANIZATION" PHASE

This first phase has been characterized by a move of manufacturing plants away from the central cities of the old traditional manufacturing centers of the Northeast and Northcentral regions towards their suburbs. Examples of suburban manufacturing development abound, from the development of the Northern Jersey petrochemical industry (away from New York City) to that of the Dearborn automobile industry (away from Detroit). These developments are part of an explanation of pre- and postwar suburban development in the United States. Evidence of this trend, which is felt most strongly from the 1940s until the mid-1960s, is presented in Table 5.2. The table shows annual rates of growth of manufacturing employment in the suburbs of eight of the largest metropolitan centers consistently higher than those of their central cities throughout the decades of the 1940s, 1950s and 1960s.

THE "REGIONALIZATION" PHASE

This second phase has been dramatized by the move of manufacturing towards the Sunbelt metropolitan centers. The development of military and aerospace industries in the South (Los Angeles, Atlanta, San Diego) during the various war efforts of the past 40 years is illustrative of this period, as is the more recent development of the electronics industry in southern cities (San Jose, Phoenix, Dallas). In cases such as that of the relocation of the textile industry away from New England or Pennsylvania to the Piedmont Southern Region, the "regionalization" phase goes quite far back—at least to the 1920s. In general, however, this phase seems to have had the greatest impact on the economy from the late 1950s on to the early 1970s.

Recent regional shifts in the nation's manufacturing base are summarized in Table 5.3 in terms of a simple, two-region (Sunbelt vs. Snowbelt) analysis of the evolution of each 2 digit SIC manufacturing industry during the period 1959–1976. Only the Snowbelt's share of the nation's employment in each industry is shown here, since the Sunbelt's respective share is simply its complement—the residual which adds to 100 percent.

For purposes of presentation, the 20 industries are divided into two groups. The first group, which is presented in the upper half of the table, includes those industries that have undergone the least regional shift over the last two decades. As can be seen from this table, the Snowbelt has maintained or increased its relative level of specialization in these industries, as measured by the location quotients of employment (columns 4 and 5)—though not its shares (columns 1 and 2). These are industries traditionally associated with the old manufacturing base of the Snowbelt (primary metals, fabricated metals and transportation equipment), often strongly unionized, and usually heavily dependent on well paid (column 9) and relatively skilled blue collar workers. For the most part, these are also among the slowest growing manufacturing industries (column 8).

The second group of industries, or "fast shifting industries" (lower half of the table), includes those industries that have experienced the greatest regional shift over the last two decades, and can be differentiated in terms of two subgroups. The first subgroup includes the apparel, furniture, textile, and tobacco industries

Table 5.2   Average Annual Rates of Growth of Employment in
            Retailing and Manufacturing in the Central Cities
            and Suburbs of Eight Large Metropolitan Areas,
            1940-1970

Decade	Central Cities Modified Average[a]		Suburbs Modified Average[a]	
	Ret[b]	Mfg[c]	Ret[b]	Mfg[c]
Forties	4.74	10.39	8.40	12.16
Fifties	-0.52	-1.13	7.69	5.02
Sixties	-1.33	-0.04	7.48	4.21

Note: The eight metropolitan areas are Baltimore, Boston,
        Cleveland, Denver, New Orleans, New York, Philadelphia
        and St. Louis.

[a]Unweighted modified average of the average annual rates of
growth of employment in the eight places.

[b]Respectively 1939-48 (Forties), 1948-58 (Fifties),
1958-67 (Sixties).

[c]Respectively 1939-47 (Forties), 1947-58 (Fifties),
1958-67 (Sixties).

Source: U.S. Department of Commerce, Bureau of the Census,
          1939, 1947, 1958 and 1967 Census of Manufactures and
          1939, 1948, 1958 and 1967 Census of Businesses (Retail
          Trade Statistics). From Table 3.1, Thomas M.
          Stanback, Jr. and Richard V. Knight, Suburbanization
          and the City, Montclair, NJ: Allanheld, Osmun, 1975.

which, while continuing to move south, had already shifted considerably prior to
the 1960s.[4] The second subgroup, which ranges from "machinery" to "electrical appliances and electronics" industries, represent industries that have shifted
more recently and includes many of the fastest growing manufacturing
industries.[5]

   In general, while many of the "fast shifting industries" are characterized by
low wage structure (column 9), thus giving some credence to the argument often
put forth that the low wage characteristic of the Sunbelt labor market has been a
strong attraction in the southward shift of manufacturing, the shift demonstrated
by some relatively well paying industries (e.g., machinery, electrical appliances)

Table 5.3 Sunbelt-Snowbelt Shifts in Manufacturing: Snow-
belt Shares of Employment in Each Two-Digit SIC
Manufacturing Industry, Shifts in Shares, and
Analysis of Change, 1976-1959

	Snowbelt Employment in Two-Digit Industry as Share of US Total in Industry[a]		Shift in Share
	1976	1959	1959-1976
"Slow Shifting Industries"	(1)	(2)	(3)
33 Primary Metals	73.66	80.51	-6.85
34 Fabricated Metals	68.07	73.72	-5.65
37 Transportation	61.55	66.80	-5.25
26 Paper	60.41	68.19	-7.78
32 Stone, Clay & Glass	57.08	64.24	-7.16
20 Food	53.42	61.38	-7.96
28 Chemicals	52.83	60.44	-7.61
29 Petroleum	39.07	44.00	-4.93
24 Lumber & Wood	28.48	25.87	+2.61
"Fast Shifting Industries"			
35 Machinery	70.12	84.27	-14.15
31 Leather	69.83	87.15	-17.32
39 Misc. Manuf.	69.79	84.98	-15.19
38 Instruments	69.71	84.67	-14.96
30 Rubber & Plastics	66.25	82.82	-16.57
27 Printing & Publish.	65.96	74.00	- 8.04
36 Elec. App. & Electronics	63.88	82.14	-18.26
27 Apparel	46.84	69.72	-22.88
25 Furniture	41.29	53.98	-12.69
22 Textile	22.84	37.28	-14.44
21 Tobacco	8.93	26.78	-17.85
All Manufacturing Industries	59.61	68.84	-9.27

[a]Sunbelt share for each year equals 100 percent minus
Snowbelt share.
[b]Share of Snowbelt employment in two-digit SIC industry as a
percent of US employment in same industry divided by share of
Snowbelt employment in all manufacturing industries as a
percent of US employment in all manufacturing (multiplied by
100).
[c]Eight largest employment sectors underlined for emphasis.
[d]Six fastest growing manufacturing industries underlined
for emphasis.

Analysis of Change

Snowbelt Location Quotient of Employment in Two-Digit Industry[b]		Gains(+) Losses(-) in Loc. Quo.	Industry As Share (%) of all US Manufacturing[c]	Rate of Growth of Industry[d]	Wage Characteristic[e]
1976	1959	1976-59	1976	1959-76	1976
(4)	(5)	(6)	(7)	(8)	(9)
123.6	117.0	+	5.81	-8.42	H
114.2	107.1	+	7.60	9.67	H
103.3	97.0	+	8.85	1.99	H
101.3	99.1	+	3.24	9.84	H
95.8	93.3	+	3.06	4.41	H
89.6	89.1	+	7.81	-7.89	M(H)
88.6	87.8	+	4.52	16.90	H
65.5	63.9	+	0.76	-18.56	H
47.8	37.6	+	3.34	9.29	M(L)
117.6	122.4	-	10.50	42.02	H
117.1	126.6	-	1.34	-27.59	L
113.7	123.5	-	2.29	17.67	M(L)
116.9	123.0	-	2.75	78.87	H
111.1	120.3	-	3.42	80.52	L
110.7	107.5	-	5.71	26.18	M(H)
107.2	119.3	-	8.49	36.09	H
78.5	101.3	-	6.98	11.27	L
69.3	78.4	-	2.30	21.43	M(L)
38.3	54.2	-	4.66	-0.93	L
15.0	38.9	-	0.33	-21.94	L
100.0	100.0		100.00%	17.02%	

[e]L=Low wage: 60 percent or more workers earn less than 125% of poverty level; M(L)=Mixed (Low) wage: 60 to 50 percent earn less than 125% of poverty level; M(H)=Mixed (High) Wage: 50 to 60 percent workers earn more than 125% of poverty level; H=High wage: 60 percent workers earn more than 125% of poverty level.

Source: County Business Patterns, 1959 and 1976. Wage characteristics of two-digit SIC industries are from Patricia Wilson-Salinas, Subemployment and the Urban Underclass, Working Paper, Austin: Department of City and Regional Planning, University of Texas, 1980.

suggests that the process of shift may have been somewhat more complicated. We return to this point shortly.

THE "DECENTRALIZATION" PHASE

This third and relatively more recent phase has been characterized by a general move away from very large or large centers—almost regardless of regional consideration—towards smaller metropolitan centers and non-metropolitan counties. This is best seen in the case of the electrical equipment and electronics industries, where the most recent trend has been for expanding production in small urban places or even rural counties: for example, Digital Equipment in Colorado Springs, or General Electric in rural Vermont. But the same trend is in evidence in other industries as well: for example, in the automobile industry Volkswagen has opened shop in New Stanton, Pennsylvania, while in machinery and parts, Cummins Engine and TRW were setting up new facilities in Jamestown, New York. Meanwhile, cities such as Atlanta or Los Angeles, whose manufacturing had grown substantially until the late 1960s, have experienced dramatic losses during the early 1970s.

Evidence to that effect is presented in Table 5.4 in which the 1970–1976 growth experience of the suburban counties of the 36 largest SMSAs of the nation (including many Sunbelt metropolises) is contrasted with that of all non-metropolitan counties of the nation. At a time when manufacturing stagnated in the nation as a whole, manufacturing employment declined in the suburbs of the largest centers—thus reversing the earlier trend (see Table 5.2)—but increased noticeably in non-metropolitan counties. Table 5.5 complements this finding by showing that not only has that growth been particularly healthy among some of the least urbanized non-metropolitan counties (largest city in county characterized by less than 20,000 population), but that, in that case too, there has been well-marked regional differences: non-metropolitan counties of the West, South and North Central States have made strong gains, while small cities and towns of the Northeast have performed poorly on the whole.

THE "INTERNATIONALIZATION" PHASE

Finally, the transformation of the manufacturing landscape has also been strongly affected by the more recent tendency to relocate certain production facilities abroad, and, perhaps more interestingly, low level assembly work in low wage areas of Third World nations. While this development has had and may continue to have major implications for the domestic economy, we do not attempt to identify it here in any detail.[6] It must be noted, however, that such development bears strong similarities to the three phases outlined earlier.

The Dispersion of Manufacturing Production: The Underlying Factors

The trends discussed above have come about in two ways: as a result of decisions made initially in new industries, as they emerged, to locate away from the traditional centers of production (e.g., petrochemical or electronics), and as a result

Table 5.4   Employment Growth in Suburban Counties of Large
            Metropolitan Areas and in Non-Metropolitan
            Counties by Sector, 1970-1976

	Suburban Counties		Non-metropolitan Counties	
	Net Job Increases (thousands)	Percent Growth	Net Job Increases (thousands)	Percent Growth
Total Employment[a]	1,364.5	16.7%	2,535.5	12.0%
Manufacturing	-7.3	-0.4%	335.7	7.7%
Wholesale Trade	146.2	47.8%	292.4	63.5%
TCU	47.3	13.6%	64.0	8.4%
FIRE	111.8	44.3%	142.8	34.7%
Other Services	426.0	35.7%	470.3	18.5%
Retail Trade	338.8	27.0%	436.7	18.1%

Note: Tabulation includes suburban counties in metropolitan
        areas greater than one million population (36 SMSAs in
        all); not included are suburban communities of large
        metropolitan areas which are in the same county as the
        central city.

[a]Excludes government; includes mining, construction and
   agriculture.

Source: U.S. Department of Commerce, Bureau of Economic
          Analysis. From Tables 7.1 and 8.1 of U.S.
          Department of Housing and Urban Development, The
          President's National Urban Policy Report, 1980.

of the decisions of older industries to expand away from the centers where they had originally grown.

These developments would not have occurred, however, if it had not been for some major changes in the economics of the factor inputs which bear most heavily on the location of industrial facilities: transportation, technology, land, and labor in particular. In a very broad sense, what is observed during the postwar

Table 5.5 Employment Growth in Non-Metropolitan Counties by Region and Size of Largest Place, 1970-1976

	Total Employment		Manufacturing		Non-Manufacturing	
	Net Job Increases[a]	Percent Growth	Net Job Increases[a]	Percent Growth	Net Job Increases[a]	Percent Growth
Total Non-metropolitan	2,535.6	12.0%	335.7	7.7%	2,199.9	13.2%
Region						
Northeast	204.5	8.1	-36.7	-5.6	241.2	13.0
North Central	715.0	10.0	85.7	6.1	629.3	10.9
South	1,009.1	11.5	221.0	11.0	780.1	11.7
West	607.0	23.5	65.7	22.8	541.3	23.5
Population Size of Largest Place in County						
Less than 2,500	257.3	11.5	43.5	15.9	213.8	10.9
2,500-19,999	1,274.8	12.7	234.9	11.6	1,040.0	13.0
20,000 or More	1,003.4	11.4	57.3	2.8	946.1	14.1

[a] In thousands.

Source: U.S. Department of Commerce, Bureau of Economic Analysis; employment data compiled by the Center for Social Data Analysis, Montana State University. From Table 8.1 of U.S. Department of Housing and Urban Development, The President's National Urban Policy Report, 1980.

period is a gradual tendency towards a weakening of many of the economies of agglomeration that once tended overwhelmingly to favor large urban centers over alternative locations.

Thus, construction of the interstate highway system, the rise of the trucking industry with the parallel decline of the railroads, the increased routinization and simplification of production processes through new and improved machinery, and the application of automated control systems opens up a new range of opportunities for the siting of production away from more central locations. Furthermore, the development of new production technologies calls for a much more intensive (horizontal) use of land which can no longer be met by the old, congested (vertical) cities. Last and perhaps most importantly, the intensification of competition brought about by the general opening of nationwide markets (see Chapter 2) becomes such that firms are now compelled more than ever before to devise ways by which they can escape the high blue-collar labor costs that prevail in certain areas as a result of unionization and/or labor unrest, whether they be densely populated labor markets (large metropolitan centers) or regional labor markets (Snowbelt). Indeed, there seems to be a widespread consensus among economists that labor cost considerations may have constituted the most important factor in pushing for a rapid decentralization of manufacturing facilities through much of the postwar period.[7]

Despite such a widespread consensus, the evidence remains partly ambiguous. At a minimum, the data presented in Table 5.3 (column 9) suggest instances where relatively well-paying industries may have taken anchor in the South. There are two possible explanations: either these industries have been shifting south only that component of their manufacturing operations that is more sensitive to labor costs (for example, due to a large reliance on low skilled workers or to less influence of unions), or there have emerged cores of better skilled workers in the Sunbelt regions. In more general terms, the question thus becomes whether or not forces other than simple labor cost considerations have influenced the location of production establishments that remain dependent on relatively skilled and well-paid labor.

The Location of High Value Added Production

Some light may be shed on this question by distinguishing and observing locational patterns of processes which are essentially "routine" in nature (e.g., final assembly of parts), tend to call for low skilled labor, and yield (relatively speaking) low value added, from those which are "less routine" (e.g., batch production of parts), tend to be more capital intensive, call for a higher skilled labor force, and yield greater value added.

As we attempt to demonstrate in the following paragraphs, in the case of high value added production, not only is there a greater need for skilled blue collar workers in the factory, but also for a closer relationship among workers on the shop floor, engineers in the drafting rooms, and white collar technicians and professionals in offices, whose skill may be needed as problems crop up, production schedules are changed, new techniques are experimented with or experimental models are introduced. The location of high value added production establishments appears to be determined by a rather different set of considerations than those guiding the siting of assembly plants and to be strongly influenced by proximity to pools of skilled labor and the availablility of specialized, engineering-oriented, service-like inputs (whether in-house or from producer service firms). While there is evidence that such agglomerations of skills and service inputs have developed in some key Sunbelt centers, it appears that they still favor the older Snowbelt centers overwhelmingly.

A CASE STUDY OF FOUR MANUFACTURING INDUSTRIES

To assess the validity of such a proposition, we have analyzed four industries that are important in terms of the regional shift issue summarized in Table 5.3: motor vehicle and part supplies (SIC 371), aerospace and ordnance (SICs 372 through 376), electrical appliance and electronics (SICs 365, 366 and 367), and office, scientific and measuring equipment (SICs 357 and 381 through 387). The first industry remains a mainstay of the U.S. economy, and its fate is strongly associated with that of the manufacturing base of the Snowbelt; the last three are newer and are usually associated with postwar growth and the rise of manufacturing in the Sunbelt.

For each industry we proceeded to rank SMSAs in terms of their importance as centers of administration and management, as centers of research and development, and in terms of value added in production, respectively. The ranking of cities in terms of administration and management is based on a composite index accounting for the presence of headquarters and major divisional offices of the largest firms in the industry (i.e., those ranked among the Fortune 1000 industrial firms); the ranking in terms of research and development, on a composite index accounting for the presence of R&D facilities of the largest firms in the industry; and the ranking in terms of value added in production, on the measure of value added per production worker. These rankings were developed for the most recent possible year—1977. Their formulation is explained in much greater detail in Appendix C, as are the limitations on the number of metropolitan centers for which consistent rankings could be developed. The appendix also explains why we deal with many of the East and West Coast SMSAs as part of larger megalopolises,[8] rather than individually.

The numbers of metropolitan centers for which full disclosure is available simultaneously as regards the three functions of administration and management, research and development, and production for each of the four industries is shown in the following text table.

Fortune Code	Industry	SIC Code	Number of Metropolitan Centers with full disclosure
40	Motor Vehicle and Parts	371	30
36	Electrical Appliances and Electronics	365-366, 367	20
41	Aerospace and Ordinance	372-376	22
38, 44	Office, Scientific and Measuring Equipment	381-387, 357	28

To investigate the relationship between value added per production worker in manufacturing establishments of metropolitan centers and the importance that they play as centers of administration and management or as centers of research and development functions of the industry, we summarized, for each of the four industries, the rankings established for these three functions by listing in a single tabulation the metropolitan centers in the *upper tier of the array developed for each function*. For example, in the case of the Motor Vehicle and Parts industry, we list in the same table the 10 (top third) most important centers in administration, the 10 most important centers in research and development, and the 10 centers with the highest value added per production worker, showing each with its respective rank order. Since many centers rank high on more than one of these functions, the combined list numbers only 18 metropolitan centers (Table 5.7 below).

Evidence of correlation of functions in terms of location is shown in Table 5.6 for each of the four industries. The four-industry tabulations upon which Table 5.6 is based are presented in Tables 5.7 through 5.10. The degree of correlation among the three functions is calculated in terms of the number of "high" rankings (i.e., upper tier of each of the three arrays) occurring jointly (i.e., in more than one type of specialization in the same location): for example, "high administration, high research, and high value added per production worker," or "high administration and high value added per production worker only"). Numbers of joint "high" rankings are then translated into percentages, including those cases when high rankings occur in isolation.

Table 5.6 supports our basic thesis by showing correlation between "high" value added and "high" administration and/or "high" research considerably higher than would be expected on the basis of chance alone. In the four industries, high rankings in value added per production worker occurs jointly with high rankings in administration, research, or both (columns 1, 2, and 3 combined) in at least 45 percent of all cases of high rankings. This is well above what might be expected on the basis of chance alone (18.5 percent—columns 1, 2, and 3 combined in last line of Table 5.6). In the strongest case of all—that of the Office, Scientific and Measuring Equipment industry—this association occurs in 82 percent of the cases.

The simultaneous occurrence of high rankings in both administration and research (regardless of their coincidence with high rankings in value added per production worker—columns 1 and 4 combined), is also very high (52 percent for Motor Vehicle, the lowest; 70 percent for Office, Scientific and Measuring Equipment, the highest), and indicates simply that most corporations tend to concentrate both their administrative and research staffs in a fairly restricted number of locations. The fact that for all four industries, the simultaneous occurrence between high research capacity and high value added per production worker (column 3) is greater than that between high administrative capacity and high value added per production worker (column 2) seems to indicate that when corporations do tend to have more decentralized research and administrative staffs, the spatial proximity between research facilites and key production establishments remains the most important consideration.

The detailed tables (Table 5.7 through 5.10) shed additional light. First, in almost every industry, Greater New York, Greater Los Angeles, Greater San

Table 5.6 Correlations among High Administration, High Research and/or High Value Added per Production Worker in Key Centers, Four Selected Industries, 1976

| Industry | Percentage of High Rankings Occurring Jointly | | | | Perc. High Rankings Occurring in Isolation of Others | All Cases |
	Administration Research and VAPPW[a]	Administration and VAPPW Only	Research and VAPPW Only	Administration and Research Only		
Motor Vehicle and Parts	19.4%	6.5%	19.4%	32.3%	22.4%	100.0%
Electrical Appliances, Electronics	52.2%	-	-	8.7%	39.1%	100.0%
Aeronautic and Ordnance	42.8%	9.5%	19.1%	9.5%	19.1%	100.0%
Office, Scientific, Measuring Equipment	63.6%	6.6%	12.1%	6.1%	12.1%	100.0%
(Random Correlation)	(5.3%)	(10.5%)	(10.5%)	(10.5%)	(63.2%)	(100.0%)

[a]Value added per production worker.

Note: The degree of correlation among the three functions is calculated as the number of observations falling within each possible combination, with the list of centers arranged within the upper tier of each functional ranking counting as an independent set of observations. These numbers are then translated into percentages (see text). The "random correlation" line shows correlation, if characteristics of "High" Administration, "High" Research and "High" Value were distributed purely randomly among cities. Probability of random occurrence of the various combinations of high rankings is computed and translated into percentages, including those cases when high rankings would occur in isolation.

Source: Based on Tables 5.7 through 5.10.

Table 5.7 Major Centers of Administration, Research and Production in the Motor Vehicle and Parts Industries with Metropolitan Centers Ranked According to Their Respective Importance for Each of the Three Functions, 1976

	Administration	Research	VAPPW[a]
Detroit	1	1	8
Cleveland	2	5	
Chicago	3	4	
Greater Los Angeles	4	2	
Los Angeles	*		
Toledo	5	9	
Greater New York	6		
New York	*		
Philadelphia	7	7	
Dayton	8	3	7
Minneapolis	9		
Greater San Francisco	10		1
San Francisco	*		*
Dallas			10
Grand Rapids		6	
Milwaukee		8	4
St. Louis		(10)	3
Akron		(10)	9
Cincinnati			2
Columbus			5
Lima			6

[a]Value added per production worker in SIC #371.

Note: Table shows ranks, with highest ranking center shown as #1. Only upper tier ranking centers are shown for each of the three functions. In the case of greater metropolitan areas, rank is shown for the area as a whole and principal location within the area is identified with asterisk. Parentheses indicate that several metropolitan centers rank equally.

Source: Appendix C.

Table 5.8 Major Centers of Administration, Research and
Production in the Electrical Appliance and
Electronics Industries with Metropolitan Centers
Ranked According to Their Respective Importance for
Each of the Three Functions, 1976

	Administration	Research	VAPPW[a]
Greater New York	1	1	
New York	*		
Bridgeport	*		
Nassau Suffolk		*	
Newark		*	
New Brunswick		*	
Chicago	2	2	6 /
Greater Los Angeles	3	3	3 / 5
Los Angeles	*	*	* / *
Anaheim	*		* /
Greater San Francisco	4	4	4 / 1
San Jose	*	*	* / *
San Francisco	*		
Cleveland	5		
Dallas	6	5	1 /
Boston	7		/ 4
Milwaukee		7	
Washington, DC		6	
Ft. Lauderdale			2 / 6
Miami			5 / 7
Tampa			/ 2
Phoenix			/ 3

[a]Value added per production worker in SIC 365-66 and SIC
367. Rankings are established separately for SIC 365-66 and
SIC 367. For explanation see Appendix C.

Note: Table shows ranks, with highest ranking center shown as
#1. Only upper tier ranking centers are shown for each
of the three functions. In the case of greater metropolitan areas, rank is shown for the area as a whole,
and principal location within the area is indentified
with an asterisk.

Source: Appendix C.

Table 5.9 Major Centers of Administration, Research and Production in the Aerospace and Ordnance Industries with Metropolitan Centers Ranked According to Their Respective Importance for Each of the Three Functions, 1976

	Administration	Research	VAPPW[a]
Greater Los Angeles	1	1	3
Los Angeles	*	*	*
Seattle	2	7	7
Greater New York	3	4	6
Newark		*	
Nassau-Suffolk	*	*	*
Bridgeport	*		*
Pittsburgh	4		
Hartford	5		
St. Louis	6		5
Greater Washington, DC	7	6	
Washington, DC	*	*	
Boston		2	4
Greater San Francisco		3	1
San Jose		*	*
Philadelphia		5	
Dallas			2

[a]Value added per production worker for SIC 372-376.

Note: Table show ranks, with highest ranking center shown as #1. Only upper tier ranking centers are shown for each of the three functions. In the case of greater metropolitan areas, rank is shown for the area as a whole, and principal location within the area is identified with an asterik.

Source: Appendix C.

Table 5.10   Major Centers of Administration, Research and
             Production in the Office, Scientific and Measuring
             Equipment Industries with Metropolitan Centers
             Ranked According to Their Respective Importance
             for Each of the Three Functions, 1976

	Administration	Research	VAPPW[a]
Greater New York	1	1	7 /
New York	*	*	
Nassau Suffolk			* /
Paterson		*	
Bridgeport	*		
New Brunswick			* /
Minneapolis	2	7	10 / 3
Rochester	3	2	1 /
Boston	4	5	3 / 4
Chicago	5	6	9 /
Greater Los Angeles	6	3	
Los Angeles	*	*	
Anaheim	*	*	
Greater San Francisco	7	8	4 / 2
San Jose	*	*	* / *
Detroit	8		6 /
Dayton	9		
Philadelphia	10	4	5 /
Dallas		(10)	/ 1
San Diego		9	/ 5
Erie		(10)	2 /
Buffalo			8 /

[a]Value added per production worker for SIC 38 and SIC 357.
 Rankings are established separately for SIC 38 and SIC 357.
 For explanation see Appendix C.

Note: Table shows ranks, with highest ranking center shown as
        #1. Only upper tier ranking centers are shown for each
        of the three functions. In the case of greater
        metropolitan areas, rank is shown for the area as a
        whole and principal location within the area is
        identified with an asterisk. Parentheses indicate that
        several metropolitan centers rank equally.

Source: Appendix C.

Francisco and Chicago stand out as strong leaders of administration and/or research, pointing to the key role played by the four national nodal centers in the complexes of corporate activities of the nation. Second, Snowbelt centers show up remarkably well in terms of administration, research, and high value added production, even in those industries which are traditionally considered as part of the Sunbelt growth story. This raises some doubts as to whether or not the Sunbelt regions and metropolises have been as successful as is sometimes assumed in attracting those key service or service-like functions which are at the leading edge of the current economic transformation. Third, the weaker spatial correlation demonstrated by the Motor Vehicle and Parts Industry between key production establishments and key service facilities may indicate that the relationship between high value added and high level services is a relatively new one, akin to high technology oriented industries in which greater amounts of human and financial resources are spent on key managerial and developmental resources and in which day to day linkages between engineers and technicians and shopfloor workers must be closely maintained. This suggests that, as the program of rejuvenation of the U.S. auto industry progresses (with its expanded emphasis on developing new technologies, new organizational matrixes or, more simply, new in-house service-like activities), the same kind of spatial relationships is likely to develop: high value added production establishments will become more dependent on the producer service-like facilities of the firm; and more routine assembly-type facilities, more footloose.

GENERALIZING THE FINDINGS ON HIGH VALUE ADDED TO THE LARGER SYSTEM OF CITIES AND TO ALL MANUFACTURING INDUSTRIES

The previous analysis focused on *intra-industry* variations in value added per production worker as they relate to specialization of metropolitan centers in administration and research. But there are important *inter-industry* variations in value added as well. In order to generalize these findings to the larger urban system and to all manufacturing industries we used a more general measure which merges both types of variation in value added (inter- and intra-industry).

We arrayed the 140 largest places according to value added per production worker for all manufacturing industries combined and distributed them by quintiles. We then sought to determine the extent to which high or low quintile ranks in value added per worker in manufacturing were associated with certain types of SMSAs by comparing the distribution of different type groups of SMSAs along the five quintile array. Simply, this analysis tried to determine whether or not centers characterized by specialization in the complex of corporate activities (principally, nodal and functional nodal centers) tended also to be characterized by high value added per production worker in manufacturing.

Table 5.11 summarizes the results of this analysis which is based on the 1972 *Census of Manufactures*[9] and shows differences which are quite consistent with those suggested by the earlier four-industry study. Metropolitan centers that have well developed corporate complexes (first two major groups in the table), tend to show an above average concentration of high value added production; those with

Table 5.11 Percentage Distribution of SMSAs by Type and by Quintile of Value Added per Production Worker, All Manufacturing Industries Combined, 140 Largest SMSAs, 1972

| | Percentage Distribution by 1972 Quintile of Value Added | | | | | |
	Highest Quintile 1	2	3	4	Lowest Quintile 5	# of SMSAs
140 Largest SMSAs	20	20	20	20	20	(140)
Diversified Service Centers[a]	13	31	26	15	15	(39)
National Nodal	25	25	25	25	-	(4)
Regional Nodal	21	32	32	11	5	(19)
Subregional Nodal	-	31	19	19	31	(16)
Specialized Service Centers						
Functional Nodal	33	17	21	21	8	(24)
Government-Education	27	27	20	20	7	(15)
Education-Manufacturing	-	-	-	80	-	(5)
Consumer Oriented Centers						
Residential	33	-	33	33	-	(3)
Resort-Retirement	11	22	11	22	33	(9)
Production Centers[a]	17	13	17	17	35	(46)
Manufacturing	12	4	28	12	44	(25)
Industrial-Military	23	15	8	31	23	(13)
Mining-Industrial	29	43	-	-	29	(7)
Range of 1972 VAPPW (in dollars)	from 32,789 to 52,474	29,036 32,615	26,662 29,016	22,839 26,601	14,966 22,547	

Note: Each line adds to 100 percent.

[a]Group average.

Source: Census of Manufactures, 1972.

relatively underdeveloped corporate complexes (last two groups of the table) an above average concentration of low value added production. Thus, functional nodal centers (the largest grouping among the specialized service centers) show an overconcentration of high value added centers, with 33 percent of these SMSAs found in the upper quintile (as against 20 percent for the overall distribution of the 140 large and medium size SMSAs), and diversified service centers an overconcentration in quintiles 2 and 3 (respectively 31 and 26 percent). On the contrary, production centers are overconcentrated in the lowest quintile (35 percent as against the 20 percent average).

Among these places, mining and industrial military centers display a more favorable distribution than manufacturing centers, which simply says that they tend to be specialized in industries which, on the average, have a higher value added than those of the manufacturing centers.

In short, this analysis strongly suggests a widespread tendency for production establishments characterized by high value added, and most likely high requirements for producer services, to retain locations in urban centers with developed complexes of corporate activities and for establishments with low requirements to be more footloose.

Conclusion

While we must guard against making too strong a concluding statement on the basis of these limited probes, the trends revealed in this chapter shed important light on current changes in the geography of manufacturing.

The postwar era has been characterized by a general widening of markets for manufactured goods (increasingly from regional to national and, lately, international markets) and by renewed competition (especially during the 1970s as major foreign firms penetrated vigorously the U.S. markets). To respond to the need for greater economies of scale and better control over direct production costs, many firms have developed greater integration of the manufacturing process among their various establishments[10] and relocated part of their production operations in low wage areas, whether they be in the newer regions of the country or in Third World nations as well. Clearly, developments in production technologies have been instrumental in permitting this redeployment of routine or readily controlled processes in low wage areas. At the same time, however, the increasing need for producer services (both in-house and free-standing) in association with more specialized production processes seems to have opened new opportunities for metropolitan centers that have traditionally been well endowed with a highly skilled blue-collar labor force and have been the most successful in cultivating a whole range of developmental services. An important finding of this chapter is that while there is evidence of the formation of agglomerations of highly skilled labor and producer service inputs in some of the Sunbelt centers, many among the larger and older Snowbelt manufacturing centers seem particularly well positioned for high value added production because of their past and current developmental history.

The other side of this development is that there is likely to be increased competition among places with poor factor endowment to attract the more footloose, low value added production establishments of large manufacturing firms. Since the terms of this competition are increasingly defined by the overall wage level of the labor market area, centers with less economic base sophistication than the nodal or functional nodal places but with a long established history of manufacturing (the manufacturing centers) must increasingly compete with low skilled areas (industrial-military, mining-industrial, residential-resort-retirement centers, as well as smaller places of the national urban system and Third World production platforms). Indeed, it is not farfetched to hypothesize that this intensification of competition with low wage areas explains in large part the poor performance of the manufacturing centers in the past two decades.

In short, the transformations identified in this chapter hold at once promises for some places and ominous implications for others in both the older and more recently developed areas of the American economy. We return to some of these important issues in the last chapter of this book.

Notes

1. In our data base, this latter grouping includes also employment in the CAO&A establishments of non-manufacturing firms. However, close to 70.0 percent of this employment represents employment in the CAO&A of manufacturing firms. Furthermore, CAO&A establishments tend to behave the same way, locationally, regardless of the industry of origin.

2. The reader will undoubtedly note the 1959–1976 drop in the location quotient of CAO&A employment among size 1 and size 2 functional nodal centers. A likely explanation is that it reflects structural and cyclical adjustments (1976 is the trough of a recession) in places where major firms' headquarters are in industries such as automobile, steel, or heavy machinery that have been under considerable stress throughout the 1970s, resulting in layoffs of white collar employees at headquarters. The sharpness of the drop in the 1976 quotient for size 2 functional nodal places appears somewhat spurious, however, and is likely to originate from data reporting problems. For unexplained reasons, reported employment in CAO&A establishments in Milwaukee declines drastically between 1959 and 1976—a development that does not seem to check with that indicated by data reported in the *Directory of Corporate Affiliations* (see next chapter).

3. For an extensive description of these four phases, see *The 1980 President's National Urban Policy Report*, U.S. Department of Housing and Urban Development, Washington, D.C.: US GPO 1980, esp. Chapters 1, 3, 7 and 8.

4. Except for apparel, 1959 Snowbelt location quotients were already well under 100.

5. In these industries, Snowbelt location quotients have fallen but are still over 100.

6. For a more detailed analysis, see Barry Bluestone and Bennett Harrison, *The Deindustrialization of America*, New York: Basic Books, 1982.

7. See for example, several of the articles in George Sternlieb and James W. Hughes, editors, *Post Industrial America: Metropolitan Decline and Inter-Regional Job Shifts*, New Brunswick, NJ: The Center for Urban Policy Research, 1975, or David Gordon, "Capitalist Development and the History of American Cities," in William Tabb and Larry Sawers, *Marxism and the Metropolis*, New York: Oxford University Press, 1978.

8. We define four such megalopolises: Greater New York (includes New Brunswick, Long Branch-Ashbury, Newark, Jersey City, Patterson, Passaic, New York, Nassau Suffolk, and Bridgeport); Greater Los Angeles (Los Angeles, Anaheim, Riverside); Greater San Francisco (San Francisco, San Jose); and Greater Washington D.C. (Washington D.C., Baltimore).

9. Publication of the 1977 Census was not completed by the time we carried out this test.

10. Once largely local market oriented, factories are now increasingly integrated into a nationwide, if not multi-nationwide, system of facilities where the output of one facility is shipped to and assembled in another (often located far apart) for the purpose of selling final products on consumer markets that are themselves conceived increasingly on a nationwide or worldwide basis.

CHAPTER SIX

The Rise of the Complexes of Corporate Activities: The Role of Corporate Offices

The rapid buildup of employment and output in the corporate complexes has been a hallmark of the development of many large and medium size U.S. cities during the past two decades. City after city has had to manage its way through difficult transitions as factories and warehouses were cleared from the old urban cores to make room for office construction, and as an increasing number of white collar employees were called upon to replace the blue collar workers of an earlier era. At the core of this development is the rising importance of producer service-type inputs in the operation of industrial corporations, manifested by the multiplication of corporate offices and other service-like establishments and by the growth of attending producer service firms.

This chapter identifies agglomeration tendencies among the three basic managerial units of large corporations—national headquarters, divisional head offices and regional sales headquarters. The next examines selected financial institutions and corporate services firms, the linkages that have developed between them and the major offices of corporations, and the resulting need (or lack thereof) for spatial proximity between the two.

R&D establishments of large corporations as well as private and public sector laboratories are studied in Chapter 9 along with key nonprofit and public sector institutions because of close linkages among them.

Special Problems Associated with the Study of the Complexes of Corporate Activities

Traditionally, there has tended to be a clear-cut distinction between services that corporations produce in-house and those they purchase from producer service firms. For example, since the breakup of the corporate giants of the late 19th and early 20th century, financial services have been rendered by firms independent of industrial corporations. In addition, since the 1933 Glass-Steagel Act, investment banking services, related to bond and stock offerings, have been rendered by specialized banking institutions (''investment banks'') distinct from those which provide for short and medium term loans (''commercial banks'').

More recently, however, the relationship between many in-house and free-standing services has been in flux, with industrial corporations moving into territories that were once the sole domain of independent producer service firms. For example, while insurance services were traditionally offered by specific financial institutions, corporations have now begun to meet a variety of their insurance needs within the boundaries of their own institutions (namely, the rise of the so-called "captive" insurance subsidiaries). In addition, whereas short term lending to non-financial firms long remained the prerogative of commercial banks, the late 1970s have witnessed the development of short term lending by cash-rich industrial firms to cash needy corporations. Likewise, there are indications that if some of the new S.E.C. rules go into effect, corporations will be able to market directly their own securities.

Several implications follow. Corporate offices and producer service firms need to be examined in conjunction with one another, because of strong complementarity and substitutability between their outputs. At the same time, because of substitutability, it is often difficult to carry out studies in which producer services output can be neatly identified. In management consulting, for example, the market for advisory services is characterized by strong competition among independent management consulting firms, the management advisory service divisions of the accounting firms, individual consultants, and "internal consultants" (management consulting units set up within large industrial corporations). In public relations, firms can either provide for their own needs or get help from public relation or advertising firms. The consequent limitations for data analyses become readily apparent. Most conventional government data, whether relating to employment or output, often lack the level of detail required to clearly identify and measure producer services.

This is not the only data limitation, however. As has been noted in Chapter 1, the empirical category that is used here to define complexes of corporate activities include economic institutions which, while strongly oriented to the needs of the large corporation, serve also those of smaller businesses, government, and individuals. The implication, when examining employment or output data, is that it is difficult to distinguish between those activities included in the complexes that cater mostly or exclusively to firms and those that serve a much larger public.

The following example illustrates this point. While the 250 largest commercial banks of the nation provide for a very large share of "Commercial and Industrial Loans" (well over 90 percent),[1] there are roughly 13,000 additional commercial banking institutions which cater to the more mundane banking needs of Americans and American institutions. In locational terms these 250 largest banking institutions are highly concentrated in a few cities of the urban system. There is no simple way, however, by which one can use government data to distinguish the employment they generate from that of their smaller counterparts.

The third order of difficulty lies in developing measures which, despite their imperfection, can help identify major functional differences among corporate complexes. In spatial terms, it is clear that there is considerable specialization among complexes of corporate activities for at least three reasons. First, different functional levels of corporate offices (e.g., national headquarters, regional sales headquarters or divisional head offices) deliver different types of services, need to be served by different types of producer service firms, and tend to locate in different types of places (see Chapter 2 and below). Second, different types of corporations tend to locate their headquarters and other major offices in different types of places so that there tend to be "industry-oriented" specializations of the complexes of corporate activities. Thus, variations in both the functional and industrial mixes of corporate offices which concentrate in different places promote variations among the producer service firms that develop in those places. Lastly, the size of the corporate complex tends to influence the level of sophistication available locally from producer service firms. Some producer services are so specialized, sophisticated or unique in nature as to be found only in the largest corporate complexes.

Because of the many limitations inherent in employment and output measures drawn from conventional government data, we have developed analyses based largely on industry data. Despite their own imperfections, the latter are superior in describing patterns of specializations on spatial, industrial, and functional bases. Nevertheless, we do not completely abandon government data. They are used in the next short section to establish some key observations that set the terms of the detailed analyses which follow.

A Second Look at the Employment Data

As has been noted in Chapter 4, the complexes of corporate activities constitute perhaps the most geographically specialized employment sectors, when compared to other major sectors, with the share of employment accounted for by the corporate complex of individual cities strongly influenced by both size and type of SMSA. Table 6.1 amplifies these key observations by reviewing the geographical concentration of the sector in the most important diversified and specialized service centers.

In 1976, size 1 to 4 nodal and functional centers—63 of the 276 SMSAs of the urban system—accounted for close to 65 percent of the nation's employment in the corporate complexes, as against 49 percent of the nation's employment in all industries. Such a share represented a slight decline over 1959, when the same 63 SMSAs accounted for 68 percent of the employment in the corporate complexes, but a relatively smaller one than the decline in their share of all industries' employment (from 54 percent in 1959 to 49 percent in 1976).

In addition to emphasizing the continuing concentration of corporate complex employment in a restricted number of cities, Table 6.1 indicates shifting among certain size groups. National nodal centers lost part of their earlier share between 1959 and 1976 (from 28.5 percent in 1959 down to 22.2 percent in 1976), while regional and subregional nodal centers improved their relative standing (from 25.7 percent in 1959 up to 31.9 percent in 1976). Functional nodal centers as a group showed little change, although there was shifting among size groups with gains reported in the smaller centers (sizes 2, 3 and 4) compensating for the losses in the larger ones (size 1).

Table 6.2 provides additional breakdown of these employment data, measured in terms of location quotients. This table permits additional observations. More

Table 6.1   Employment in the Corporate Complexes of Nodal
            and Functional Nodal SMSAs as Shares of All U.S.
            Employment in the Corporate Complex, 1976 and 1959

	SMSA Size	# of SMSAs	Corporate Complex		All Industries	
			1976	1959	1976	1959
			(percentages)			
National Nodal	1	4	22.2	28.5	13.1	18.1
Regional Nodal	1	8	14.3	13.5	11.7	12.1
	2	11	9.1	7.4	7.6	6.7
Subregional Nodal	3	10	4.3	3.7	3.8	3.4
	4	6	1.2	1.1	1.0	0.9
Functional Nodal	1	3	5.9	6.9	4.3	5.1
	2	3	2.2	2.1	2.0	1.3
	3	12	4.6	4.1	4.4	4.7
	4	6	1.2	1.0	1.2	1.2
All Nodal and Functional Nodal SMSAs Combined		63	64.8	68.4	49.0	54.0
United States			100.0	100.0	100.0	100.0

Source: County Business Patterns, 1959 and 1976.

importantly perhaps, the table shows changes in the values of location quotients in FIRE and corporate services (CS) between 1959 and 1976 which suggest a tendency for diffusion of some of these services throughout the system of cities, especially among government-education, residential and resort-retirement centers. Clearly, the increasing need for interaction between corporations and the public sector has resulted in the growth of producer service firms located in government-education centers (e.g., legal counsel, public relations or accounting), and the increasing complexity of many government programs is generating a growing demand on the part of public sector agencies for professional services of producer service firms. Accounting firms, for example, have made major inroads in the market for accounting and consulting services for the government sector. More generally, the growth of financial and corporate services in government, residential, and resort-retirement places also indicates that, in addition to corporate customers, many producer firms cater to a consumer base (namely the booming market for individual income tax services), or that certain producer service firms must continuously keep in touch with both the corporate and the consumer ends of their market. Thus, brokers need offices not only near the major stock exchanges but also close to important concentrations of individual customers in markets as distant as New Mexico, Florida, or Arizona.

In part then, the declining share of corporate complex employment in the largest SMSAs is both a concomitant of the declining share of total U.S. employment accounted for by these metropolitan centers and a result of the tendency for certain producer services to become more dispersed. Still, during the last two decades, corporate complexes have grown relatively faster in medium size nodal SMSAs than in the largest centers because they have benefited from the rapid growth of certain offices of the large corporations which did not require highly central locations (see below). At the same time, the relative decline in the share of corporate complex employment in national nodal centers does not necessarily indicate a loss of clout. There is evidence that the level of expertise of specialized services has increased in the largest centers (e.g., banking, see next chapter). The analyses which follow in this and the next chapter should help clarify these opening observations.

Corporate Offices

This section identifies locational patterns of major corporate offices: national headquarters, divisional head offices and regional sales headquarters. After specifying the various samples of firms utilized in our analyses, we review major locational tendencies among these three major types of offices. We then examine the spatial behavior of regional headquarters in more detail. This examination is followed by an analysis of geographical shifts in the location of national headquarters of Fortune 500 firms during the 1959–1976 period. Lastly, we investigate the tendency for national headquarters and divisional offices of major firms in related industries to agglomerate in selected metropolitan areas.

DATA SOURCES

Listings of major U.S. firms, with proper identification of the location of their national headquarters, are available from various business sources. We follow tradition, and use Fortune's lists of the largest publicly held corporations, concentrating in most of our analyses on Fortune's 500 largest industrial firms, 50 largest transportation companies, 50 largest utilities and 50 largest retailing firms (hereafter the Fortune 650s). In a few tabulations, we also use the list of Fortune's second 500 largest industrial firms. The Fortune lists have been available for a number of years, although only the 500 largest industrial firms were identified in 1959, the third year such a list was published. One of the tabulations

Table 6.2 Location Quotients of Employment in the Corporate Complex and Its Subsectors by Type and Size of SMSA, 1976 and 1959

	SMSA Size	# of SMSAs	Corp Complex 1976	Corp Complex 1959
Diversified Service Centers				
National Nodal	1	4	149.7	157.5
Regional Nodal	1	8	122.6	112.1
	2	11	119.7	111.6
Subregional Nodal	3	10	114.6	109.8
	4	6	125.8	127.8
Specialized Service Centers				
Functional Nodal	1	3	135.4	134.4
	2	3	111.9	116.9
	3	12	105.7	89.3
	4	6	96.6	82.8
Government-Education	1	1	138.2	123.3
	3	2	90.1	88.1
	4	12	92.3	91.6
Education-Manufacturing	1-4	5	85.1	79.2
Consumer-Oriented Centers				
Residential	1-4	3	102.9	80.8
Resort-Retirement	1-4	9	98.1	93.7
Production Centers				
Manufacturing	2	1	89.5	83.5
	3	8	74.6	72.0
	4	17	68.4	68.2
Industrial-Military	2	1	96.1	77.4
	3	2	89.0	89.5
	4	9	67.0	61.8
Mining-Industrial	4	7	81.7	86.1
Size 5 SMSAs and Non-metropolitan Areas			59.7	60.3
Share of U.S. Employment in Sectors and Subsectors			14.7	10.2

Column heads: Same as Table 2.2.

Note: Location quotients are unweighted modified averages for major type-size groups.

CAO&A		FIRE		CS	
1976	1959	1976	1959	1976	1959
159.5	145.2	154.4	155.2	141.2	166.3
148.7	119.1	112.6	111.9	120.2	109.2
116.3	90.2	124.7	119.8	116.6	109.8
104.6	102.0	123.8	124.9	110.8	92.2
56.3	58.7	148.1	164.5	135.9	107.3
254.0	294.0	111.2	94.8	105.9	118.0
87.8	145.6	125.2	122.6	110.3	96.1
200.2	151.2	79.3	72.7	88.5	81.5
141.6	106.9	87.4	79.9	85.4	76.1
81.9	49.7	102.0	111.0	194.9	173.7
80.9	99.5	76.7	79.9	105.9	94.4
56.7	88.0	97.5	92.0	103.0	92.9
60.8	44.5	86.9	83.3	93.9	88.4
81.8	36.4	101.0	78.8	113.6	103.5
44.8	24.9	109.1	101.1	111.2	114.4
67.3	88.4	79.9	74.5	107.7	93.8
57.3	57.0	78.4	78.6	78.7	69.4
56.8	41.9	69.2	72.8	72.6	73.6
45.8	16.2	96.8	84.2	171.1	95.3
48.9	44.1	100.6	102.2	95.9	92.1
31.5	39.2	71.2	69.7	78.2	60.8
72.9	124.7	79.3	75.2	87.7	83.9
36.6	48.1	65.4	66.1	63.4	58.1
2.7	1.6	5.7	5.0	6.3	3.6

Source: County Business Patterns, 1976 and 1959.

presented in this chapter involves tracing corporations that have recently joined the ranks of the Fortune 500s or that have disappeared from the list because of mergers or rank downgrading. We have used *Moody's* and *Standard and Poor's* Industrial Manuals when additional information was required to identify changes in the Fortune 500s.

Listings of the major industrial divisions of the largest U.S. firms has been available for nearly a decade now from the *Directory of Corporate Affiliations*. However, only since the mid-1970s has the Directory consistently published the location of the divisional head offices. The 1976 Directory was used here to determine the locational pattern of the divisional head offices of the Fortune 650s at that time.

Listings of the major regional sales headquarters of firms are extremely difficult to come by. The *Directory of Corporate Affiliations* does not report such facilities except in an extremely limited number of cases (largely because the Directory is designed primarily as a guide to supplier firms). When the Directory lists regional administrative facilities, the reporting is often incomplete. To the best of our knowledge, a full census of such facilities for a large sample of firms would require a case-by-case research of individual corporations, involving a study of *Annual Reports* and other corporate materials. Here we have settled for a sample of eight Fortune 650, drawing on three secondary sources.[2]

Employment levels in national headquarters, divisional offices or regional headquarters are not available in any systematic way from any single source. On the basis of a few corporations for which we were able to find fairly detailed data, we estimate that employment in the national headquarters of a typical Fortune 650 may involve anywhere between 2 to 5 percent of the *corporation*'s total labor force (i.e., usually several hundred people) and in the divisional head office, up to 10 or 15 percent of the *division*'s labor force (at times, several thousand people may thus be involved). Employment in regional head offices is even more difficult to estimate—ranging from relatively small numbers to perhaps several hundred people per regional office, depending on the product and merchandising strategy as well as size of the region.[3]

NATIONAL HEADQUARTERS, DIVISIONAL HEAD OFFICES, AND REGIONAL SALES HEADQUARTERS OF LARGE CORPORATIONS: MAJOR TRENDS

Table 6.3 presents for 1976 the numbers and shares of national headquarters, divisional head offices, and regional sales headquarters of the major Fortune firms sited in the 51 largest nodal and functional nodal centers (size 1 through size 3).

Included in this tabulation are the national headquarters of the Fortune 500 industrial firms, the "second" Fortune 500, and the Fortune 50 transportation, 50 utilities and 50 retailing firms (hereafter Fortune 150), the divisional offices of the Fortune 650 (Fortune 500 and Fortune 150 combined), as well as the regional sales headquarters of our sample of eight Fortune 650.[4] Appendix D presents additional place-by-place detail .

Table 6.3 shows very strong concentration of national headquarters and other

Table 6.3 Distribution (numbers and shares) of the National Headquarters, Divisional Head Offices and Regional Sales Headquarters of the Largest U.S. Corporations among the Largest Nodal and Functional Nodal Centers, 1976 and 1959

	SMSA Size	# of SMSAs	Hqs Fortune 500		Hqs 2nd Fortune 500		Hqs Fortune 150		Regional Sales Hqs sample: Fortune 650		Divisional Head Off. Fortune 650		Pop. Share	Hqs Fortune 500 (1959)	
			#	%	#	%	#	%	#	%	#	%		#	%
National Nodal	1	4	179	35.8	140	28.0	51	34.0	16	12.5	2,840	24.7	12.42	217	43.4
Regional Nodal	1	8	83	16.6	95	19.0	33	22.0	31	24.2	1,792	15.0	10.38	78	15.6
	2	11	30	6.0	36	7.2	18	12.0	32	25.0	868	7.6	6.72	21	4.2
Subregional Nodal	3	10	14	2.8	20	4.0	7	4.7	12	9.8	410	3.6	2.94	13	2.6
Functional Nodal	1	3	35	7.0	24	4.8	8	5.3	9	7.0	651	5.7	4.05	44	8.8
	2	3	16	3.2	13	2.6	0	-	6	4.7	260	2.3	1.72	10	2.0
	3	12	53	10.6	37	7.4	15	10.0	3	2.3	782	6.8	4.02	31	6.2
Summary: All Size 1 through 3, Nodal and Functional Nodal		51	410	82.0	365	73.0	132	88.0	109	85.2	7,603	66.3	42.25	414	82.8
All Remaining SMSAs and Non-metropolitan Areas		90	90	18.0	135	27.0	18	12.0	19	14.8	3,874	33.7	57.75	86	17.2
Total		500	500	100.0	500	100.0	150	100.0	128	100.0	11,477	100.0	100.00	500	100.0

Source: Fortune (national headquarters); Directory of Corporate Affiliations (divisional head offices); various sources (regional headquarters); see Table D.1.

corporate offices among the 51 largest nodal and functional nodal centers at mid-decade (1976). Concentration is particularly high among the national headquarters of the Fortune 500 and Fortune 150, and among the regional sales headquarters of our sample of Fortune 650: 82.0, 88.0 and 85.2 percent, respectively, are seated in one of these 51 centers compared to a 42.3 percent share of the nation's population. Concentration is slightly less among the national headquarters of the second Fortune 500, and the divisional head offices of the Fortune 650: 73.0 and 66.3 percent, respectively.

The differences in the levels of concentration between the headquarters of the very large corporations (Fortune 500 and Fortune 150) and those of relatively smaller firms (the second Fortune 500) simply indicates differences in market orientation: more national among the former; more regional among the latter. The remarkably strong concentration of regional sales headquarters in regional nodal centers, and the relatively diffused distribution of divisional offices among a large number of places, seems to point to differences in the attractiveness of various types and size of metropolitan centers for the several types of corporate offices.

Finally, the comparison of the location of the national headquarters of the Fortune 500 firms in 1976 and 1959, made possible by the data presented in Table 6.3, shows almost no overall change—410 firms in the 51 SMSAs in 1976 as against 414 in 1959—but a good deal of shifting among these 51 largest centers: major losses among the national nodal and size 1 functional nodal centers, relatively little change among the size 1 regional nodal centers, and gains everywhere else.

In Table 6.4, these distributions are normalized by computing the ratio of the percentages of headquarters and head offices in a given type-size group of SMSAs to the percentage of the nation's population in the same type-size group of SMSAs. Data presented are for 1976 only, but are extended to other major types of centers.

In addition to reemphasizing the tendency for head offices of all types to concentrate heavily in the very large or large, nodal or functional nodal centers, the table sheds interesting additional light. The size 2 regional nodal and size 3 subregional nodal centers—mostly Sunbelt places—are shown to be weaker in attracting the national headquarters of the Fortune 650 or second Fortune 500 than either the size 1 national and regional nodal centers or the size 1 through 3 functional nodal centers—mostly Snowbelt places. Among divisional head offices of the Fortune 650, the tendency is again heavily in favor of a siting in the older Snowbelt centers (national nodal, size 1 regional nodal centers, and all functional nodal centers). Finally, among regional sales headquarters, the tendencies are quite different. Concentration of regional sales headquarters appear to be strong in the regional and subregional nodal centers, the largest (size 1 and 2) functional nodal centers, and in the large government-education (size 1 and 3) and resort-retirement (size 2 and 3) centers, but relatively weak in the national nodal centers, and smaller (size 3) functional nodal centers.

In short, the locational tendencies of each type of central administrative offices seem to differ sufficiently to require additional investigation.

REGIONAL SALES HEADQUARTERS

The very strong concentration of regional sales headquarters in regional and subregional nodal centers, when compared to other types and sizes of places (Table 6.4), underscores the role such centers have come to play in the market strategy of large U.S. corporations. The relatively weaker standing of the functional nodal centers, especially that of size 3 functional nodal places whose 1976 normalized share of regional head offices is 57 percent of the nation's average as against 333 percent for size 3 subregional nodal centers, seems to indicate that the former are lacking in the service infrastructure necessary to serve as sites from which to oversee regional consumer markets.

The distinction is less clear between the largest functional nodal centers and the regional nodal centers, however. The detailed information on regional sales headquarters presented in Appendix D indicates that among the size 1 and 2 functional nodals, Pittsburgh, San Jose and Hartford appear to have a weak regional orientation; Detroit, Newark and Milwaukee, a somewhat stronger one. This may be reflecting a sorting out of role among large Snowbelt centers, between those that are keeping a strong regional market orientation (mostly classified as regional and subregional nodal centers) and those that are losing it (mostly classified as functional nodal centers). It seems very likely that the growing size of the large corporation and the development of modern communication technologies are increasingly making it possible for large firms to oversee wider markets than formerly from relatively distant centers, thereby bringing about some degree of redundancy among certain Snowbelt places.

These measures also point to one of the ways in which the large and medium size Sunbelt regional and subregional nodal centers have come to gain importance: by becoming centers in which large corporations—often headquartered in the Snowbelt—have established regional sales headquarters to penetrate the South's consumer markets.

The strong showing of the largest government places (Washington, Albany and Sacramento) and some of the resort-retirement centers (particularly Tampa, Orlando, and Honolulu) suggests that these metropolitan economies may be building up strength as centers of regional markets.[5] This interpretation seems consistent with one of our earlier findings, showing that these places have been strengthening their producer service base (finance and corporate services).

Finally, the case of the national nodal centers deserves additional comment. The relatively weaker concentration of regional sales headquarters in these places (Table 6.4) suggests that such centers have become relatively less involved with the overseeing of hinterland markets and more with broader functions such as corporate-wide planning, financing or overseeing of international markets. Evidence presented below and in the next chapter strongly supports this hypothesis.

NATIONAL HEADQUARTERS: 1959–1976 GEOGRAPHICAL SHIFTS

The earlier analysis has indicated a high concentration of national headquarters of Fortune 500 firms in large and medium size nodal and functional nodal centers

Table 6.4   Normalized Shares of National Headquarters,
            Divisional Head Offices and Regional Sales
            Headquarters of the Largest U.S. Corporations by
            Size and Type of SMSA (size 1 to 3 only), 1976

	SMSA Size	# of SMSAs	Fortune 650 Ntl Hdqs	2nd Fortune 500 Ntl Hdqs
Diversified Service Centers				
National Nodal	1	4	294.4	233.4
Regional Nodal	1	8	185.3	197.3
	2	11	102.6	100.0
Subregional Nodal	3	10	98.7	122.3
Specialized Service Centers				
Functional Nodal	1	3	168.2	122.0
	2	3	136.9	144.6
	3	12	224.6	158.9
Government-Education	1	1	76.1	28.3
	3	2	20.8	20.8
Education-Manufacturing	3	2	114.8	119.4
Consumer Oriented Centers				
Residential	1-2	2	27.9	90.8
Resort-Retirement	2-3	5	41.2	35.7
Production Centers				
Manufacturing	2	1	25.1	25.1
	3	8	40.5	80.9
Industrial-Military	2	1	40.7	40.7
	3	2	43.0	43.0
Size 4 and 5 SMSAS and Non-metropolitan Areas			22.9	42.4

Note: Normalized shares are ratios of national headquarters,
        divisional head offices or regional sales headquarters
        in type-size groups of SMSAs to the percentage of the
        nation's population in same type-size group of SMSAs.
        Based on a full count of national headquarters and
        divisional head offices. Regional sales headquarters
        measures are based on an eight-firm sample (see text).

Fortune 650 Div. Head Off.	Fortune 650 Reg'l Sales Hdqs (Sample)	1976 SMSA Group Pop. as Share of US Pop.
201.7	100.7	12.42
150.6	233.4	10.38
113.1	372.1	6.72
122.3	333.1	2.94
142.8	172.7	4.05
134.2	274.3	1.72
175.6	57.2	4.02
73.3	165.1	1.42
45.2	195.3	0.80
120.4	0.0	0.64
59.2	75.5	2.07
58.2	175.2	2.23
87.4	126.0	0.62
105.2	29.3	2.67
30.0	102.8	0.76
47.2	94.1	0.83
55.0	8.5	45.71

Source: Same as Table 6.3.

during the past two decades. In this section we explore this finding in greater detail.

Table 6.5 shows the tally of gains and losses and the resulting net change in the number of Fortune 500s headquartered in each nodal and functional nodal center between 1959 and 1976. Causes for change are shown in Tables 6.6 and 6.7. The procedure used in these tabulations consists of identifying changes in the 1959 and 1976 lists of Fortune 500 headquartered in each SMSA due to acquisitions, departures (headquarters move-out) and rank downgradings ("losses"), or new arrivals (headquarters move-in) and rank upgradings ("gains").

Table 6.5 shows that the magnitude of *net changes* between 1959 and 1976 has tended to be relatively small in most places (at most, a net gain or a net loss of a couple of headquarters—column 3), except for a selected number of metropolitan centers which have experienced major changes. New York (with a net loss of 37), Philadelphia (8), Pittsburgh (8), Chicago (6) and St. Louis (6) were among the major net losers; Bridgeport-Stamford-Greenwich (with a net gain of 20), Houston (9), Minneapolis (6), Portland (5), Milwaukee (5), Atlanta (4) and Los Angeles (4), among the major net gainers.

It is important to observe, however, that, in many instances, the net change statistic (column 3) tends to hide considerable transformation in the pool of firms headquartered, with relatively sizeable gains (column 4) and relatively sizeable losses (column 5) occurring during the period. Since the patterns of change seem to differ markedly among major types of places, a few key observations are worthy of note.

Among the group of national nodal centers (gains and losses not computed separately in Table 6.5), overall changes tend to be influenced overwhelmingly by New York's large net loss of headquarters. Relative to New York, the three other national nodal centers show much less transformation over the 1959–76 period.

As a group, the "older" regional nodal centers (mostly Snowbelt places) display a substantial net loss of headquarters between 1959 and 1976, a result of their inability to offset major losses by comparable gains of new headquarters. The noticeable exception is Boston, which registers a net gain of two headquarters of Fortune 500s during the period, by way of three losses and five gains. (Cleveland and Baltimore register a net gain of one major headquarters.) Among the "newer" regional nodal centers (mostly Sunbelt places) the rule is reversed: gains largely surpass losses. In the aggregate, these two opposite tendencies result in a shift in the number of Fortune 500s headquartered away from the older centers towards the newer ones, with a more even distribution among the two groups by 1976.

Interestingly, subregional nodal centers show little net change, with very limited gains or losses throughout the period, the exceptions being Richmond (two gains, three losses) and Omaha (two gains, two losses). As a whole, this group of SMSAs remains fairly peripheral throughout the period in terms of the number of Fortune 500s which it hosts.

Lastly, functional nodal centers show limited net changes during the entire period, although this relative stability results largely from their ability to offset losses by gains of comparable magnitude. The case of the "New York related" functional nodal centers (Newark, Bridgeport and Paterson) is somewhat exceptional and is discussed below in greater detail.

In short, what this tabulation indicates is that most metropolitan centers have had to rejuvenate continuously their base of headquarters if they were to maintain their original strength. Failure to do so has translated into major losses, and some places have clearly fared better than others.

The way in which this process of transformation has occurred is shown in Tables 6.6 and 6.7, where the causes for individual losses and gains are identified in each place in terms of the categories indicated earlier:

> Losses: departure of headquarters (move-out), firm acquired by another corporation, and rank downgrading of firm (firm too small by 1976 to be classified among the Fortune 500).
>
> Gains: arrival of headquarters from another SMSA (move-in), and rank upgrading of firm (firm added to list of Fortune 500 since 1959 due to increase in size).

A residual category, "undetermined," is used for those cases in which we were unable to identify the reason for the loss or the gain.

In Table 6.7, this procedure is not developed for the national nodal centers since most of the major changes have arisen from losses in the New York SMSA and since the nature of these losses has been identified in an earlier study of the *Corporate Headquarters Complex in New York City*.[6] Findings from this study are shown in Table 6.6. Between 1965 and 1975, New York City lost a total of 66 headquarters, 38 as a result of headquarters relocating to other SMSAs,[7] 21 as a result of acquisition and 7 as a result of rank downgrading. By comparison New York City gained only 28 headquarters, 22 of which as a result of rank upgrading of firms.

Table 6.7 shows the main tendencies for other types and sizes of cities. Among the "older" regional centers (mostly net losers), losses have tended to result, first, from firms being acquired by other corporations and, second, from rank downgrading with the exception of St. Louis, where corporate headquarters move-outs have been substantial. Causes for gains seem to have been associated mostly with rank upgrading of local firms. (There is a large number of gains whose origins remain undetermined.)

Among the "newer" regional centers (mostly net gainers), gains have been associated, primarily, with headquarters moving in from other SMSAs, and, to a lesser extent, with rank upgrading, with the exception of Minneapolis, where rank upgrading of local firms has constituted an important source of gains. Causes for losses have been mostly due to acquisitions.

The functional nodal centers—excluding the New York-related SMSAs—display little overall net change yet substantial gains and losses. Losses result mostly from acquisitions, and gains mostly from rank upgrading among local firms, with the exceptions of Detroit and Pittsburgh, which benefit also from corporate move-ins. Among the New York-related SMSAs, gains are mostly due to corporate move-ins and losses to acquisitions.

This analysis suggests several conclusions. First, the major cause for losses of

Table 6.5   Gains and Losses of Fortune 500 National
            Headquarters among Nodal and Functional Nodal
            Centers, 1959-1976

	1976	1959	Net Change	Gains	Losses
National Nodal	179	217	-38		
New York (-)	100	137	-37		
Los Angeles (+)	21	17	+4		
Chicago (-)	44	50	-6		
San Francisco	14	13	+1		
Regional Nodal					
Older Regional Centers	62	74	-12	+22	-34
Philadelphia (-)	12	20	-8	+4	-12
Boston	9	7	+2	+5	-3
St. Louis (-)	12	16	-4	+4	-8
Baltimore	2	1	+1	+2	-1
Cleveland	18	17	+1	+7	-6
Cincinnati	3	4	-1	0	-1
Kansas City	2	4	-2	0	-2
Indianapolis	3	4	-1	0	-1
Columbus	1	1	0	0	0
Newer Regional Centers	51	23	+28	+39	-11
Dallas	8	8	0	+4	-4
Houston (+)	10	1	+9	+10	-1
Minneapolis (+)	12	6	+6	+8	-2
Atlanta (+)	4	0	+4	+4	0
Miami	2	0	+2	+2	0
Denver	3	4	-1	+2	-3
Seattle	2	2	0	0	0
Phoenix	2	0	+2	+2	0
New Orleans	2	1	+1	+2	-1
Portland (+)	6	1	+5	+5	0
Subregional Nodal	11	12	-1	+5	-6
Memphis	1	0	+1	+1	0
Salt Lake City	0	0	0	0	0
Nashville	1	1	0	0	0
Oklahoma City	1	2	-1	0	-1
Syracuse	2	2	0	0	0
Richmond	3	4	-1	+2	-3
Charlotte	1	1	0	0	0

	1976	1959	Net Change	Gains	Losses
Omaha	2	2	0	+2	-2
Little Rock	0	0	0	0	0
Des Moines	0	0	0	0	0
Spokane	0	0	0	0	0
Jackson	0	0	0	0	0

Functional Nodal
<u>All places except</u>
<u>New York related</u>

	1976	1959	Net Change	Gains	Losses
New York related	<u>85</u>	<u>82</u>	<u>+3</u>	<u>+31</u>	<u>-28</u>
Detroit	16	15	+1	+5	-4
Pittsburgh (-)	14	22	-8	+2	-10
Milwaukee (+)	12	7	+5	+6	-1
San Jose	1	1	0	+1	-1
Hartford	4	2	+2	+2	0
Rochester	4	2	+2	+3	-1
Louisville	0	0	0	0	0
Dayton	4	3	+1	+1	0
Toledo	7	6	+1	+2	-1
Greensboro	5	3	+2	+3	-1
Akron	4	4	0	0	0
Allentown	1	2	-1	0	-1
Tulsa	3	2	+1	+3	-2
New Brunswick	2	1	+1	+1	0
Jersey City	0	2	-2	0	-2
Wilmington	3	3	0	+1	-1
Knoxville	0	0	0	0	0
Wichita	2	2	0	+1	-1
Fort Wayne	1	2	-1	0	-1
Peoria	1	2	-1	0	-1
Kalamazoo	1	1	0	0	0
<u>New York related</u>	<u>33</u>	<u>12</u>	<u>+21</u>	<u>+29</u>	<u>-8</u>
Newark	6	7	-1	+3	-4
Bridgeport (+)	23	3	+20	+22	-2
Paterson	3	2	+1	+3	-2
Total 59 centers	420	420	0		

(-) Major net losers of Fortune 500 headquarters.
(+) Major net gainers of Fortune 500 headquarters.

Source: <u>Fortune</u>, 1976 and 1959.

Table 6.6   Causes for Change in the Number of Fortune 500
            Firms with National Headquarters in New York City,
            1965-1975

Fortune 500 Headquarters in New York City, 1965   128

Losses, 1965-1976   -66

   Moved to Suburbs   -25
   Moved out of New York Area   -13
   Acquired by Other Corporations   -21
   No Longer Fortune 500   - 7

Fortune 500 Headquarters in New York City
      in both 1965 and 1975   62

Gains, 1965-1975   +28

   Moved to New York City   + 6
   Added to Fortune List Since 1965 Because of
         Size or Reclassification   +22

Fortune 500 Headquarters in New York City, 1975   90

Source: The Corporate Headquarters Complex in New York City,
         New York: Conservation of Human Resources, 1977.

---

headquarters in most SMSAs has stemmed from acquisitions of local Fortune 500s by outside firms.

Second, the next most important cause of losses has been rank downgrading of local Fortune 500s—in many instances, that of steel companies (see "Remarks on Losses due to Rank Downgrading" in Table 6.7). Not noted in the table is the fact that many acquisitions during the period have consisted in the takeover of failing steel (and fabricated metal) companies by other firms. This explains why Philadelphia and Pittsburgh have been so strongly affected by losses during the 1959–1976 period.

Third, only in New York (and St. Louis, on a much smaller scale) have corporate headquarters move-outs been the principal cause for losses. This large exodus of corporate headquarters out of New York is important in explaining the overall transformation. It is almost exclusively in those places which have benefited from the relocation of former New York-based firms (mostly the New York-related functional nodal centers and the newer regional nodal centers) that one can identify substantial net gains in the number of headquarters between 1959 and 1976. In most other places net gains have been more limited, with the vast majority of gains resulting from rank upgrading among firms in rapidly growing industrial sectors—particularly electronics, food, energy and motor vehicle part supplies (in the latter case, rank upgrading resulted usually from consolidations of smaller firms into sizeable corporate enterprises rather than from rapid internal growth of individual firms).

In light of the above it seems reasonable to argue that, since the shakeout among the New York firms appears to be substantially completed, the newer regional nodal centers (strong beneficiaries of New York City's corporate exodus in the past) will increasingly be forced to compete with other nodal and functional nodal centers on a more equal footing: that is, by nurturing their own large firms. In this respect, there is no clear evidence from our analysis of the 1959–76 period that these newer centers have been or will be any more successful than the older ones.

A last comment is warranted as regards centers that have failed to maintain their overall position. As we have seen, this phenomenon has tended to be restricted to a few cities and has often been closely associated with the decline of a single industry: steel. It is quite possible that the phenomenon will repeat itself in a few other older industries, but the more general outlook is that headquarters location will tend to stabilize as the U.S. economy completes its adjustment to the new economic order.

DIVISIONAL HEAD OFFICES AND NATIONAL HEADQUARTERS:
INDUSTRIAL SPECIALIZATION OF THE COMPLEXES OF
CORPORATE ACTIVITIES

The previous analyses have examined the patterns of concentration of national headquarters, divisional head offices and regional sales headquarters among different types and sizes of SMSAs, with little regard to the industrial specialization of the firms whose central administrative offices were being investigated. In the present section, we analyze location of national headquarters and divisional head offices in terms of the industry in which they are specialized. The analysis is carried out for 40 selected nodal and functional nodal centers using 11 broad industry groupings.[8]

The industrial specialization of the complexes of national headquarters and divisional head offices of the 40 selected SMSAs is identified on the basis of the industry of specialization of the Fortune 650 firms present in the SMSA either through their national headquarters or through divisional offices. The procedure developed to measure strength of places in each of the 11 industry groupings is explained in Appendix E. In Table 6.8 which summarizes the findings of this analysis, "S" indicates a strong local presence of Fortune 650 firms in a given industry grouping, either through their national headquarters or through divisional head offices, "M" indicates a moderate presence, and a blank cell a weak or nonexistent presence.

National headquarters and divisional head offices in foods and beverage, and

Table 6.7 Causes for Change in the Number of Fortune 500 with National Headquarters in Regional Nodal, Subregional Nodal and Functional Nodal Centers, 1959-1976

	Fortune 500 Hdqtrs in SMSA in both '59 & '76	Losses					Gains				Remarks on Gains (losses) due to Rank Upgrading (downgrading)
		All	Move-out	Ac-quired by Other Firm	Rank Down-grad-ing	Un-deter-mined	All	Move-in	Rank Up-grad-ing	Un-deter-mined	
	(1)	(2)	(3)	(4)	(5)	(6)	(7)	(8)	(9)	(10)	(11)
Regional Nodal Centers											
"Older Regional Centers"											
Philadelphia	8	12	1	4	3	4	4	–	–	4	(3 steel)
Boston	4	3	–	3	–	–	5	–	3	2	1 elect., 1 sci.eqpt., 1 movies
St. Louis	8	8	3	2	2	1	4	1	–	3	(1 brewer), (1 steel)
Baltimore	0	1	1	–	–	–	2	–	–	2	
Cleveland	11	6	1	3	1	1	7	–	1	6	(1 steel), 1 motor veh.
Cincinnati	3	1	–	1	–	–	0	–	–	–	
Kansas City	2	2	–	1	1	–	0	–	–	–	(1 steel)
Indianapolis	3	1	–	–	1	–	0	–	–	–	(1 elect.)
Columbus	1	0	–	–	–	–	0	–	–	–	
"Newer Regional Centers"											
Dallas	4	4	–	3	–	1	4	3	–	1	
Houston	0	1	1	–	–	–	10	5	2	3	
Minneapolis	4	2	1	1	1	–	8	1	3	4	(1 paper), 1 computer, 2 food

Atlanta	0	0	–	–	–	4	2	–	2	
Miami	0	0	–	–	–	2	–	–	2	
Denver	2	3	–	2	1	2	1	1	–	(1 cement), 1 brewer
Seattle	2	0	–	–	–	0	–	1	–	
Phoenix	0	0	–	–	–	2	1	1	–	1 diversified
New Orleans	0	1	–	1	–	2	–	2	–	1 oil expl., 1 not prior in F1000
Portland	1	0	–	–	–	5	1	1	3	1 elect.
Subregional Nodal Centers										
Memphis	0	0	–	–	–	1	–	–	1	
Salt Lake City	0	0	–	–	–	0	–	–	–	
Nashville	1	0	1	–	–	0	–	–	–	
Oklahoma City	1	1	1	1	–	0	–	–	–	
Syracuse	2	0	–	–	–	0	–	–	–	
Richmond	1	3	1	1	1	2	–	2	2	(1 elect.)
Charlotte	1	0	1	1	–	0	–	–	–	
Omaha	0	2	–	–	–	2	2	–	–	2 food
Little Rock	0	0	–	–	–	0	–	–	–	
Des Moines	0	0	–	–	–	0	–	–	–	
Spokane	0	0	–	–	–	0	–	–	–	
Jackson	0	0	–	–	–	0	–	–	–	
Functional Nodal Centers										
"All places except NY related"										
Detroit	11	4	1	3	–	5	2	3	–	3 auto parts
Pittsburgh	12	10	–	5	4	2	2	–	–	(1 steel)
Milwaukee	6	1	–	–	–	6	1	1	4	(1 auto parts) 1 brewer

(continued on next page)

Table 6.7 (continued)

	(1)	(2)	(3)	(4)	(5)	(6)	(7)	(8)	(9)	(10)	(11)
San Jose	0	1	1	-	-	-	1	-	1	-	1 elect.
Hartford	2	0	-	-	-	-	2	-	1	2	1 sci. eqpt.
Rochester	1	1	1	-	-	-	3	-	1	2	
Louisville	0	0	-	-	-	-	0	-	-	1	
Dayton	3	0	-	1	-	-	1	-	-	-	
Toledo	5	1	1	-	-	-	2	-	2	-	2 auto parts
Greensboro	2	1	1	-	-	-	3	-	3	-	3 textile
Akron	4	0	-	-	1	-	0	-	-	-	
Allentown	1	1	-	-	-	-	0	-	-	-	
Tulsa	0	2	-	2	-	-	3	1	2	-	2 oil industry
New Brunswick	1	0	1	-	-	-	1	1	1	-	1 chemical
Jersey City	0	2	1	1	-	-	0	-	-	-	
Wilmington	2	1	1	-	-	-	1	-	1	-	
Knoxville	0	0	-	-	-	-	1	-	-	-	
Wichita	1	1	1	-	1	-	1	-	1	-	(1 aerospace), 1 food
Fort Wayne	1	1	1	-	1	-	0	-	-	-	
Peoria	1	1	-	-	-	-	0	-	-	-	(1 steel)
Kalamazoo	1	0	-	-	-	-	0	-	-	-	
"New York Related"											
Newark	3	4	1	1	-	2	3	3	-	-	
Bridgeport	1	2	-	2	-	-	22	14	-	8	
Paterson	.0	2	1	1	-	-	3	2	-	1	

Note: Last column (11) indicates industry of firms gained or lost due to rank upgrading or downgrading.
Losses due to rank downgrading are shown in parentheses.
Sources: Fortune, 1976 and 1959; Directory of Corporate Affiliations, various years; Moody's Industrial Manual, various years; Standard and Poor's, various years.

in retail and distributive services show strong tendencies to agglomerate in the regional and subregional nodal places. In foods and beverage, they are overwhelmingly concentrated in the regional nodal centers. They are found only selectively in some of the subregional nodal and functional nodal centers, usually in those places that have clear ties to agricultural markets (e.g., Memphis, Syracuse, and Omaha among the subregional nodals, or Wichita and Fort Wayne among the functional nodals). In retail and distributive (transportation and utility) services, they are found in large numbers of both regional and subregional nodal cities. By comparison, functional nodal places tend to remain weaker centers of management in this group of industries.

Among the nine other industry groups, the administrative facilities of major firms show a much greater tendency to agglomerate in a very restricted number of centers. The two size 1 regional nodal centers show administrative strength in a majority of these nine industry groups, reflecting their long-standing involvement in the management of many of the key industries of the nation. But among the size 2 regional nodal centers, only 4 out of the 11 places studied show strong or moderate administrative capacity in three or more of these 9 industry groups: Atlanta (2 strong, 2 moderate), Denver (3 strong, 2 moderate), Cincinnati (3 strong, 2 moderate), Columbus (1 strong, 3 moderate); among size 2 functional nodals, 1 out of 3 places: Milwaukee (3 strong).

Among the size 3 subregional nodal centers, only 1 of the 7 centers studied shows strong or moderate administrative capacity in two or more of the 9 industry groups: Richmond (3 strong, 1 moderate). As for the lone size 4 subregional nodal center, it is weak in every industry group. By comparison, 10 of the 11 size 3 functional nodal centers studied show strong or moderate administrative capacity in two or more of the 9 industry groups and each of the 4 size 4 functional nodal centers studied show strong or moderate administrative capacity in at least one industry.

This analysis is important in at least two respects. First, it confirms our earlier impression (based on the four industry analyses presented in the previous chapter) that most of the industries of the nation continue to be administered, in large measure, from the older Snowbelt centers—whether they are managed from the large (size 1) regional nodal centers, which tend to retain administrative control in many major industry groups, or from the functional nodal centers, which hold management control more selectively. Only in foods and beverage and in retail and distributive service industries have a majority of the (mostly Sunbelt) size 2 and 3 nodal centers made major inroads, and only in a few cases have some of the Sunbelt centers seemed to gain control in any of the 9 other major industry groups.

Second, this analysis clarifies the position which functional nodal centers occupy in the system of cities. In addition to their continued specialization in manufacturing production, a large measure of their strength resides in their ability to manage and administer, selectively, groups of industries. Thus we find examples of strongly specialized corporate complexes in almost all of these cities: San Jose in the electronics industry, Rochester in office and scientific equipment, Akron in the tire industry, Toledo in the motor vehicle parts industry, Greensboro-High

Table 6.8 Industrial Specialization of the Complexes of National Headquarters and Divisional Head Offices of Selected SMSAs as Shown by Their Relative Strength in Eleven Broad Industry Groups, 1976

Regional, Sub-regional Nodal	SMSA Size	Food &Bev	Ret Dist Serv	Pap& Cons Mat	Prin Publ	Met Mfg	Tran Equip	Elec Mach Elec	Petr Chem	Phar Cosm	Tbco	Text Appl Furn
Philadelphia	1	S	S	S	S	S	S	S	S	S		S
Cleveland	1		S	S		S	S	S	S			
Atlanta	2	S	S	S				M	M			S
Miami	2	S	S		S							S
Denver	2	S	M	S	S	S	S	M	M			
Seattle	2	S	S				S					
Cincinnati	2	S	S	S				M	M			
Kansas City	2	S	S				M			S		
Phoenix	2	S										
Indianapolis	2	S	M				M		M			
New Orleans	2	M	S			S			M			
Portland	2	S	M	S			M					
Columbus	2		M			S		M	M			
Memphis	3	S										
Nashville	3	S	M									S
Oklahoma City	3		M						S			
Jacksonville	3		M				M		S			
Syracuse	3	S	S	S		S						
Richmond	3		M						M		S	
Charlotte	3		M									S
Omaha	3	S							M			
Des Moines	4											

Functional Nodal

Milwaukee	2	S	M			S		S	S
San Jose	2	M				S		S
Hartford	2					M	S	
Rochester	3	M					S	M
Louisville	3		S		S		S	S
Dayton	3		S		S		S	S
Bridgeport	3	S	S	S	S		S	S
Toledo	3		S		S		S	S
Greensboro	3					S		S
Akron	3	M	S	S	S		S	
Allentown	3	S		S	M		M	
Tulsa	3	M			S		S	
New Brunswick	3	S			M		M	S
Wilmington	3	S	S				S	M
Paterson	4		S		S		S	M
Wichita	4	S					S	
Fort Wayne	4	S					M	M
Peoria	4						M	

Other Types

Buffalo	2	M			S		S	S
San Diego	2		M		M			
Providence	3			S	S		S	M
New Haven	3				M	S		S

Note: Based on a survey of Fortune 650 firms. Basis for measuring relative strength is explained in Appendix E. "S" indicates strong local presence of Fortune 650s either through national headquarters or through divisional head offices; "M" indicates medium local presence; blank indicates weak or nonexistent local presence.

Source: Fortune, 1976, and Directory of Corporate Affiliations, 1976. Appendix E.

Point in the textile and furniture industries, Wilmington in the petrochemical industry, Wichita in the aerospace industry, and Fort Wayne and Peoria in the farm equipment industry. Such development is clearly a result of historical factors, since the management strength of these functional nodal centers tends to be in the very same industries in which they have long specialized in manufacturing production, and is usually closely related to the development of large, locally based corporations.

Conclusion

While we must await the analyses presented in the next chapter to establish fully the nature of differences that exist among major metropolitan corporate complexes, the present chapter suggests important differences in the forces of agglomeration at work among key corporate offices and a resulting tendency for specialization among these complexes.

Despite a relative loss in share during the past two decades, the national nodal centers remain a privileged headquarter location for the largest U.S. firms or some of their largest industrial divisions: nearly 40 percent of the Fortune 1150 firms, and 25 percent of the industrial divisions of the Fortune 650 were located in these four major urban centers in 1976. As various studies have shown[9] and as the next chapter confirms, these firms and divisions are typically among the most heavily involved in international markets as they find in these centers the best and most sophisticated infrastructure of producer services conducive to this kind of activity.

Regional nodal centers and, to a lesser extent, subregional nodal and large government centers appear to offer some of the most favorable locations from which corporations operating nationwide can oversee the major regional consumer markets (resulting in large concentrations of regional sales headquarters in such centers), and in which large, yet more regional, consumer-oriented firms (foods, beverage, retailing, distribution) can seat their corporate headquarters.

The relatively more "off-centered" functional nodal places seem characterized most importantly by their strong managerial control over specific industry lines (e.g., automobile, computer, office equipment, semiconductor, and so forth) through both national headquarters and major divisional offices, while showing a more peripheral involvement in regional consumer markets.

A last major finding is that when the locational concentration of both national headquarters and divisional offices of large U.S. firms is used as an indicator of the extent of metropolitan economies' control over industrial sectors, it shows that a great deal of the control of the major industrial sectors of the economy remains sited in the nodal and functional nodal centers of the Snowbelt.

In the next chapter, we investigate locational tendencies among selected financial institutions and corporate service firms in order to identify further structural differences that differentiate corporate complexes.

Notes

1. Federal Reserve Board's estimate.

2. See source to Appendix Table D.1.

3. In Subcommittee on the City, *Large Corporations and Urban Employment*, U.S. House of Representatives, 95th Congress, 1978.

4. For 1976, *The Directory of Corporate Affiliations* shows a total of 11,477 divisions for the Fortune 650, an average of 18 divisions per firm, and the 8-firm sample of Fortune 650 yields 128 regional sales headquarters, an average of 16 regional sales headquarters per firm. See Appendix D.

5. Miami, today a major regional nodal center, would appear to be an example of a city in which this transition has already taken place.

6. Op. cit., New York: Conservation of Human Resources, 1977.

7. Of the 38 corporations that moved out of New York City, 26 relocated in its vicinity—mostly in the Greenwich-Stamford-Bridgeport SMSA. To a very large extent, such a move reflected their need or desire to maintain close business relationships with the New York City-based producer service firms. More on this in the concluding section of the next chapter.

8. Most of the size 1 nodal and functional nodal centers were not analyzed because of the complexity involved in working up the tabulation.

9. Conservation of Human Resources, 1977, op. cit. and Robert Cohen, "The Internationalization of Capital and U.S. Cities," Ph.D. Dissertation, New School for Social Research, 1980.

CHAPTER SEVEN

The Rise of the Complexes of Corporate Activities: The Role of Financial Institutions and Corporate Service Firms

In this chapter, we continue our investigation of the firms and institutions that have shaped the growth of corporate complexes. The analysis is organized in two major sections. In the first section we examine three groups of financial institutions: commercial banks, life insurance, and financial subsidiaries of industrial firms; in the second, two major corporate services: accounting and advertising.

Financial Institutions

In their drive for expansion, large firms can raise new capital in several ways besides reinvesting their own yearly profits. They can issue equity (stocks) or long term bonds (debentures) through underwriters or private placement, establish long term credit lines (revolving credit agreements) with consortia of domestic commercial banks, sell long-term notes to domestic private non-bank lenders—traditionally insurance companies but increasingly other industrial corporations, or raise funds from the Eurodollar markets (either in the form of Euro loans or Euro debentures). The issuance of stocks and domestic bonds entails relationships with U.S. investment banks; that of notes, Euro notes or Euro bonds with U.S. commercial banks and non-bank financial intermediaries or U.S. and foreign, commercial and investment banks in the case of Euro funds.

Since the late 1960s, there has been a powerful trend among large corporations to rely increasingly on domestic commercial bank credit and Euro funds compared to an earlier, more traditional dependence on stock and bond issues. In general, this trend has resulted in a strengthening of the relationships between large commercial banks and large corporations. Thus, while in 1970 domestic loans from commercial banks represented only 6 percent of the long term financial resources of industrial firms, their share reached well over 25 percent by the mid-1970s.[1] In addition, the increasing importance of Euro loans and Euro bonds as sources of funds has further reinforced the relationships developing between U.S. industrial corporations and U.S. commercial banks on the basis of domestic lending. This has been so because, the Euro dollar markets being beyond the reach of federal regulators, U.S. commercial banks have been free to act as investment bankers on these markets—a role from which they are still excluded in the domestic financial markets.[2]

This and the proliferation of other types of services provided nowadays by commercial banks (leasing, cash management, foreign exchange trading, factoring and so forth) appear to have been moving the economy rapidly into an era of "one-stop banking," in which large commercial banks and the emerging giant investment bank-insurance company-money market funds conglomerates[3] are increasingly competing to provide a wide range of financial and non-financial services to their corporate customers. What is also becoming apparent is that these developments are not only further propelling the larger financial institutions to center stage, largely at the expense of smaller institutions, but that they are reinforcing the trend towards concentration of financial resources in a very restricted number of metropolitan centers. Thus, while we do not attempt to map out the position of the emerging giant financial hybrids vis-à-vis that of the very large commercial banks in this chapter (for reasons explained below), we do take a close look at the latter and demonstrate that, in relative terms, contrary to a common impression, it has been the first tier banking institutions (the so called "money center banks") which have grown the fastest during the 1960s and 1970s, not the second tier banks (the so called "regional banks").

In the first half of this chapter, we focus on (1) commercial banks, (2) life insurance companies and (3) financial subsidiaries of non-financial firms. By the late 1970s, commercial banks were the largest holders of assets among financial institutions, with roughly 40 percent of all assets, and life insurance firms the third largest, with approximately 13 percent.[4] Savings and loan associations—not studied here—were the second largest, with 17 percent, while the financial hybrids *a la* Merrill Lynch or American Express/Shearson, with the ir money market funds, were rapidly closing ranks on the life insurance firms.[5] Summary data covering the assets of the financial subsidiaries of non-financial firms are not readily available since these are not subject to systematic reporting to financial regulatory agencies.

Financial subsidiaries of non-financial firms are studied here, however, for several reasons. Although they find their origins in different kinds of companies (mostly industrial corporations), they are rather similar to the financial hybrids mentioned above which are being built through mixed mergers of financial institutions (investment banks, life or property and casualty insurances, consumer credit companies and so forth). Indeed the growing importance of both types of institutions is related to the same general forces which are breaking open the entire financial markets. Thus the largest financial subsidiaries of non-financial firms have become sizable competitors in areas such as credit to consumers (Sears, GM, Ford), insurance (Sears, J.C. Penney), leasing (International Harvester, IBM, ITT and a number of office equipment firms), short term loans to cash needy corporations (Exxon, IBM), or even money market funds (Sears), and there is evidence that, in a rapidly changing financial environment, their importance will continue to grow.

In the absence of satisfactory listings of the financial hybrids, we found in the *Directory of Corporate Affiliations* a reasonable way of examining what is happening to some of the most important financial subsidiaries of non-financial firms. The evidence gleaned from these records shows that these financial subsidiaries are strongly drawn to the nation's financial markets and especially to the money centers, thereby further bolstering the latter's increasing prominence.

COMMERCIAL BANKS

Our analysis of the geography of commercial banking in the United States proceeds in three steps. It opens with an examination of the locational concentration of the deposits of the major commercial banks, proceeds with a study of the geography of major domestic corporate loans, and concludes with a survey of foreign trade related, bank-corporation linkages.

Locational concentration of banking deposits. As has been suggested in the previous chapter, U.S. commercial banking can be viewed as a system in which the "Top 250" commercial banks play the major role and all other 13,000 or so institutions, a much more peripheral one. This view still leaves out fundamental differences which exist among these very large banks, between those located in New York and the three other national nodal centers (San Francisco, Chicago and Los Angeles), and those found in other centers.

Table 7.1 distributes the deposits of the 137 "Top 250" commercial banks that are headquartered in the 27 largest banking centers. This table shows the very high degree of concentration of commercial banking deposits in a few metropolitan centers, as well as the evolution of trends over the period 1960–1976.

New York's dominance is truly overwhelming. By 1976, the 20 "Top 250" commercial banks headquartered in New York City had come to control close to a quarter of all U.S. commercial banking deposits—a huge increase over 1960 (15 percent). As a whole, the 41 "Top 250" commercial banks headquartered in the four national nodal centers were overseeing a staggering 42 percent of the nation's deposits in 1976, compared to 28 percent in 1960. The other metropolitan centers with sizable concentrations of large commercial banks—16 regional and subregional nodal centers, 6 functional nodal centers, one government-education center and 2 production centers—were controlling an aggregate share of 19.3 percent, compared to 17.5 percent in 1960. By comparison, deposits in smaller banks and smaller banking centers had registered a sharp decline over the period: from 54 percent in 1960 down to 39 percent in 1976.

On a place-by-place basis, the growth of deposits in these major banking centers displayed substantial variation between 1960 and 1976. This is shown in the last column of Table 7.1, where the ratio of the rate of growth of deposits in locally based "Top 250" banks to the rate of growth of all U.S. deposits is presented for the period 1960–76. A ratio above 1.0 indicates that these deposits have grown faster than the average for the nation; below 1.0, slower.

As these ratios indicate, deposits in the larger banks of the national nodal centers) have grown much faster than the national average—particularly among the

New York banks (ratio of 1.80). Among other major banking centers, experiences have been much more varied. Among the regional and subregional nodal centers, Charlotte (ratio 4.25), Phoenix (1.74), Houston (1.41), Philadelphia (1.34), and Atlanta (1.25) have performed particularly well, followed by Seattle (1.21), Dallas (1.16), Indianapolis (1.13), and Baltimore (1.07). Cleveland (0.58) and St. Louis (0.59) have done particularly poorly.

Among the specialized service centers, growth has been poorer on average, ranging from Washington (highest, with a ratio of 1.26) to Milwaukee (lowest with 0.64).

Among the two production centers with a large banking capacity, the growth of commercial banking deposits has been particularly vigorous in Buffalo (ratio 2.78). This, however, has resulted from banking consolidations in upper New York State, whereby Buffalo's largest banks have taken over a number of the region's banks.

These ratios suggest several observations. First, they suggest that the presence of a regional center of the Federal Reserve Bank in a particular locale (name of city followed by asterisk in Table 7.1) has neither deterred nor particularly favored the growth of its banking sector (for that matter, two of the Federal Reserve Bank centers—Richmond and Kansas City—do not even rank among these 27 largest banking centers).

Second, and perhaps more importantly, they suggest that despite some relationship between regional growth and the growth of deposits—as underscored by the growth of banking in Charlotte, Phoenix, Houston, Atlanta or Dallas—the correlation has not been straightforward. Clearly, the particular growth dynamics of individual local banks has been a major factor in explaining the growth of banking deposits in specific places in both Snowbelt and Sunbelt regions.[6] One must recognize, however, that in their pursuit of growth, regional banks have often had to follow strategies putting them at greater risks than the money center banks. Thus, several of Atlanta's major banks suffered major setbacks during the 1973–75 recession, as did First Pennsylvania and some of the other Philadelphia banks in the late 1970s, or Seafirst in Seattle in the early 1980s.

On the whole, banks in the regional, subregional or functional nodal centers have usually been hard pressed to keep up with New York and the money centers, suggesting that maturity, experience, and size of assets of individual institutions remains a considerable comparative advantage in the banking business.[7] This theory is partly corroborated by the fact that the older regions, which benefited from an earlier start, continue to host close to two-thirds of the large regional banking centers.

To understand better the dominance of the largest banks, we investigated two types of relationships: major credit lines established by banks for the domestic funding needs of major industrial firms and bank-corporation linkages arising from corporate needs to finance foreign trade or foreign investments.

The geography of major domestic corporate loans. Major domestic relationships between commercial banks and industrial corporations are illustrated in Table 7.2. This table shows, for the first half of the 1970s, the number of cases in

Table 7.1 Total Deposits and Growth of Total Deposits in the 137 "Top 250" Commercial Banks Located in the 27 Largest Banking Centers, 1976 and 1960

	SMSA Size	Top 250 Com. Banks # 1976	Top 250 Com. Banks # 1960
DIVERSIFIED SERVICE CENTERS			
National Nodal			
New York*	1	20	22
San Francisco*	1	7	8
Chicago*	1	9	12
Los Angeles	1	5	5
Regional/Subregional Nodal			
Philadelphia*	1	12	7
Dallas*	1	5	5
Boston*	1	5	5
Seattle	2	5	4
Cleveland*	1	5	5
Houston	1	5	4
Phoenix	2	3	3
Atlanta*	2	4	4
Portland	2	2	2
Baltimore	1	4	6
Charlotte	3	2	2
Minneapolis*	1	3	3
Indianapolis	2	3	2
St. Louis*	1	3	4
SPECIALIZED SERVICE CENTERS			
Functional Nodal			
Detroit	1	7	6
Pittsburgh	1	4	4
Newark	1	5	3
Hartford	2	2	2
Milwaukee	2	3	3
Greensboro	3	1	2
Government-Education			
Washington, DC	1	7	4
PRODUCTION CENTERS			
Buffalo	2	3	3
Providence	3	3	2

Residual
All U.S. Commercial Banks[a]

*Federal Reserve Bank Center.
[a]SMSAs are listed by major type and are ranked, within type, according to the volume of deposits in the "Top 250" commercial banks headquartered in the SMSA. This listing shows the 27 largest U.S. banking centers. Deposits in all Top 50 commercial banks, 37 of the second Top 50, and 70 of

Top 250 Deposits $ Billions		Top 250 Deposits % U.S.		Growth Deposit Ratio: Local "250" to U.S.
1976	1960	1976	1960	
198.045	34.176	23.44	14.83	1.80
86.619	16.631	10.25	7.22	1.58
40.235	8.271	4.76	3.59	1.45
26.886	5.611	3.18	2.43	1.42
18.146	3.981	2.15	1.73	1.34
10.546	2.585	1.25	1.12	1.16
9.901	2.759	1.17	1.20	0.97
8.699	2.056	1.03	0.89	1.21
8.366	3.281	0.99	1.42	0.58
7.919	1.662	0.94	0.72	1.41
5.851	1.035	0.69	0.45	1.74
5.635	1.299	0.66	0.56	1.25
5.149	1.698	0.61	0.74	0.76
4.919	1.276	0.58	0.55	1.07
4.885	0.396	0.58	0.17	4.25
3.990	1.238	0.47	0.54	0.83
3.667	0.916	0.43	0.40	1.13
3.414	1.468	0.40	0.63	0.50
14.128	4.078	1.67	1.78	0.92
11.675	2.880	1.38	1.25	1.15
4.012	1.221	0.47	0.53	0.86
3.138	0.807	0.37	0.35	1.08
3.120	1.148	0.37	0.50	0.64
2.846	0.744	0.34	0.32	1.06
5.244	1.203	0.62	0.52	1.26
10.875	1.294	1.29	0.56	2.78
3.219	0.760	0.38	0.33	1.21
333.961	126.020	39.52	54.69	0.62
845.100	230.500	100.00	100.00	1.00

the next 150 banks are accounted for by the deposits of the metropolitan centers shown in table. Deposits in the 113 remaining "Top 250" commercial banks are included in the residual with those of the 13,000 or so smaller banks.

Source: Moody's 1960 and 1976 lists of the 250 largest Commercial Banks. Federal Reserve Board list of the Federal Reserve Bank centers.

which a commercial bank acted as the "lead" bank (largest long term lender) or held the second or third largest long-term lending position to a selected number of major firms in the four industries studied in the previous chapter.[8] For example, it shows that Chase Manhattan was "lead bank" to two of the 9 aerospace firms, and second or third largest lender to three among them.

The position of "lead bank" is a key one, as it denotes not simply the largest long-term lender but also the bank in charge of organizing consortia of banks willing to provide for multi-year, multi-million dollar credit lines to the corporation. Second and third largest lenders do not play as strategic a role as the lead bank does. Still, second and third largest lenders—like the lead bank—may often hold several tens of millions of dollars in long-term notes issued by the borrowing corporation under revolving credit agreements, not to mention larger amounts of short-term notes (e.g., overnight paper, 10 or 60 day notes) which they may own independently from these long-term agreements.

The data presented in Table 7.2 are extracted from a sample survey of about 250 Fortune 500 industrial firms conducted for the *UN Center on Transnational Corporations*.[9] Because the U.N. study from which the data are drawn is a partial survey of the largest Fortune firms, information is available for only 48 of the Fortune firms included in the four selected industries (14 in motor vehicle, 9 in aerospace and ordnance, 14 in electrical appliances and electronics, and 11 in office, scientific and measuring equipment). In addition, because of disclosure problems, only 40 of the 48 lead banks are identified and only 60 of the 96 second and third largest lenders. The results of the probe remain highly indicative, however.

The lead bank measure shows an overwhelming dominance of the New York banks (particularly Citibank, Chase Manhattan, and Morgan): 60 percent of the lead positions (24 out of 40) are occupied by the New York banks. The industry breakdown does show some bank specialization along business lines, however. Thus, National Bank of Detroit stands out as a strong leader in the motor vehicle industry, Citibank in aerospace, Morgan in electrical appliance and electronics, and Manufacturers Hanover in office equipment.

The tabulation of the second and third largest bank lenders brings out the importance of the other national nodal centers, particularly that of San Francisco. Not surprisingly, both the lead bank measure and the second and third largest lender measures point also to the relative weakness of the banks located in other than the four national nodal centers in the market for major long-term corporate loans, indicating only very limited activity on their part.

Most important, perhaps, is the fact that only 8 among the 24 firms using a New York bank as a leader and 5 among the 8 firms using either a San Francisco, a Chicago or a Los Angeles bank as a leader are headquartered in the same city as their lead bank, indicating that most major U.S. firms, depend heavily on New York and the three other national nodal centers for their major banking, regardless of the location of their headquarters.

Corporate banking relationships of such a nature were traditionally carried out by executives from the firm or the bank shuttling back and forth to arrange the terms of loan contracts. As of 1968, however, banks were allowed to set up "loan production offices" in major metropolitan centers as a means of tightening up contacts with their key corporate customers. Up until the late 1970s, however, with interstate banking regulations forbidding formal banking outside a bank's home state, loan production offices were limited in the kind of business they could conduct. They could not accept deposits, sign loan agreements, or disburse funds. In most states, however, they could carry out loan negotiations and proposal formulations, short of the formal signing of the agreement which must be done in the bank's home office.[10] The first loan production offices remained, however, an important indication of a bank's will to strengthen its presence in major regional markets.

Not suprisingly, most of the loan production offices in existence by 1975 had been opened by banks headquartered in the national nodal centers. This is shown in Table 7.3 which presents the location of the 36 loan production offices opened by 12 of the top 50 commercial banks at mid-decade (1975).[11] This table indicates that national nodal center banks had, by then covered rather thoroughly each other's home territory. Los Angeles and Chicago seemed to be particularly favored targets for out-of-town national nodal center banks; New York and San Francisco somewhat less so, probably because the near-monopoly position of their local banks was so strong. There were also scattered efforts on the part of a few large regional banks to establish their presence in the national nodal centers. Lastly, while several national nodal center banks had already begun establishing offices in key regional nodal centers, none of the regional banks had attempted to reciprocate. Obviously, the latter were too busy protecting business on their own turf.

The geography of foreign trade-related, bank-corporation linkages. Another important area of finance in which the services of large commercial banks have been increasingly called upon by industrial corporations is foreign trade (export-import) and foreign investment. To lend corporations *domestic* funds needed to finance such transactions, banks are required, by U.S. law, to set up special financial units—Edge Act Bank Subsidiaries—whose sole purpose is to engage in the financing of foreign-related business.[12] One peculiarity of these Edge Act subsidiaries is that they can be set up in cities outside the home state of the parent commercial bank. During the early part of the 1970s, the number of Edge Act corporations grew very rapidly—from 29 in 1965 to 113 in 1976—largely in response to the increasing volume of foreign business handled by domestic corporations.[13] In most cases, these Edge Act subsidiaries were opened by large and very large regional and national nodal center banks.

The location of these subsidiaries is shown in Table 7.4 for both 1965 and 1976, pointing once again, to some very important dimensions of the geography of banking within the United States. The table shows that during the 1970s, many regional nodal center banks were attempting to follow the earlier lead of the national nodal center banks by opening their own Edge Act subsidiaries—a sure indication of their increased involvement in a business which was once handled almost exclusively by the national nodal center banks. In addition, the table indicates that by the mid-1970s six metropolitan centers had become characterized by a strong presence of Edge Act subsidiaries from non-local banks: New York with 24, Los Angeles and Miami with 9 each, Chicago and Houston

Table 7.2 Lead Bank and Second and Third Largest Lenders to 48 Fortune 500 in Four Selected Industries, 1969-1976

MONEY CENTERS	Lead Bank					Second and Third Largest Lenders				
	Motor Vehicle (14 Firms)	Aerospace (9 firms)	Elec'l App. & Elect. (14 firms)	Office Equip. (11 firms)	All Firms All Industries	Motor Vehicle	Aerospace	Electrical App. & Elect.	Office Equip.	All Firms All Industries
New York Banks	3	8	8	5	24	9	10	9	8	36
Citibank	1	3		1	5	2	4	2	2	10
Chase Manhattan		2	2	1	5	4	3	1	2	9
Morgan		1	4		5	1		1	1	3
Manufacturers Hanover	1		1	2	3	2	2	1	1	6
Chemical	1		1	1	3		1	3	1	5
Irving Trust					1					0
Bankers Trust		2			2			1		1
European American					0			1	1	2
Bank of New York			1		1					
San Francisco Banks	0	0	1	1	2	4	4	2	1	11
Bank of America	0	0	1	1	2	3	4	2	1	10
Crocker				0	0	1	0	3	1	4
Chicago Banks	1	0	2	0	3	1				1
Continental Illinois	1		1		2	0	0	2		0
F.N.B. Chicago	1		1		1					
Harris Trust					0					0
Northern Trust				0	0			1	1	1
Los Angeles Banks	2	0	1	0	3	2	0	1	2	4
Security Pacific	2	0	1	0	3	2	0	0	2	4

REGIONAL BANKING CENTERS

	Lead bank					Second or third largest lender				
	Motor Vehicle	Aerospace and Ordnance	Electrical Appliance and Electronics	Office Equipment	Total	Motor Vehicle	Aerospace and Ordnance	Electrical Appliance and Electronics	Office Equipment	Total
Philadelphia Banks	0	0	0	0	0	0	2	0	1	3
Girard	0	0	0	0	0	0	1	0	1	1
First Pennsylvania						0	1	0	0	1
Philadelphia N.B.						0	0	0	0	1
Detroit Banks	4	0	0	0	4	3	0	1	0	0
N.B. of Detroit	3	0	0	0	3	1	0	1	0	0
Detroit Bank and Trust	1	0	0	0	0	1	0	0	0	0
Boston Banks	0	0	0	0	0	1	0	1	0	0
F.N.B. of Boston	0	0	1	0	0	1	0	1	1	1
Dallas Banks	0	0	0	0	0	0	0	1	0	1
Republic N.B. of Dallas	1	0	1	1	0	1	0	1	0	1
Pittsburgh Banks	0	0	0	1	0	0	1	0	0	1
Mellon	0	0	0	0	0	1	0	0	0	1
Cleveland Banks	1	0	1	0	0	0	0	0	0	0
N.B. of Cleveland	1	0	1	0	0	1	0	0	0	0
OTHERS	0	0	1	1	1	1	0	0	0	0
Disclosed	11	9	12	8	40	17	15	16	12	60
Not disclosed	3	0	2	3	8	11	3	12	10	36

Note: This table shows the number of times a bank is the lead bank (left hand side of table) and second or third largest lender (right hand side of table) to 48 of the largest firms in Motor Vehicle, Aerospace and Ordnance, Electrical Appliance and Electronics and Office Equipment Industries. Lead banks are identified for only 40 of the 48 firms; second and third largest lenders in only 60 of the 96 possible cases.

Source: Lending by Transnational Banks and other Financial Institutions to Transnational Corporations, United Nations Centre on Transnational Corporations, 1977.

Table 7.3 Loan Production Offices of Twelve of the Top 50 Commercial Banks, 1975

SMSAs with Loan Production Offices	New York			San Fr	Chicago			Philadelphia		Atlanta	Greensboro	Charlotte
	Citi corp	Chase Manh	Banker Trust	B of A	FNB Chic Ill	Cont Ill	Exch Chic	First Penn	Fidel	Citi & South	Wach	NCNB
National Nodal												
New York	X			X	X	X				X	X	X
Los Angeles		X	X		X	X			X	X		
Chicago			X	X				X		X		
San Francisco		X	X		X			X				
Regional Nodal												
Philadelphia	X											
Boston					X							
Houston	X	X	X		X	X						
Baltimore					X	X						
Cleveland	X				X							
Atlanta	X				X							
Miami							X					
Kansas City					X							

Source: American Banker, July 18, 1975.

Table 7.4 Metropolitan Centers with Edge Act Bank Subsidiaries, 1976 and 1965

	1976		1965	
	Total # of Edge Acts	# of Edge Acts with Parent Outside SMSA	Total # of Edge Acts	# of Edge Acts with Parent Outside SMSA
DIVERSIFIED SERVICE CENTERS				
National Nodal				
New York	36	24	15	7
Los Angeles	12	9	0	0
Chicago	9	6	2	0
San Francisco	6	4	2	0
Regional/Subregional Nodal				
Miami	9	9	0	0
Houston	7	6	0	0
Boston	4	0	2	0
Philadelphia	3	0	3	0
Cleveland	3	0	0	0
Dallas	2	0	1	0
Atlanta	2	0	0	0
Seattle	2	0	0	0
Portland	2	0	0	0
Minneapolis	1	0	0	0
Baltimore	1	0	1	0
St. Louis	1	0	0	0
Indianapolis	1	0	0	0
New Orleans	1	1	0	0
Charlotte	1	0	0	0
Richmond	1	0	0	0
SPECIALIZED SERVICE CENTERS				
Functional Nodal				
Detroit	3	0	2	0
Pittsburgh	2	0	1	0
Greensboro	1	0	0	0
PRODUCTION CENTERS				
Buffalo	2	0	0	0
Norfolk	1	0	0	0

Note: This table accounts for all existing Edge Act Bank Corporations as of 1965 and 1976.

Source: American Banker, February 1977.

with 6 each, and San Francisco with 4. This unusual concentration of Edge Act subsidiaries in the six cities reflected the key role these cities had, by then, come to play in international trade, either along market or product lines: New York for Western Europe, Los Angeles for the Pacific Region, Miami for Latin America; Houston for energy and energy-related equipment, and Chicago and San Francisco for somewhat less clearly defined markets. Miami and Houston are interesting because these cities were not particularly strong banking centers in their own right (although Houston had undoubtedly a much stronger local banking capacity than Miami). The smaller number of Edge Act subsidiaries in Chicago and San Francisco compared to New York and Los Angeles was a reflection of the relatively weaker international market orientation of the former vis-à-vis the latter.

To explore the degree to which the spatial distribution of Edge Act subsidiaries and that of the foreign trade facilities of large corporations were becoming increasingly related to one another, we went back to the *Directory of Corporate Affiliations* and identified for each of the Fortune 500 industrial firms the divisions and subsidiaries listed by their parent company as facilities specialized in foreign trade, in foreign investment or in the oversight of world markets (in the case of worldwide integrated corporations). In all, approximately 200 of the Fortune 500 reported 298 such facilities with about a fourth among them reporting more than one such facility per corporation. One limitation in this probe is that many firms have international head offices of the type which does not have a divisional or a subsidiary status and are not recorded by the *Directory of Corporate Affiliations*. Nevertheless, the tabulation presented in Table 7.5 is a fair indication of major patterns.

As of 1976, the managerial control of U.S. firms' foreign business remained heavily concentrated in a relatively small number of SMSAs. Of the 298 divisions and subsidiaries recorded for this tabulation (column 4 and 6 combined), 109 (or 36 percent) were headquartered in the four national nodal centers, 75 (or 25 percent) in 9 functional centers, 53 (or 18 percent) in 10 regional nodal centers and the remaining 61 (or 21 percent) in 50 less important SMSAs. New York and Chicago together attracted almost a third of all such divisions and subsidiaries: 22 and 10 percent respectively.

Still, close to 80 percent of these divisions (256 of a total of 298) remained directly attached to their parent's headquarters (column 4). It is then of particular interest to examine the ratio of the number of local Fortune 500 firms with a foreign-trade facility (column 2) to the total number of locally headquartered Fortune 500s (column 1) (ratios are shown in column 3), as it gives a rough idea of the degree of involvement of local Fortune 500s in foreign business at that time. The differences displayed among the 23 most important centers, between national and regional nodal centers on one hand and functional nodal centers on the other, are quite revealing. On average, close to 50 percent of the firms headquartered in the latter reported foreign-trade subsidiaries, whereas little more than 30 percent of the firms headquartered in the former reported such subsidiaries. While such a measure is too crude to permit estimates of foreign business activity generated in each city (dollar measures would be necessary here), it seems rather consistent with our earlier analysis of corporate office specialization among types of SMSAs (Chapter 4). What is being observed is that many national and regional nodal centers are characterized by concentrations of large, but often regional firms, whereas most functional nodal centers are characterized by the presence of very large, product-oriented firms that are more likely to be already heavily involved in foreign markets.[14]

The location of the remaining 20 percent or so divisions (42 of the 298)—those not located near their parent's headquarters (column 6)—emphasize the special role played by a few SMSAs in handling foreign trade. In this respect, the strength demonstrated by New York, followed by Miami, Houston, and Chicago, with 17, 5, 3 and 3 such divisions, respectively, is highly consistent with the locational tendencies of Edge Act subsidiaries illustrated earlier. Additional information gained from the *Directory of Corporate Affiliations* in preparing this tabulation indicates, not surprisingly, that the 17 divisions found in New York represent a wide array of industries and products traded worldwide, the 5 found in Miami conduct most of their business with Latin America, and the 3 found in Houston are international divisions of oil companies. The relative weakness of San Francisco seems to corroborate our earlier findings from the tabulation of Edge Act subsidiaries.[15]

Finally, the observation that many among the corporations opening a foreign trade facility outside their hometown tend to be located in relatively weak metropolitan centers (column 7) reinforces the notion that only a relatively restricted number of centers provides the kind of specialized producer services necessary to the conduct of foreign business.

The major conclusion here is that, even though sizable activity on foreign markets tends to originate from a limited number of very large corporations operating out of a restricted number of locations and, while institutions equipped to finance foreign activity tend to be highly concentrated in the national and regional nodal centers, the managerial handling of foreign business is not the exclusive domain of these most central places. The relatively high concentration of foreign business related facilities of industrial corporations in a number of functional nodal centers suggests that active involvement in foreign markets can, to a reasonable extent, be administered away from the major centers of finance.

This analysis concludes our review of the impact of commercial banks and commercial bank-corporation linkages on the system of cities. The main finding is that the geography of commercial banking can be seen as a three tier system in which the upper two tiers (the money centers and the regional banking centers) have encroached sizably upon the domain of the lower tier (the remainder of the system) in recent decades. In effect, this process of encroachment has been most formidable among the national nodal center banks whether the process is measured in terms of deposits, leadership in domestic corporate lending, or leadership in the financing of international trade. In terms of the system of cities, the unrelenting competition among commercial banks coupled with the rising importance of foreign trade and investment has clearly resulted in a strengthening of the financial capacity of the four national nodal centers (especially, New York) to the expense of most other centers. A few additional centers have also preserved a sizable banking capacity (mostly regional nodal centers but including a restricted number of functional nodal, subregional nodal and otherwise classfied centers),

Table 7.5 Twenty-three Metropolitan Centers Most Favored by the International Divisions of Large Corporations, 1976

	# Local Fortune 500 (1)	# Local Fortune 500 Reporting Int'l Div. (2)	Ratio (1)-(2) (3)	# Local Int'l Div. of Local Fortune 500 (4)	# Nonlocal Fortune 500 Reporting Local Int'l Div. (5)	# Local Int'l Div. of Nonlocal Fortune 500 (6)	Headquarters Location of Nonlocal Fortune 500 Reporting Local Int'l Div. (7) (see column 5)
DIVERSIFIED SERVICE CENTERS							
National Nodal(total)	179	56	31%	89		20	
New York	100	31	31%	49	16	17	Chicago(4), Bridgeport(3), Detroit(1), L.A.(1), Greensboro (1), Minneapolis(1), Newark(1), Cleveland(1), Greenville(1), Corning NY(1), Ft Mill NC(1)
Chicago	44	16	36%	28	1	3	
San Francisco	14	5	36%	6	0	0	
Los Angeles	21	4	19%	6	0	0	L.A.(1)
Regional Nodal(total)	88	27	31%	37		16	
Miami	2	0	0%	0	5	5	Pittsburgh(2), S.F.(1), Minneapolis(1), Phoenix(1)
Houston	10	2	20%	3	3	3	Pittsburgh(1), N.Y.(1), Bridgeport(1)
Boston	9	3	33%	7	2	2	not tabulated
Minneapolis	13	4	31%	4	1	1	not tabulated

Cleveland	18	5	28%	8	0	0	
St. Louis	12	4	33%	4	0	0	
Philadelphia	11	4	36%	4	0	0	
Columbus	1	1	100%	2	2	2	Dallas(1), Ashland KY(1)

SPECIALIZED SERVICE CENTERS

Functional Nodal(tot.)	86	41	48%	69	2	6	
Detroit	15	7	47%	14	2	2	Toledo(1), Pittsburgh(1)
Bridgeport	23	8	35%	12	1	1	New York(1)
Wilmington	3	3	100%	7	2	2	Memphis(1), Elkhart IN(1)
Toledo	7	5	71%	7	0	0	
Newark	6	5	83%	10	0	0	
Pittsburgh	14	3	21%	7	1	1	Dallas(1)
Akron	4	4	100%	6	0	0	
Milwaukee	11	3	27%	3	0	0	
Wichita	3	3	100%	3	0	0	

GRAND TOTAL 256 42

Note: This tabulation is based on a survey of the 298 international divisions disclosed by the Fortune 500s. SMSAs shown in the table are grouped by major types and are listed, within type, according to the number of Fortune 500s reporting international divisions in the SMSA (columns 2 and 5 combined). In addition to the 23 SMSAs presented in this table, there are another 50 SMSAs (not shown) with international divisions of two Fortune 500s or less per SMSA. The 61 international divisions, which these 50 SMSAs account for, are all local divisions of local Fortune 500s. They are included in the grand total figure shown at the bottom of column 4. Lastly, note that column 4 may exceed column 2, and column 6, column 5, because firms may have several international divisions in the same location.

Source: Directory of Corporate Affiliations, 1976.

but the gap between them and the national nodal centers has, in most cases, widened.

LIFE INSURANCE COMPANIES

As noted earlier, life insurance companies are the third largest holder of assets among the nation's financial institutions, next to the commercial banks and the savings and loans institutions. Casual observation, alone, suggests that three factors are likely to influence the locational behavior of the industry.

First, life insurance companies derive the largest share of their financial resources from engaging in business with individual, as distinguished from corporate, customers. In 1976, 66.9 percent of their sales originated from "ordinary" insurance policies, 31.8 percent from "group," and 2.0 percent from "industrial." Proximity to customers is thus likely to be a strong influencing variable, if only in determining the location of sales offices.

Second, life insurance companies are sizable investors on financial markets. In 1976, 48.2 percent of their assets were invested in corporate stocks and bonds and 28.5 percent in mortgages. Hence, one can expect the location of the headquarters of life insurance firms or of some of their in-house financial offices to be influenced by proximity to major financial markets.

Third, life insurers are also highly dependent on major pools of white collar workers who must process policy forms and, more generally, keep up with the routine of a heavily paper-oriented business. In the case of the life insurance industry, such work—which often accounts for the efforts of over half of the total labor force of a life insurer—is usually concentrated in a single or, at most, a couple of major offices at or near headquarters. At the same time, because it is largely routine and does not require highly skilled labor, it is unclear whether or not it needs to be carried out within the largest places.

Which locational forces prevail, and to what degree, is investigated in the following paragraphs. The analysis proceeds by examining, first, the locational characteristics of the headquarters of the major life insurers and, second, those of their workforce. The analysis is facilitated by the fact that life insurance is a heavily concentrated business with the Top 50 firms controlling 80.0 percent of the assets of the industry in 1976 (as against 86.0 percent in 1960) (see Table 7.6).

Headquarters location of the largest life insurance companies. In 1976, the seven largest life insurance centers were home to 20 of the 50 largest life insurance firms, accounting for 82.0 percent of their assets (New York, alone, accounting for 34.7 percent). The other 18.0 percent were distributed among 25 additional metropolitan centers.

While headquarters of the major firms in the industry are obviously highly concentrated geographically, examination of the type and size of SMSAs included in these two layers points immediately to locational characteristics which are strikingly different from those observed in commercial banking.

Among the seven largest life insurance centers, three are nodal centers (New York, Boston and Des Moines), while three are functional nodal places (Newark,

Table 7.6 Distribution of Assets and Headquarters of the
Top 50 Life Insurance Companies, 1976 and 1960

| | Headquarters of Top 50 Life Insurance | | Assets of Top 50 | | | |
| | | | $ Billions | | Share of Top 50 (%) | |
	1976	1960	1976	1960	1976	1960
Top 50 Life Insurance	50	50	256.9	100.0	100.0	100.0
New York	7	7	88.1	38.0	34.7	37.9
Newark	2	2	47.5	17.5	18.5	17.5
Hartford	5	5	35.3	11.6	13.7	11.5
Boston	2	2	19.0	8.0	7.9	7.0
Milwaukee	1	1	8.5	4.1	3.3	4.0
Springfield, MA	1	1	6.4	2.3	2.5	2.3
Des Moines	2	2	5.3	1.7	2.1	1.7
25 other SMSA[a]	30	30	46.8	17.1	18.2	17.1
Assets of All US Life Insurance			321.1	116.2		

[a]Combined assets of Top 50 Life Insurance companies
headquartered in these 25 centers range from $5.2
(Philadelphia) to $0.7 billion.

Source: Moody's Manuals, 1976 and 1960.

Hartford, Milwaukee) and one, an education-manufacturing SMSA (Springfield, Mass.). In addition, two (Springfield and Des Moines) of these seven major insurance centers are relatively small SMSAs (size 3 and 4, respectively).

Among the 25 other large insurance centers, the breakdown by type and size of SMSAs (not shown in Table 7.6) indicates, again, substantial diversity. Fourteen centers are diversified service centers (national, regional or subregional nodal), five are specialized service centers (functional nodal) and six are classifed under other types. In addition, 12 among these 25 centers are size 3 or smaller.

Thus, if both size and type of place are used as indicators of ''centeredness'' (to use Dunn's terminology) with the largest nodal places regarded as most centered, the location of the headquarters of the Top 50 life insurance firms clearly demonstrates a dual, somewhat contradictory tendency, with some insurance firms seeking centralized locations in diversified service centers and others, off-centered locations primarily, but not exclusively, in specialized service centers.

An additional striking feature of the geography of life insurance headquarters is the predominance of the Northeast-New England corridor—New York, Newark, Hartford, Boston, Springfield (Massachusetts), Philadelphia[16]—a phenomenon which historians of the industry attribute to the fact that for years these largest insurance markets made it impossible for firms to operate within their boundaries, unless the firm or a specially established subsidiary were headquartered within their state.

Locational tendencies of the workforce of life insurance firms.   While the previous analysis shows tendencies pertinent to geographical concentration of the headquarters of life insurance firms, it is incomplete as regards the locational tendencies of their workforce. The key distinction here is between home offices and major processing centers where large pools of clerical workers are employed, and field offices where salespersons are to be found, usually with a small back office staff.

Needless to say, detailed data on the labor force of life insurance companies are hard to come by. We found published data for one major company, however—Aetna Life & Casualty (6th largest life insurance firm) headquartered in Hartford.[17] We have reason to believe that the behavior demonstrated by Aetna is not unlike that of other large firms in the industry.[18]

In 1977, Aetna employed 25,905 persons in its combined U.S. operations. Of these, 10,207 were employed in Aetna's Hartford headquarters. The 15,698 others were dispersed in field offices in 65 SMSAs with employment ranging from slightly less than 100 to slightly above 400—except in New York City, where Aetna employed 1,100 persons. The large number of employees in New York seems due to the presence of some of Aetna's brokers and other financial personnel in the city.

Table 7.7 distributes Aetna's 65 field offices by type and size of SMSAs. If both type and size of places are used, again, as indicators of "centeredness," this distribution indicates a strong attraction of field offices towards centers of large consumer markets. As regards *types* of places, while field offices are found in almost all national and regional nodal centers (21 out of 23 SMSAs), other field offices are more irregularly distributed among other types of urban centers: in 10 of the 16 subregional nodal centers, in 9 of the 24 functional nodal centers, in 6 of the 15 government centers, and so forth. As regards *size* of place, field offices are found in 16 of the 17 size 1 SMSAs, and 15 of the 19 size 2 SMSAs, but only in 18 of the 39 size 3, 9 of the 65 size 4, and 5 of the 126 size 5 SMSAs. In a tabulation not shown here, we also computed the number of employees in field offices per capita in the SMSA of the field office. The measure showed that "off-centered" field offices tend to employ larger numbers of employees per capita than "central place" offices, indicating very likely that it takes proportionately more people to sell insurance in less dense markets.

To conclude, this analysis of the spatial behavior of life insurance firms seems

Table 7.7 Distribution of Aetna Life and Casualty's Field Offices by Type and Size of SMSA, 1977

	SMSA Size	# of SMSAs	# of SMSAs with Aetna's Field Offices
Diversified Service Centers			
National Nodal	1	4	4
Regional Nodal	1	8	8
	2	11	9
Subregional Nodal	3	10	6
	4	6	4
Specialized Service Centers			
Functional Nodal	1	3	2
	2	3	2
	3	12	4
	4	6	1
Government-Education	1	1	1
	3	2	2
	4	12	3
Education-Manufacturing	3	2	1
	4	3	0
Consumer-Oriented Centers			
Residential	1	1	1
	2	1	1
	3	1	0
Resort-Retirement	2	2	2
	3	3	0
	4	4	0
Production Centers			
Manufacturing	2	1	1
	3	8	3
	4	16	1
Industrial-Military	2	1	0
	3	2	2
	4	10	0
Mining-Industrial	4	7	0
Size 5 SMSAs and Non-metropolitan Areas	5	126	5
Total		266	65

Source: Subcommittee on the City, Large Corporations and Urban Employment, Committee on Banking, Finance and Urban Affairs, House of Representatives, 95th Congress, Second Session, February 1978.

to show evidence of the influence of both centrifugal and centripetal locational forces on the industry.

In terms of the sales force of the industry, locational forces are market-determined, as the industry tries to reach, above all, the largest and most densely populated areas.

In terms of the headquarters of life insurers, there appears to be a dual locational pull at least between diversified and specialized service centers. In that sense, life insurance is much more similar to manufacturing industries for which national headquarters and divisional head offices tend to be distributed among various diversified and specialized service centers, than to commercial banking which is becoming increasingly concentrated in the largest diversified service centers. Admittedly, these data still fall short of reflecting what is truly happening at headquarters. Interviews with specialists of the insurance industry point to the existence of very strong decentralization tendencies at work, resulting from possibilities opened by new computer and communications technology, from the relative tightening of the supply of both system analysts and computer operators in cities where the industry has traditionally concentrated, and from an increased availability of skilled clericals and computer technicians in other regions and cities. Thus, several of the largest life insurers have begun relocating part of their data processing operations away from their original headquarters location, and many of the property and casualty insurers (not studied here)—which are, relatively speaking, even more data generating than the life insurers (since there are frequent revisions of coverage, rates, and so on)—have now set up several regional processing centers to shift part of the workload from headquarters.

What this indicates is that there is increasing pressure and willingness on the part of this quintessential white-collar industry to locate the most free-standing parts of its operations away from the largest, and most congested centers. This suggests a type of service activity which some "off-centered" places might be well positioned to attract in the future.

FINANCIAL DIVISIONS OF NON-FINANCIAL FIRMS

To prepare the third and final probe of our study of financial services, we surveyed the financial divisions (and subsidiaries) of the Fortune 500, recorded by the *Directory of Corporate Affiliations*. To recall, a number of industrial firms have recently moved forcefully into certain areas of financial intermediation, usually by way of specialized financial divisions or subsidiaries. One of our major concerns here is to determine the extent to which the location of such divisions follows that of other key financial institutions, or that of the headquarters of their parent industrial corporations.

Our survey of the Fortune 500 uncovered nearly 120 firms reporting 169 financial divisions. Their location is shown in Table 7.8. This tabulation indicates a very high concentration of such divisions (column 3 and 5 combined) in the four national nodal centers, followed by 12 regional nodal and 6 functional nodal centers with 36, 22, and 18 percent respectively of all financial subsidiaries. The remaining 24 percent are widely dispersed among 38 less important centers.

The first interesting finding is the strong showing of Chicago next to New

York and the weak showing of San Francisco and Los Angeles (columns 3 and 5) among the national nodal centers. New York and Chicago alone attract 17 and 15 percent each of all such divisions.

The second important finding is that, contrary to what was found among foreign trade facilities, financial subsidiaries of industrial firms are more likely to be located away from their parents. Thus, more than a third (61 out of 169) are located in cities other than those of their parents' headquarter, being drawn in most cases to either a national nodal or a regional nodal center. In most instances, these relatively footloose financial subsidiaries are those of firms headquartered in places with weak financial resources (column 6).

In short, the major conclusion here is the strong tendency for financial subsidiaries of industrial firms to be found in the major financial centers of the nation: principally, in national nodal and key regional nodal centers. This suggests that such financial subsidiaries need this kind of strong financial environment to operate and prosper and that, they in turn, contribute to the continuing strengthening of the major financial centers of the nation—New York and Chicago, in particular.

This concludes our third and final probe of the geography of financial intermediaries. In the next major section of this chapter, we examine locational patterns among corporate services.

Corporate Services

In this section, two corporate service industries have been selected for detailed analysis: accounting and advertising. These two industries were chosen for several reasons, including their importance in employment terms, the relatively clear cut nature of their output, the availability of reasonably good data, and the sharp differences displayed by their locational tendencies.

ACCOUNTING

Accounting is a highly concentrated industry. It is dominated by eight very large firms (the "Big Eight": Arthur Andersen & Co., Arthur Young & Co., Coopers & Lybrand, Ernst & Ernst, Haskins & Sells, Peat, Marwick, Mitchell & Co., Price Waterhouse & Co., and Touche Ross & Co.) which overshadow a second layer of seven smaller firms, followed by a plethora of small partnerships.

Traditionally, very little information had been available on the industry from the public domain until a study of the "accounting establishment" (i.e., the "Big Eight") was undertaken by a Congressional Committee in 1977.[19] Although the primary focus of the congressional study pertained to an analysis of the "Big Eight" accounting firms only, the materials developed in the course of that investigation constitute a valuable resource for examining the linkages between accounting firms and their corporate clients. Before turning to such an analysis, it is helpful to review some of the main features of the industry.

Key characteristics of the accounting industry. The reasons for the high degree of concentration exhibited by the industry are essentially of an historical and in-

Table 7.8 Twenty-four Metropolitan Centers Most Favored by the Financial Divisions of Large Corporations, 1976

	# Local Fortune 500 (1)	# Local Fortune 500 with Local Fin'l Div. (2)	# Local Fin'l Div. of Local Fortune 500 (3)	# Non-local Fortune 500 with Local Fin'l Div (4)	# Local Fin'l Div. of Non-local Fortune 500 (5)	Headquarters Location of Nonlocal Fortune 500 with Local Fin. Div. (6) (see column 4)
DIVERSIFIED SERVICE CENTERS						
National Nodal(total)	179	18	30		31	
New York	100	9	11	4	17	Detroit(1), Akron(1), Indianapolis (1), Fremont MI(1)
Chicago	49	8	18	3	8	Pittsburgh(1), New Orleans(1), Portland(1)
Los Angeles	14	1	1	4	4	St. Louis(1), Seattle(1), Tampa(1), Bridgeport(1)
San Francisco	21	0	0	2	2	not tabulated
Regional and Sub-regional Nodal(total)	79	14	19		18	
Houston	10	2	4	2	2	N.Y.(1), Chicago(1)
Denver	3	0	0	3	4	N.Y.(1), Los Angeles(1), Chicago(1)
Portland	6	1	1	2	2	not tabulated
Minneapolis	12	2	2	1	2	not tabulated
Phoenix	2	2	4	1	1	Chicago(1)

Philadelphia	12	0	0	2	2	not tabulated
Dallas	8	0	0	2	2	not tabulated
Cleveland	18	1	1	1	1	not tabulated
Nashville	1	1	1	1	1	Detroit(1)
Cincinnati	3	2	3	0	0	
Syracuse	2	1	1	1	1	not tabulated
Seattle	2	2	2	0	0	

SPECIALIZED SERVICE CENTERS

Functional Nodal	63	13	22	0	8	
Detroit	16	5	12	0	0	
Pittsburgh	14	3	5	1	1	
Wilmington	3	0	0	3	5	Dallas(1), Philadelphia(1), N.Y.(1), Cleveland(1)
Bridgeport	23	2	2	1	1	not tabulated
Greensboro	5	1	1	1	1	not tabulated
Wichita	2	2	2	0	0	
Government-Education	2	0	0	2	2	
Washington	2	0	0	2	2	not tabulated
OTHER TYPE	1	1	1	1	1	
Nassau Suffolk	1	1	1	1	2	not tabulated
GRAND TOTAL			108		61	

Note: This tabulation is based on a survey of the 169 financial divisions disclosed by the Fortune 500s. SMSAs shown in the table are grouped by major type and are listed, within type, according to the number of Fortune 500 with financial divisions in the SMSA (column 2 and 4 combined). In addition to the 24 SMSAs presented in this table, there are another 36 SMSAs (not shown) with financial divisions of one Fortune 500 per SMSA. The 36 financial divisions, which these 36 SMSAs account for, are all local divisions of local Fortune 500s. They are included in the grand total figure shown at the bottom of column 3. Lastly, note that column 3 may exceed column 2, and column 5, column 4, because firms may have several financial divisions in the same location.

Source: Directory of Corporate Affiliations, 1976.

stitutional nature and directly related to the legally mandated certification of corporate records, required in conjunction with the issuance of publicly held securities. While these matters are somewhat beyond the scope of the present study, it is important to observe that, by 1976, the "Big Eight" accounting firms (1) provided auditing and accounting services to 85 percent of the 2,641 corporations listed on the New York Stock Exchange and the American Stock Exchange (nearly all of the Fortune firms used in this study); (2) employed over 50,000 persons, well over 20 percent of all employed by the accounting industry (although the "Big Eight" firms employed only 10 to 12 percent of the nation's estimated 160,000 certified public accountants); (3) brought in revenues of over $2 billion, close to a third of all revenues of the industry. These and other statistics are summarized in Table 7.9.[20]

On the average, the Big Eight firms received approximately 70 percent of their total revenues from performing auditing and accounting services, 18 percent from delivering tax services, and the remainder from management advisory services. Of increasing importance to the Big Eight firms were the revenues drawn from services performed for local, state, and federal government agencies. In 1975, the Big Eight firms were billing the federal government for $16.5 million worth of services, twice as much as in 1971. Although exact figures are not available for other governmental bodies, our estimate is that services delivered to local government institutions were at least twice as great ($40 million or so).[21] Thus, some of the data presented hereafter would seem to indicate that in a number of places accounting firms are able to maintain field offices primarily because of the revenues drawn from services rendered to local government bodies.

In general, corporations use the same firm for all the books they need to certify (usually those of the parent company and those of its incorporated subsidiaries). One implication is that, following a takeover, the certification of accounts of the merged firm will routinely be shifted to the accounting firm of the parent company.[22] For example, when Carborundum, a Buffalo firm which traditionally had used the services of the local office of Price Waterhouse, was taken over by Kennecott in 1977, Kennecott shifted Carborundum's account to Coopers & Lybrand (Kennecott's accounting firm) which, as a result, opened a field office in Buffalo to serve this new account.[23]

Spatially, the interindustry relationship between accounting and industrial firms is mostly a relationship between the *local* office of the accounting firm and the *headquarters* of the client corporation. As we indicate hereafter, there are important exceptions to this rule, however, as one moves down the population size hierarchy of places.

To study the spatial dimensions of the accounting industry in more detail, we have developed two sets of data. The first pertains to the location of the field offices of the Big Eight accounting firms, using the number of partners and principals in each office as a measure of the importance of individual field offices (Table 7.10). It is based on information recorded from *Employee Directories* published by each of the Big Eight firms. The second is a set of cross tabulations, showing the accounts served by the Big Eight accounting firms in their local offices (Table 7.11). These tabulations have been developed for 15 selected metropolitan centers, including 7 regional nodal centers, 2 subregional nodal centers,

Table 7.9 Employment and Revenue Statistics of the Big Eight Accounting Firms, 1975

	Arthur Andersen	Arthur Young	Coopers & Lybrand	Ernst & Ernst	Haskins & Sells	Peat, Marwick & Mitchell	Price, Water-house	Touche Ross
U.S. Employment								
Numbers of Partners and Principals in U.S.	763	464	565	504	455	881	366	484
U.S. Employees (excluding Partners and Principals)	8,554	4,800	6,189	5,795	4,798	8,227	5,933	4,219
Revenues								
Share (%) of revenue derived from[a]								
A – Auditing and Accounting	66	69	69	73	74	68	76	62
B – Tax Services	18	17	19	17	15	21	16	24
C – Service to Federal, State and Local Government	3	5–10	2	1	5	4	2	n.a.
D – Others (mostly Management Advisory Services)	16	14	12	9	11	12	6	14

[a]Columns sum up to more than 100 percent because the services provided to federal, state and local governments (C) are partly double-counted in categories A, B and D.

Source: Subcommittee on Reports, Accounting & Mergers, The Accounting Establishment, U.S. Senate, 95th Congress, Washington, D.C.: U.S. Government Printing Office, March 1977, p. 30-31.

Table 7.10 Number of Field Offices and Location Quotients
of Employment of Partners and Principals of the
Big Eight Accounting Firms by Size and Type of
SMSA (size 1 to 3 only), 1976

	SMSA Size	# of SMSAs	Average Number of Big Eight Firms with Field Office in SMSAs	Location Quotient Employment of Big Eight Partners & Principals in SMSAs
Diversified Service Centers				
National Nodal	1	4	8	174.3
Regional Nodal	1	8	8	146.3
	2	11	8	152.8
Subregional Nodal	3	10	7	144.5
Specialized Service Centers				
Functional Nodal	1	3	8	124.2
	2	3	7	144.1
	3	12	4	96.5
Government-	1	1	8	152.1
Education	3	2	4	64.7
Education- Manufacturing	3	2	3	96.6
Consumer-Oriented Centers				
Residential	1-2	2	5	22.8
Resort- Retirement	2-3	5	5	88.3
Production Centers				
Manufacturing	2	1	7	83.7
	3	8	2	54.6
Industrial-	2	1	7	79.3
Military	3	2	3	65.8

Note: Average numbers of field offices and location quotients
of employment are unweighted modified averages for
major size-type groups.

Source: Individual Directories of Big Eight accounting firms.

5 functional nodal centers and 1 manufacturing center. They are based on information collected for *The Accounting Establishment* study cited above.

Location of the field offices of the Big Eight accounting firms.   Table 7.10 summarizes the information on Big Eight field offices, and on principals and partners employed in these local offices (for size 1 through 3 SMSAs only), with place by place detail shown in Appendix F.

The column showing the average number of Big Eight firms with field offices in size type group of SMSA is extremely revealing. Only in the 4 national nodal centers, the 19 regional nodal centers, the 3 size 1 functional nodal centers and Washington, D.C. (the lone size 1 government center) had all Big Eight accounting firms opened a field office as of 1976.

The other type-size groups standing out by their concentration of Big Eight field offices are the size 3 subregional nodal and size 2 functional nodal centers in which an average of seven of the Big Eight are present locally. The experience of the size 3 subregional nodal centers is remarkable as it differed sharply from that of functional nodal centers of comparable size, where, on average, only half of the Big Eight maintained an office. This seems a rather clear indication of differences in the range of the markets that are served by those two types of places. Functional nodal centers, as we have already suggested, tend to serve rather restricted hinterlands. We may assume that the few Big Eight accounting firms that are active in these SMSAs are there primarily to serve the few large corporations headquartered locally. By comparison, subregional nodal centers serve wider hinterlands and this is reflected in a strong presence of Big Eight accounting firms which deal presumably not only with local firms but also with those located in nearby cities. Finally, in other types of centers the presence of the Big Eight accounting firms is even more uneven, being particularly sparse among production centers (with the exception of the largest two: Buffalo and San Diego).

Location quotients of employment of partners and principals in the field offices of the Big Eight accounting firms show roughly the same sharp differences among different type-size groups of SMSAs. If anything, this tabulation brings out the particular strength of the four national nodal centers when compared to other centers in which Big Eight firms are fully established.

While these measures show the importance of factors of centrality (associated with both size and type of places) in influencing the location decisions of the Big Eight accounting firms, they also reflect variations in individual firm strategies in locating field offices. For example, firms such as Arthur Andersen and Arthur Young, put a much higher limit on the volume of business they need to generate to support a field office than do Ernst & Ernst or Touche & Ross. This was confirmed in an interview we had with one of Arthur Andersen's partners in the Charlotte office of the firm. The firm handles more business from offices distant from the headquarters of corporations it serves than some of its rivals, commuting its accountants whenever necessary. Nevertheless, the more important the market, the more likely it is that the major accounting firm will see fit to establish a field office there.

The geography of accounting firm-corporation linkages.   The next table, Table 7.11, summarizes the information gathered for 15 selected metropolitan centers as regards the auditing of large, locally headquartered corporations[24] and local government bodies by Big Eight accounting firms. Because the data are based on voluntary reporting by the Big Eight accounting firms to the Senate Subcommittee Staff which produced the *Accounting Establishment* study, disclosure is at times incomplete.

Two findings are immediately apparent. The first is the sizable degree of involvement of Big Eight firms with local governmental institutions (right side of table). The second finding, perhaps more important for our purpose, is the differences shown between regional and subregional nodal centers on the one hand and functional nodal centers on the other. Whereas in only one case is a firm headquartered in a regional or subregional nodal center audited by an out-of-town office of a Big Eight firm (Great Western United, of Denver, served by Peat Marwick's Dallas office), a substantial number of large local corporations and local governmental agencies in functional nodal centers are audited by out-of-town offices of the Big Eight firms. This finding is, indeed, very consistent with the earlier one on variations in the local presence of offices of Big Eight firms.

What must be concluded from this analysis is that while the presence of the largest accounting firms is felt directly (i.e., by means of field offices) in a substantial number of large cities, it is by no means felt everywhere and/or equally. The largest nodal and functional nodal centers are clearly the main centers of activity for the Big Eight firms, while their presence is more scarce in other types of centers. Still, the field offices in the nodal centers are undoubtedly the key ones in the organizational structure of the largest accounting firms, since in many functional nodal centers—unlike in the nodal centers—accounting firms choose to serve accounts from non-local field offices.

ADVERTISING

The pattern of interindustry relationships between advertising firms and large corporate institutions differs greatly from that exhibited by the accounting industry. Advertising is principally a New York affair. The nation's largest advertising firms are New York-based firms. These firms tend to handle most of their accounts from their New York office and to be rather parsimonious in their decisions to open field offices in other cities. In a nutshell, what seems to determine much of what happens spatially is the overwhelming importance of day-to-day contacts between the advertising firms on the one hand and the national media on the other (i.e., TV, magazine, photography, etc.—all centered in New York).

Key characteristics of the advertising industry.   The advertising marketplace shows signs of a hefty concentration on both sides. On the one hand, the 100 largest corporate advertisers had an advertising and promotion budget of $7.7 billion in 1976—about 40 percent of the total billing handled by U.S. advertising firms. Mostly all are Fortune 650 firms (plus a few large foreign corporations: e.g., Volkswagen of America). On the other hand, the top 10 U.S. advertising firms captured $8.5 billion worth of advertising promotion—44 percent of the billings of the industry. The top 50 firms captured 70 percent of the industry's revenues, and the next 150 firms, an additional 20 percent. This left the plethora of small, locally based advertising firms fighting over the remaining 10 percent of the industry revenues, which they collected from serving small local accounts (independent car dealers, local department stores, food markets, etc.).[25]

Location of headquarters and field offices of advertising agencies. Table 7.12 presents the geographical distribution of headquarters and field offices of advertising agencies. This table can be looked at in conjunction with place by place detail shown in Appendix F.

Not surprisingly, this tabulation shows an industry which is highly biased spatially. In terms of the headquarters of the top 50 agencies, the great majority of the major advertising firms are New York-based: 37 of the top 50 firms in 1976. As a result, the remainder of the urban landscape is rather sparsely populated. Only Chicago (four firms), Detroit (three firms), Dallas (two firms), Los Angeles, St. Louis, Minneapolis and Pittsburgh (one firm each) are also home to one or more of the top 50 advertising firms. In terms of the headquarters of the next 150 firms, the situation is only slightly more favorable to places other than New York (the home of 59 of the next 150 firms), with the three other national nodal centers, several among the size 1 regional nodal centers and the largest functional nodal centers showing some strength (note, in particular, Chicago, Los Angeles, Philadelphia, Cleveland, Detroit, and Minneapolis).

When the location of the field offices of the 200 largest advertising firms is examined, the record shows that advertising firms are very reluctant to open offices outside a few selected metropolitan centers. It is essentially the same groups of size 1 places (national nodal, regional nodal and functional nodal) which benefit the most from the presence of field offices, accompanied by a few size 2 regional nodal centers (most notably Atlanta, Denver, and Kansas City) and Washington, D.C. All in all, then, New York is the dominant center, followed by the three other national nodal centers where a substantial number of the New York-based firms clearly find it necessary to maintain a representative office. A final observation is that among the few centers outside New York that are hosts to a respectable number of field offices, most are Snowbelt places.

The geography of advertising accounts. From the point of view of corporate advertisers, advertising may involve a split of responsibilities between the national headquarters which will typically handle the largest and most important accounts (usually consumer advertising: brand names and so forth) and the divisional head offices which will take care of smaller and more peripheral accounts (usually industrial advertising).

To try to determine how much advertising activity goes on in some of the smaller places, we investigated in some detail the advertising accounts disclosed by the national headquarters and divisional offices of Fortune 650 firms located in the following eight selected SMSAs: *Size 2* regional nodal centers: Atlanta, Denver, Phoenix, and Columbus; *Size 3* subregional nodal centers: Nashville and

Table 7.11 Auditing of Large Corporations and Services Rendered to Local Governmental Agencies by Big Eight Accounting Firms, Fourteen Selected Metropolitan Centers, 1975

| | # of Big Eight Accounting Firms with Local Field Office | Large Corporations | | | | | Local Governmental Agencies | | |
| | | Total # of Firms | # of Firms Whose Audit is Done by Big Eight | | # of Firms Whose Audit is Done by Other Local Accounting Firms | # of Firms Whose Audit is Not Disclosed | Total # of Local Gov't Agencies | # of Local Gov't Agencies Served by Big Eight | |
		#	Locally	Out of Town			#	Locally	Out of Town
Regional Nodal									
Philadelphia	8	28	17	-	3	8	26	26	-
Cleveland	8	25	19	-	-	6	14	14	-
Atlanta	8	12	9	-	-	3	10	10	-
Denver	8	9	5	1	-	3	8	8	-
Cincinnati	8	11	4	-	-	7	7	7	-
Phoenix	8	6	4	-	-	2	13	13	-
Columbus	8	5	3	-	-	2	5	5	-
Subregional Nodal									
Nashville	5	5	2	-	-	3	4	4	-
Charlotte	3	3	3	-	-	-	10	10	-

Functional Nodal

Bridgeport	2	26	5	17	–	4	5	5
Greensboro	4	10	6	1	3	–	2	2
Akron	4	6	1	4	–	1	1	1
Tulsa	6	4	2	–	–	2	3	2
Paterson	0	5	–	3	–	2	1	1

Manufacturing

Buffalo	7	4	2	–	–	2	1	–

Note: Sample of large corporations includes Fortune 500 largest industrial firms, Fortune 50 largest transportation, utilities, retail and insurance firms and Moody's 250 largest commercial banks. Sample of local governmental agencies includes local governmental agency clients disclosed by Big Eight accounting firms in the Accounting Establishment (op. cit. in text).

Source: Same as Table 7.9.

Table 7.12 Headquarters and Field Offices of the 200 Largest
Advertising Firms (size 1 to 3 SMSAs only), 1976

	# of Firms Head-quartered in SMSA		# of Firms not Headquartered with Local Field Office	
	Top 50	Next 150	Top 50	Next 150
DIVERSIFIED SERVICE CENTERS				
National				
New York	37	59	13	not tab.
Los Angeles	1	5	29	10
Chicago	4	12	20	8
San Francisco	0	3	19	12
Regional (size 1)[a]	0	4	3	3
Philadelphia	0	6	3	6
Boston	0	4	6	5
Dallas	2	0	4	2
Houston	0	2	6	5
St. Louis	1	1	1	1
Baltimore	0	3	1	3
Minneapolis	1	4	4	2
Cleveland	0	8	1	1
(size 2)	0	1	3	3
Subregional(size 3)	0	0	1	0
SPECIALIZED SERVICE CENTERS				
Functional (size 1)	2	2	4	3
Detroit	3	2	9	3
Pittsburgh	1	0	2	4
Newark	0	3	1	1
(size 2 & 3)	0	0	0	0
Government-Education				
Washington	0	1	7	2
(size 3)	0	0	0	0
Education (size 3)	0	0	0	0
CONSUMER-ORIENTED CENTERS				
Residential(size 1 & 2)	0	0	0	1
Resort Ret.(size 2 & 3)	0	0	0	1
PRODUCTION CENTERS				
Mfg. (size 2 & 3)	0	0	0	1
Military (size 2 & 3)	0	0	1	1

[a]Unweighted modifed average for size-type groups.

Source: Based on list of 200 largest Advertising agencies
established with data from Advertising Age and Directory of Advertising Agencies. Location of headquarters
and field offices is from Directory of Advertising
Agencies.

Charlotte; *Size 3* functional nodal center: Bridgeport; and *Size 2* manufacturing center: Buffalo. This investigation is based on data published by the *Standard Directory of Advertisers* and the *Standard Directory of Advertising Agencies.* The findings are summarized in Table 7.13.

Part II of the table presents a simple disclosure measure and gives the reader an indication of the difficulties met in carrying out this probe.[26]

Part I of the table breaks down the advertising accounts, disclosed by the Fortune 650 in each of the eight SMSAs on the basis of where they are being served. The main tendencies indicated by these breakdowns seem highly consistent with what is suggested by the data presented in Table 7.12. Denver (70.0 percent) and Atlanta (62.0 percent) show large shares of advertising accounts served locally, followed by Buffalo and Nashville; the other SMSAs show much weaker local advertising activity. In Atlanta, the role of locally headquartered, "next 150" advertising firms stands out markedly, while it is field offices (branches) of non-local "Top 50" advertising firms which seem particularly active in Denver. In Buffalo and Nashville, the influence of small local advertising firms (below rank 200) stands out, somewhat unexpectedly. Although there are 17 local accounts from major corporations in these two SMSAs combined, none are served by any of the top 200 advertising firms. We can only conclude that, in both centers, a few local advertising firms have been able to survive, if not thrive, by keeping some large accounts away from the large advertising firms, possibly because there are industrial rather than consumer advertising accounts.

The bottom half of Part I of the table shows the breakdown of accounts served "out of town." It shows the heavy advertising dependency of the eight SMSAs on New York and to a much lesser extent, Chicago. In a few cases, however, additional regional influences can be detected: Los Angeles on Phoenix, Cleveland on Columbus, Rochester on Buffalo. Bridgeport's dependence on New York is rather overwhelming.

In the end, the major conclusion from this short analysis of advertising remains quite straightforward. The industry is an extreme example of a producer service activity which is highly biased spatially. The overwhelming dominance of New York forces most corporations to establish direct linkage with advertising agencies in that city, and only a very limited number of places seem to avoid falling completely under New York's umbrella.

Conclusion

The implications of the case studies presented in this chapter are numerous, and can be summarized in terms of the light they shed both on the spatial behavior of specific producer service industries and on specialization tendencies of corporate complexes in different types and sizes of places.

Key findings as regards the spatial behavior of individual producer service industries have been established as we progressed through the presentation. In these last paragraphs we concentrate on the specialization tendencies of corporate complexes in the various metropolitan economies.

In general, findings related to all five groups of institutions and services studied in this chapter (commercial banks, life insurance companies, financial divi-

Table 7.13 Cross-Tabulation of Advertising Accounts Disclosed by National Headquarters and Divisional Head Offices of Fortune 650 and Advertising Agencies Serving Those Accounts, Eight Selected SMSAs, 1976

PART I: CROSS-TABULATION	Regional Nodal		
	Atlanta	Denver	Phoenix
# Adv. Accounts Disc. by Local Nat'l Hdqtrs and Div's of Fortune 650[a]	29(100.0%)	20(100.0%)	23(100.0%)
Account Served Locally	18 (62.0%)	14 (70.0%)	9 (39.0%)
Adv. Done Directly[b]	6	2	1
Adv. Done by			
-Local Top 50[c]	0	0	0
-Local Next 150[d]	8	0	0
-Nonlocal Top 50 (branch)	1	8	5
-Nonlocal Next 150 (branch)	1	0	0
Adv. Done by Small Local Adv. Firms (main or branch off.)	2	4	3
Account Served Out of Town	11 (28.0%)	6 (30.0%)	14 (30.0%)
Top 50 Firms	7[e]	3	6
	N.Y.(6)	N.Y.(3)	N.Y.(4)
	Detroit(1)		Pittsburgh(1)
			Chicago(1)
Next 150 Firms	2	0	5
	N.Y.(1)		L. Angeles(2)
	Chicago(1)		Bridgeport(1)
			Rockford(1)
			Greensboro(1)
Others	2	3	3

PART II:DISCLOSURE STATISTICS[f]			
1. # Local Nat'l Hdqtrs and Div's of Fortune 650	110	137	50
2. # Local Nat'l Hdqtrs and Div's of Fortune 650 Disclosing Adv. Accounts	21	17	12
Disclosure ratio (2 1)	19%	13%	24%

[a]Several divisions and national headquarters disclose several advertising accounts.
[b]Advertising is done by the head office itself.
[c]50 largest advertising firms.
[d]150 next largest advertising firms.
[e]Indicates that 7 accounts are served by 6 N.Y. adv. firms in their N.Y. office and 1 account by a Detroit firm in Detroit.

	Subregional Nodal		Funct'l Nodal	Manufacturing
Columbus	Nashville	Charlotte	Bridgeport	Buffalo
18(100.0%)	13(100.0%)	11(100.0%)	81(100.0%)	18(100.0%)
$\frac{7}{1}$ (39.0%)	$\frac{7}{2}$ (54.0%)	$\frac{3}{0}$ (27.0%)	$\frac{15}{8}$ (18.5%)	$\frac{10}{0}$ (55.5%)
0	0	0	0	0
0	0	0	0	0
0	0	0	0	0
0	0	0	0	0
6	5	3	7	10
$\frac{11}{2}$ (61.0%)	$\frac{6}{2}$ (46.0%)	$\frac{8}{2}$ (73.0%)	$\frac{65}{30}$ (81.5%)	$\frac{8}{4}$ (44.5%)
N.Y. (2)	N.Y. (1)	N.Y. (2)	N.Y. (29)	Rochester (2)
	Evansville(1)		Minneapolis(1)	Chicago (1)
				New York (1)
3	1	3	13	3
N.Y. (1)	Louisville(1)	Greenville(1)	New York(8)	Chicago (1)
Cleveland(2)		Hartford (1)	Newark (1)	New York(1)
		Greensboro(1)	Seattle (1)	Rochester(1)
			Hartford(1)	
			Paterson(1)	
			Cleveland(1)	
6	3	3	23	1
81	66	43	182	63
17	13	10	50	18
21%	20%	23%	27%	29%

fFor analysis of disclosure ratio, see text.

Source: List of 50 and next 150 largest adv. firms derived
from Advertising Age (1977) and Standard Directory of
Advertising Agencies (1977); cross-tabulation of accounts
based on Standard Directory of Advertising Agencies and
Standard Directory of Advertisers, 1977.

sions of industrial firms, accounting firms and advertising agencies) concur in establishing a clear hierarchical structure among major complexes of corporate activities, in which size is an important yet not fully explanatory variable. The four national nodal centers stand at the top of this hierarchy, with New York at the apex, offering both the most diversified and the most specialized producer services. The regional nodal centers constitute the next layer of the structure, offering a somewhat less specialized and diversified mix of services. On the whole, SMSAs included in this group seem well equipped to provide a wide range of basic services in each of the five service industries examined, although there are indications that some cities fare better than others in the group, particularly in the case of commercial banking and advertising. Among cities of the third layer, the subregional nodal centers, there is a great deal of unevenness in the extent to which producer services have "filtered down" to these smaller corporate complexes. In each of the five industries studied here, there are indications of sharp differences from city to city. For example, some subregional nodal centers have a strong banking sector, others have not; some benefit from a full presence of the Big Eight accounting firms, others do not.

The case of the functional nodal centers (and to a varying extent that of government and education centers) is extremely interesting because it does not fit well into this three layer hierarchy. While many among these cities have attained a size comparable to the regional and subregional nodal centers, their corporate complexes are not as fully developed, despite instances of cities showing strength in specific producer service areas. Thus, in banking, accounting and advertising, there is strong evidence that in many instances major corporations headquartered in the functional nodal centers must go out of town to obtain the services they need, except for those headed in the largest centers. To repeat, this must be seen as an indication that the corporate complexes of functional nodal centers are aimed at restricted clientele, with smaller numbers of customers available to producer service firms than in comparable nodal centers. This is a very important observation which generalizes a finding established in an earlier study on a more restricted basis. In their *Corporate Headquarters Complex in New York City*,[27] the authors found that the New York corporations that had relocated to outlying SMSAs—such as Bridgeport or Patterson (two functional nodal centers in our typology)—remained highly dependent upon New York City's producer service firms. The present study indicates that such finding extends well beyond these two, perhaps special cases, to an entire group of SMSAs—the functional nodal centers—which, while major sites for the headquarters of large industrial corporations, have remained relatively poorly endowed in producer services.

Finally, this chapter emphasizes that with a few exceptions (Buffalo, San Diego, and some of the largest consumer oriented centers) advanced producer services have remained conspicuously absent from either the production or the consumer oriented centers. While we have not screened the full range of producer services, there seems little reason to believe that analyses of additional producer services would alter fundamentally our findings.[28] In the end, only in the case of the life insurance firms did we find locational tendencies departing from the hierarchical structure suggested above, with the headquarters of major firms behaving more like those of manufacturing firms and showing attraction for both diversified and specialized service centers.

Notes

1. Federal Reserve Board, *Flows of Funds*, various years.
2. See mention in the previous chapter of the Glass Steagel Act. This Act required a clear institutional separation between commercial and investment (or "merchant") banking.
3. E.g., Bache-Prudential, American Express/Shearson or Merrill Lynch.
4. Federal Reserve System, *Flow of Funds Accounts*, 1976.
5. Ibid.
6. For example, Philadelphia National Bank, Girard and First Pennsylvania in Philadelphia (a slow growing SMSA), Marine Midland in Buffalo (another slow growing SMSA), Valley National Bank in Phoenix (a fast growing SMSA) or NCNB in Charlotte (another fast growing SMSA).
7. There is evidence that in the early 1980s, the gap between banking assets and deposits in the four national nodal centers and in other large banking centers has even further widened (see, for example, *Business Week*'s 1982 list of the 200 largest banking corporations).
8. Motor Vehicle and Parts, Aerospace and Ordnance, Electrical Appliance and Electronics, Office, Scientific and Measuring Equipment.
9. Robert Cohen, *Lending by Transnational Banks and Other Financial Institutions to Transnational Corporations*, UNCTC, New York: 1977.
10. *American Banker*, July 18, 1975. Both state and federal banking regulations have changed rapidly in recent years and many restrictions in effect in the early 1970s do not apply any longer.
11. The tabulation is based on a survey presented in the *American Banker*, July 18, 1975. The 36 loan production offices represent the total number existing at that time.
12. Banks can also finance international trade and investment with non-domestic funds through their foreign-based branches and offices, which are not subject to U.S. rules and regulations. Indeed as Cohen, op. cit., 1979, has shown, a good deal of the internationalization of U.S. banks in the 1970s related to the foreign expansion of U.S. firms and their resulting need for financial resources abroad.
13. Based on a survey conducted by the *American Banker*, February 1977. Consistent time series for the capitalization of these Edge Acts could not be found.
14. This finding is to be compared with that from Conservation of Human Resources, op. cit., 1977 (page 48) showing that the Fortune 500s headquartered in 12 SMSAs accounted for over 75 percent of the foreign sales of all Fortune 500s as of 1974: 54.3 percent in the national nodal centers (New York, 40.5 percent; San Francisco, 5.4; Chicago, 4.6; and Los Angeles 3.8), 17.9 percent in four functional nodal centers (Detroit, 8.8; Pittsburgh, 6.2; Akron, 1.7; Paterson, 1.2) and 6.4 percent in four regional nodal centers (Houston, 2.8; Minneapolis, 1.3; St. Louis, 1.2; Cleveland, 1.1). In the case of the national nodal centers, our finding is consistent with the aforementioned finding if one observes that while such places have a very large number of Fortune 500s with very limited foreign sales, the few firms that have foreign sales account for a very large share of total foreign sales of all Fortune 500s.
15. The weak showing of Los Angeles is somewhat surprising, perhaps due to the problems in sampling technique mentioned previously.
16. Philadelphia, not shown in Table 7.6, ranks as the nation's 8th largest insurance center.
17. In Subcommittee on the City, *Large Corporations and Urban Employment*, House of Representatives, 95th Congress: February, 1978.
18. Based on additional information published in ibid.
19. *The Accounting Establishment*, Staff Study by the Subcommittee on Reports, Accounting & Mergers, U.S. Senate, March 1977, 95th Congress.
20. From *The Accounting Establishment*, op. cit.
21. Assuming that 3 percent of the $2 billion revenues (i.e., $60 million) of the Big Eight are derived from services rendered to federal, state and local government bodies (see line C, Table 7.9).
22. Federal Trade Commission, *Conglomerate Merger Performance*, Washington, D.C., Government Printing Office, 1972.

23. Interview with a partner in one of the Big Eight accounting firms.

24. Including Fortune 500 largest industrial firms, Fortune 50 largest transportation, utilities, retail and insurance firms and *Moody's* 250 largest commercial banks.

25. These data are from *Advertising Age* and *Standard Directory of Advertising Agencies*.

26. On average, in only 22 percent of the cases were we able to identify the advertising accounts of the Fortune 650 headquarters or divisional offices located in a given SMSA (13 percent in the lowest case; 29 percent in the highest case). This difficulty occurred partly because divisions do not always have an advertising budget separate from that of their parent, but mostly because many of the firms are not covered by the directories used in this probe. The difference between the number of headquarters, divisions (or subsidiaries) disclosing advertising accounts (line 2-Part II of the table) and the number of advertising accounts disclosed (line 1-Part I of the table) simply reflects the fact that several divisional offices or headquarters report several accounts.

27. Op. cit., Conservation of Human Resources: New York, 1977.

28. Indeed, Cohen's analysis of legal and investment banking services tend to support such an assertion. See R. Cohen, op. cit.

CHAPTER EIGHT

Changes in Distributive Service Networks

The previous three chapters have focused in some detail on the role played by the manufacturing sector and the complexes of corporate activities in structuring the system of cities. In the next two chapters, we investigate, somewhat more concisely, distributive services, nonprofit institutions and the government sector. This chapter identifies some key changes in distributive service networks; the next evaluates the importance of major nonprofit and governmental institutions in the economic base of cities.

As defined in this monograph, distributive services include industries which are primarily specialized in the distribution of goods and services to user firms and institutions, and are, accordingly, mostly producers of intermediate services. In reality, such a grouping of industries remains largely heterogeneous. Many distributive service firms serve both producers and final consumers. Thus, railroads continue to carry passengers next to their mainline business, the transport of freight; electric utilities distribute energy to both households and firms; telephone companies serve individual customers in addition to providing communications services to firms; and the large passenger bus companies transport small packages for businesses throughout the nation.

Moreover, some of the distributive services are geared to distributing goods and services largely within the goods sectors of the economy; others to serving mostly its service sectors. Thus, ships and railroads carry raw materials to production establishments, trucks carry parts from supplier firms to their customer firms, and air cargo is used to transport partly assembled semiconductors from Southeast Asian plants back to U.S. facilities. Communication companies transmit data from centralized mainframe computers to dispersed terminals, and airlines provide transportation for scores of employees, professionals, executives, businessmen who must meet with others for business purposes.

Finally, some distributive services are closer to the final stages of distribution (grocery wholesaling, for instance) than others. In short, it is easy to hypothesize how various distributive service networks might be influenced differently by three sets of factors: by the location of production facilities, by the location of corporate complexes and nonprofit or governmental institutions, or by the location of consumer markets.

In this chapter we attempt to evaluate the influence of these three sets of factors on the geography of distributive services through detailed analyses of three industries: air transportration, communications, and wholesaling. The locational behavior of the first two is expected to be strongly influenced by the presence of vigorous corporate complexes and dense consumer markets; that of the last, by proximity to production sites and consumer markets. We first review the more general employment trends.

Locational Trends of Employment in the Distributive Services

Table 8.1 shows the location quotient of employment in the distributive service sector and some of its component industries for 1959 and 1976 by type and size of SMSA.

The first and most remarkable observation is the lack of major overall change in the location of distributive service employment during the entire 17-year period. Between 1959 and 1976, employment in the distributive services has remained overconcentrated in the diversified service centers; underconcentrated everywhere else. Admittedly, these measures represent averages for component industries whose behavior may differ sharply and we must move on to more specific measures if we are to understand the dynamics at work.

Employment in air transportation—one of the nation's fastest growing industries through much of the 1960s and early 1970s—has remained remarkably concentrated in national nodal, size 2 regional nodal and resort-retirement centers (also Washington, D.C., shown here as the lone size 1 government SMSA), despite noticeable changes in these and other size-type groups. Thus, sizable gains in location quotients are recorded in national nodal, size 1 regional nodal and size 1 functional nodal centers, while size 2 regional nodal centers, resort-retirement centers, and Washington, D.C. lose part of their earlier (1959) locational advantage. It is likely that the gains shown by size 1 regional nodal and size 1 functional nodal centers reflect the attempt by large, mostly Snowbelt centers to strengthen their position in the nation's network of large airports, and to catch up with large Sunbelt centers (mostly size 2 regional nodals), which were quicker to enter the race for commercial jet air connection (see below). The sharp drop in the location quotient of employment in the resort-retirement centers, is somewhat surprising in light of the fact that data presented below (Table 8.5) show that air traffic has continued to grow vigorously in these centers. A likely explanation is that while such airports have benefited from the growth of vacation-related traffic, they are not the kind of facilities in which major airlines have established the bulk of their maintenance crews or other ground-based workforce.

In 1976, the communications sector showed relatively heavy employment in nodal, government-education, education-manufacturing, resort-retirement, industrial-military, and mining-industrial centers, and relatively light employment in functional nodal, manufacturing, and smaller size (size 5 and below) centers. Among centers characterized by an overconcentration of communications employment at the start of the period, the largest nodal centers (size 1 and 2) have tended to lose slightly (in terms of location quotients) while other centers have tended to gain; among the relatively weak functional nodal, manufacturing and size 5 centers, many functional nodal and manufacturing centers have tended to gain, most size 5 centers have tended to lose. Here we may simply be witnessing, to a certain extent, a tendency on the part of utilities to locate expanding data processing and other routine activities away from some of the major centers where labor costs tend to be higher.

Although employment in wholesaling has remained relatively over-concentrated in nodal centers throughout the 1959–76 period, especially among subregional nodals, it is showing a slight tendency to shift away from such centers, towards the group of functional nodal, government-education and education-manufacturing centers, the manufacturing and the smaller size (size 5 and below) centers. Other types of places show fewer changes, except residential places which are characterized by strong gains. The gains displayed by residential places reflect recent tendencies among shipping and warehousing activities to expand in the outer periphery of the very large nodal centers (away from congested centers) and to follow consumers in areas contiguous to major metropolises. The more general tendency, however, seems to be one in which certain wholesaling functions are moving away from traditional, distribution-oriented metropolitan centers towards production-oriented centers, thus following production facilities where they tend to concentrate. In the last section of this chapter we present additional evidence to this effect.

In short then, locational trends in several component industries of the distributive services seem to reflect certain forces at work causing services which cater to the goods side of the economy to be influenced in their location by that of manufacturing production and those which serve the producer service side of the economy to expand where corporate complexes grow. All distributive services, however, remain also influenced by the need for proximity to final consumer markets as shown by a strong positive association with population size of places.

Business Telephones

To evaluate more fully the impact of communications on the system of SMSAs, we used data published by the Federal Communications Commission on the numbers of business telephones per capita in SMSAs.[1] Table 8.2 presents unweighted modified averages for each type and size group of SMSAs for both 1969 and 1976.

An important observation is that, at the same time that the number of business telephones per capita has grown substantially everywhere throughout the 1969–76 period, differences among various types of places have become sharper. In 1976, for example, there were 32 percent more business telephones per capita in diversified service centers than in the production centers, compared to 25 percent more in 1969. The relationship between the number of business telephones and the size of white-collar, office-based employment is inescapable. On average, the diversified service centers are the largest users of business telephones (0.2485 per capita) in 1976, followed closely by the government-education centers (0.2468), the consumer-oriented centers (0.2332), and the functional nodal centers (0.2285). The production centers display a sharply lower average (0.1881 per capita), a finding that is highly consistent with the intuitive notion that it takes fewer business telephones to run a factory than an office.

Table 8.1 Location Quotients of Employment in the Distributive Service Sector and Several of Its Component Industries by Type and Size of SMSA, 1976 and 1959

	SMSA Size	# of SMSAs	Dist Serv 1976	Dist Serv 1959
Diversified Service Centers				
National Nodal	1	4	125.2	124.0
Regional Nodal	1	8	111.2	111.7
	2	11	129.8	129.4
Subregional Nodal	3	10	128.1	127.5
	4	6	129.9	127.3
Specialized Service Centers				
Functional Nodal	1	3	94.0	94.9
	2	3	85.9	77.7
	3	12	96.1	88.8
	4	6	96.5	88.1
Government-Education	1	1	68.7	79.3
	3	2	82.2	81.2
	4	12	83.9	85.6
Education-Manufacturing	1 to 4	5	80.8	79.0
Consumer-Oriented Centers				
Residential	1 to 4	3	87.8	71.3
Resort-Retirement	1 to 4	9	95.4	100.8
Production Centers				
Manufacturing	2	1	93.3	96.1
	3	8	84.7	79.5
	4	17	91.8	87.9
Industrial-Military	2	1	77.9	73.3
	3	2	100.8	107.5
	4	9	75.3	77.2
Mining-Industrial	4	7	98.6	97.0
Size 5 SMSAs and Non-metropolitan Areas			83.4	84.1
Share of U.S. Employment in Sectors and Subsectors			10.4	11.8

Note: Location quotients are unweighted modified averages for major size-type groups.

Column heads: Same as Table 2.2; Air Transp: air transportation; Comm: communications.

Source: County Business Patterns, 1959 and 1976.

TCU		Air Transp		Comm		Whl	
1976	1959	1976	1959	1976	1959	1976	1959
131.4	119.8	251.8	208.3	118.0	123.0	119.5	128.1
110.5	109.1	113.4	79.0	93.1	92.6	111.8	114.2
131.9	128.7	298.7	328.6	106.8	113.4	128.0	130.0
124.6	110.6	74.8	65.3	120.1	116.6	131.2	143.7
120.3	109.1	43.5	40.0	149.5	144.1	138.6	144.7
96.0	97.2	80.8	49.7	90.9	92.0	92.2	92.7
78.3	71.7	20.8	22.5	90.8	78.7	92.8	83.5
94.8	92.6	34.9	80.0	75.9	69.5	97.4	85.1
76.1	81.8	28.7	23.9	75.9	84.3	115.1	94.2
86.0	97.1	157.3	434.4	117.9	86.7	52.9	62.3
75.2	83.4	17.2	11.5	134.5	127.2	88.6	79.1
79.8	86.8	18.6	24.5	101.0	104.8	87.6	84.4
82.7	83.3	21.0	15.4	114.1	102.8	79.1	74.9
75.3	85.0	32.2	13.1	94.1	92.0	99.1	58.1
104.9	104.1	123.0	206.6	133.6	120.5	86.8	97.7
88.0	100.4	52.2	44.6	73.0	84.4	98.1	91.9
79.6	75.5	16.0	9.5	82.8	75.9	89.3	83.4
90.7	83.0	15.1	18.2	93.3	80.9	92.8	83.2
89.5	79.9	135.6	58.2	125.0	106.0	67.4	66.9
94.1	102.2	58.3	44.6	103.5	89.5	107.0	112.7
82.7	85.3	34.9	38.6	108.4	85.8	68.5	69.4
101.5	99.2	42.7	26.4	120.2	100.0	96.0	95.0
81.4	87.8	25.2	30.1	90.7	95.5	85.1	80.6
4.9	5.8	0.5	0.3	1.5	1.7	5.5	6.0

Table 8.2 Number of Business Telephones Per Capita by Type of SMSA, 1976 and 1969

	SMSA Size	# of SMSAs	Business Telephones Per Capita 1976	1969
Diversified Service Centers (group avg)		36	.2485	.1939
National Nodal	1	4	.2649	.2503
Regional Nodal	1	8	.2491	.2159
	2	11	.2285	.2002
Subregional Nodal	3	9	.2214	.1932
	4	4	.2544	.1808
Specialized Service Centers				
Functional Nodal (group avg)		24	.2285	.1936
	1	3	.2452	.2218
	2	3	.2602	.2253
	3	12	.2106	.1893
	4	6	.2319	.1732
Government-Education (group avg)		15	.2468	.2023
	1	1	.5797	.4040
	3	2	.2942	.2579
	4	12	.2348	.1929
Education-Manufacturing (group avg)	3,4	5	.2104	.1855
Consumer-Oriented Centers (group avg)		12	.2332	.2049
Residential	1	1	n.a.	n.a.
	2	1	.2627	.2030
	3	1	n.a.	n.a.
Resort-Retirement	2,3,4	9	.2283	.2016
Production Centers (group avg)		48	.1881	.1550
Manufacturing	2	1	.1622	.1666
	3	9	.1995	.1565
	4	19	.1852	.1560
Mining-Manufacturing	4	7	.1815	.1530
Industrial-Military	2	1	.1972	.1632
	3	2	.1680	.1336
	4	9	.1852	.1531

n.a.: not available.

Note: These measures are unweighted modified averages for major size-type groups. Number of business telephones per capita is estimated for each SMSA on the basis of area codes.

Source: Federal Communications Commission, 1976 and 1969.

Two additional observations need to be made. First, large government centers are among the heaviest users of business telephones. In Washington, the most extreme case of all, there are close to 60 business telephones per 100 people as of 1976! Understandably, this phenomenon is related to the very nature of the business that government must conduct, involving extensive dealing with people and businesses across the nation (or an entire state).

Second, while there is evidence that business telephone usage is relatively heavier the larger the place, in both nodal and functional nodal centers there is a slight tendency in 1976 for the numbers to pick up as places become markedly smaller (size 4). A possible explanation is that where such a type of place is relatively small, the diversity of services offered by their corporate complexes is likely to be quite restricted, with the result that local producer service firms or administrative offices of corporations must repeatedly contact firms in other locales to obtain some of the most basic services they need to conduct business.

Airport Capacity

The rise of commercial aviation in the postwar era is probably one of the most pervasive technological advances of the mid-twentieth century, having profoundly altered people's lives and businessmen's ways of conducting affairs. Journeys that, only 30 years ago used to take days, if not weeks (e.g., transoceanic travel) have, in a very brief span of years, been reduced to a few hours.

In terms of its overall quantitative effect on the economy, the greatest impact of aviation has come with the development of commercial jets in the late 1950s and early 1960s. Throughout the 1960s, passenger air traffic has grown by well over 10 percent annually, a staggering rate of growth indeed! The potential opened by this new jet era is a phenomenon which may have been best understood in the early 1960s by some of the Sunbelt centers (Dallas, Atlanta, Miami, Denver) as they scrambled to build huge airport capacity and attract as much traffic as they could. The result has been a surging of air traffic volume in these centers, past that in many older ones, which were often slower at responding to the shift from propeller to jet airplanes. The rapid growth of air traffic in Atlanta, Dallas, Miami, and Denver is illustrated in Table 8.3, which presents the list of the 15 largest metropolitan centers for passenger air traffic (1959 and 1976).

Data presented in Table 8.3 also indicate that not only has air traffic remained strongly concentrated in the very largest centers but that concentration has become even greater over the period. In 1976, 43.4 percent of passenger air traffic originated from the 10 largest hubs, as against 38.3 percent in 1959.

In terms of international air traffic alone, which represents, relatively speaking, a much smaller share of business (less than 3 percent of all passenger air traffic), the concentration in the key hubs is even sharper. In 1976, New York handled close to 40 percent of enplaned international passengers, and Miami 15 percent (Table 8.4). Here the picture is in large part influenced by the restrictions placed by federal regulators, which until recently limited international flights to a very selected number of airports.

What remains remarkable, however, is the highly selective impact of such a fast growing activity on individual places. This is shown in Table 8.5, which

Table 8.3   Fifteen Largest Hubs of Passenger Air Traffic
(domestic and international traffic combined), 1976
and 1959

Rank 1976	Rank 1959	SMSA	1976 Enplaned Passengers (in 1,000)	1959 Enplaned Passengers (in 1,000)
1	1	Chicago	18,143	4,535
		Greater New York	17,687	5,913
2	2	New York	14,351	4,446
(a)	7	Newark	3,336	1,467
3	11	Atlanta	13,607	1,082
4	3	Los Angeles	10,162	2,665
5	10	Dallas	7,929	1,178
6	4	Washington, D.C.	6,995	2,225
7	5	San Francisco	6,937	1,853
8	6	Miami	6,876	1,570
9	(a)	Denver	6,452	789
10	8	Boston	5,355	1,343
11	(b)	Honolulu	4,853	(b)
12	9	Detroit	4,004	1,291
13	13	Pittsburgh	3,922	978
14	15	St. Louis	3,780	875
15	14	Philadelphia	3,624	895
		Total U.S.	223,000	58,999

[a]Not classified among the top 15.

[b]Statistics not available for 1959.

Source: Civil Aeronautics Board, 1976 and 1959.

presents normalized shares of enplaned passengers (1976 and 1959) and average
annual rate of growth of enplaned passengers (two periods: 1959–69 and
1969–76) for each type-size group of SMSAs. This table suggests the following:

First, that volume of air traffic has remained overconcentrated in the nodal
centers and a few very large centers (most notably Washington, D.C., the three
largest functional nodal centers, and Buffalo) throughout the past two decades;
underconcentrated everywhere else, with one important exception—that of the
resort-retirement centers, which have clearly benefited from the expansion of
vacation related traveling.

Second, that growth in the 1970s has been slower than during the 1960s, reflecting partly the slowdown in business activity and the sharp increase in the

price of jet fuel following the first oil crisis. There has been a sharp drop in the rate of growth of air traffic volume almost everywhere, except in residential and resort-retirement places.

Last, that the high concentration of air transportation employees identified earlier among size 2 regional nodal centers (Table 8.1) is largely consistent with the tendencies indicated by the volume of traffic which they handle, confirming also our earlier impression that many of the Snowbelt regional centers—more involved in older transportation networks—may have responded more slowly to these new developmental opportunities. This may not be the only explanation, however. The fact that several of the older regional nodal centers operate under the umbrella of some of the very large hubs (Philadelphia and Boston partly under New York's, Baltimore under Washington's, and Cleveland under Chicago's) may have made it more difficult for them to expand aggressively their long-haul traffic. Evidence favoring the latter explanation is found in the events that followed the oil crisis of 1973, when many airlines curtailed some of the long-haul routes they maintained in these cities, but left intact those in New York, Washington or Chicago.

Table 8.4 Thirteen Largest Hubs of International Passenger Air Traffic, 1976

Rank	SMSA	1976 International Enplaned Passengers (in 1,000)
1	New York	2,483
2	Miami	949
3	Honolulu	417
4	Los Angeles	386
5	Boston	316
6	Chicago	272
7	Newark	227
8	Washington	189
9	San Francisco	153
10	Dallas	151
11	Atlanta	150
12	Baltimore	124
13	Seattle	119
	8 Other Centers	284
	Total U.S.	6,358

Source: Civil Aeronautics Board, 1976.

Table 8.5 Normalized Shares of Enplaned Passengers and Growth in Enplaned Passengers by Type and Size of SMSA, 1976, 1969 and 1959

	SMSA Size	# of SMSAs	# of SMSAs with Airport
Diversified Service Centers			
National Nodal	1	4	4
Regional Nodal	1	8	8
	2	11	11
Subregional Nodal	3	10	10
	4	4	4
Specialized Service Centers			
Functional Nodal	1	3	3
	2	3	3
	3	12	8
	4	5	4
Government-Education	1	1	1
	3	2	2
	4	8	8
Education-Manufacturing	3	2	0
	4	5	n.t.
Consumer-Oriented Centers			
Residential	1,2,3	3	2
Resort-Retirement	2,3,4	9	6
Production Centers			
Manufacturing	2	1	1
	3	8	7
	4	17	n.t.
Industrial-Military	2	1	1
	3	2	1
	4	9	n.t.
Mining-Industrial	4	7	n.t.

Size 5 SMSAs and Non-metropolitan Areas

n.t.: not tabulated.

Note: Normalized shares of enplaned passengers and average annual rates of growth in enplaned passengers are unweighted modified averages for major type-size groups. Shares of enplaned passengers are normalized against population shares.

Normalized Share of Enplaned Passengers		Average Annual Rate of Growth Enplaned Passengers	
1976	1959	1976-69	1969-59
179.1	168.4	2.8	12.1
138.2	114.6	3.2	13.6
284.9	213.9	4.4	12.3
141.1	156.6	3.2	10.7
146.5	181.6	5.2	12.0
124.6	139.1	1.5	10.6
75.4	71.7	5.4	11.0
49.4	61.3	2.3	10.2
60.9	59.5	4.8	10.9
221.7	321.8	2.4	10.3
58.4	78.1	2.0	9.2
77.0	74.4	5.4	12.2
0.0	0.0	0.0	0.0
n.t.	n.t.	n.t.	n.t.
6.5	0.6	8.9	14.8
214.0	n.a.	8.1	12.3
110.4	117.4	4.2	8.5
27.6	48.4	2.5	6.6
n.t.	n.t.	n.t.	n.t.
88.9	90.9	6.9	11.8
88.2	94.2	0.8	13.7
n.t.	n.t.	n.t.	n.t.
n.t.	n.t.	n.t.	n.t.
53.5	58.4		

Source: Civil Aeronautics Board, 1976, 1969 and 1959.

Wholesaling

Whereas business activity in communications and air transportation is strongly related to the centrality of urban places, wholesaling shows a more dualistic pattern. To recall, we have hypothesized above that wholesaling is subject to a double locational pull: a pull towards places which are at the center of major consumer markets, and a pull toward cities which are major centers of production, with some indication that part of wholesaling may have followed production facilities away from some of the largest markets.

To further investigate these hypotheses, we have taken a closer look at the data available from the *1972 Census of Wholesale Trade* on dollar volume of wholesaling by major types of product and by SMSA. Two limitations hinge on our analysis, however. First, because data from the *1977 Census of Wholesale Trade* were not available when we conducted this analysis, recent historical shifts were difficult to test. Second, because the Bureau of the Census publishes detailed data only for the 74 SMSAs with the largest volume of all types of wholesale trade, many smaller centers are not covered. In particular, the census data do not permit identification of many manufacturing centers which, while characterized by small volumes of wholesale trade, may be heavily specialized in the trading of one or several commodities. As a result, evidence of opposite pulls between distribution-oriented and production-oriented centers is not fully conclusive.

In addition to employment measures, there are essentially two ways of measuring the wholesaling strength of a given area: the total dollar amount and the per capita volume of wholesale trade. We have made use of both measures and broken down the data in terms of eight major product lines: motor vehicles and parts (SIC 501), metals and minerals (SIC 505), electrical goods and hardware supply (SIC 506-507), machinery (SIC 508), apparel (SIC 513), groceries (SIC 514), farm products (SIC 515), and chemical and petroleum products (SIC 516-517). As of 1972, these eight major product lines represented 76.8 percent of all wholesale trade, with groceries and motor vehicles and parts ranking the highest (15.3 and 12.0 percent, respectively), and metal and minerals and apparel the lowest (6.3 and 4.0 percent, respectively—Table 8.6).

Table 8.6 also indicates the extent to which wholesale trade, as measured by the total dollar amounts traded, is concentrated in a few places. As of 1972, concentration of the total volume of wholesale was the highest in apparel, and metals and minerals, where the 15 leading wholesale centers for each of these two product lines accounted for, respectively, 83.4 and 70.5 percent of the nation's total traded volume (71.2 percent in the 5 leading trading areas in apparel!) and the lowest in groceries and farm products with 40.9 and 34.6 percent, respectively. Overall, the dollar volume for all types of wholesale trade is clearly concentrated geographically, with 28.5 percent of all sales in the 5 largest trading centers and 47.0 percent in the 15 largest centers.

When measured in terms of per capita sales of wholesale trade, wholesaling displayed some startling differences by both type of place and type of product. This is shown in a summary form in Table 8.7, where per capita sales of wholesale trade in SMSAs are normalized to the national average to facilitate comparisons. By this measure, total wholesale trade is shown to be very strong in the nodal centers (particularly in national nodals and subregional nodals), strong in the functional nodal centers, and weaker everywhere else. On a type of product basis, the trends differ markedly, however. Thus, per capita sales of wholesale trade in apparel are well above the nation's average in the national nodal centers, well below everywhere else; in farm products, they are well above average in the subregional nodals, well below everywhere else. Per capita sales of wholesale in electrical goods, and hardware supply, and in machinery display more even distribution, at least among nodal and functional nodal centers.

These differences result, in effect, from two, somewhat distinct tendencies. On the one hand, we observe a tendency for a number of the smaller regional and subregional nodal centers to rank disproportionately high in terms of all dollar volume of wholesale trade when compared to their population rank. This is shown in the following table, where seven of the 37 (i.e., upper half of the array of the 74 leading wholesale centers) leading wholesale centers are seen to rank *much* higher in terms of wholesale sales than population:

		1972 rank according to total volume of wholesale sales	*1976 population rank*
Atlanta	(regional nodal)	9	18
Kansas City	(regional nodal)	15	28
Memphis	(subregional nodal)	17	41
Cincinnati	(regional nodal)	19	26
Portland	(regional nodal)	21	34
Charlotte	(subregional nodal)	22	66
Jacksonville	(subregional nodal)	30	56

On the other hand, there is a definite tendency for commodities to be traded where they are produced. This is shown in Table 8.8, in which we have listed for total wholesale and each major product lines the ten leading centers, with their type and size characteristics, in terms of both volume of sales (upper half of the table) and per capita sales (lower half of the table).

We observe that major centers for the apparel industry—New York, Los Angeles, Chicago, Atlanta, and Dallas—rank ahead of other centers in terms of dollar volume of apparel trade, but with other, yet smaller ones, ranking equally high in terms of per capita sales—Greensboro, Patterson, Greenville-Spartanburg, or Miami. In the area of farm products, most of the leading centers in terms of dollar volume of wholesale trade are nodal or functional nodal centers closely tied to an agricultural market (Memphis, Kansas City, Minneapolis, Dallas, etc.), including New York and Chicago which are the main platforms for the export of grain, while in terms of per capita sales, some of the smaller farm product centers rank high on the list (Memphis again, Omaha, Des Moines, etc.). To a varying extent, the same tendencies can be seen in chemical and petroleum, machinery, and metal and minerals.

Table 8.6   Dollar Volume of Wholesale Trade by Type of Product and Share of Trade in the Leading Trading SMSAs, 1972

		$ Volume of Wholesale (U.S.) (in millions)	Share(%) of $ Volume Captured by	
SIC	Name		5 Leading SMSAs	15 Leading SMSAs
50-51	Total Wholesale	695,224 (100.0%)	28.5	47.0
501	Motor Vehicle and Parts	83,015 (12.0%)	28.3	52.9
505	Metals and Minerals	43,489 (6.3%)	45.9	70.5
506-506	Elctrl Goods & Hardware Supply	67,949 (9.8%)	27.2	49.5
508	Machinery	80,692 (11.6%)	22.4	42.2
513	Apparel	27,933 (4.0%)	71.2	83.4
514	Groceries	106,457 (15.3%)	27.1	40.9
515	Farm Products	52,400 (7.6%)	24.9	34.6
516-517	Chemical & Petroleum	70,903 (10.2%)	23.5	42.8
All other products		162,386 (23.2%)		

Source: Census of Wholesale Trade, 1972.

At the other end of the spectrum, in motor vehicle or grocery wholesaling, the influence of the large population centers seems to prevail far more in determining the locational characterstics of wholesaling, if only in terms of a closer relationship between total dollar volume of sales and population of places.

In all cases, then, what remains is a certain tendency for a number of functional nodal centers and smaller subregional nodal centers to have found niches in the trading of many products, in an industry otherwise strongly dominated by the large and medium-sized nodal centers.

Table 8.7 Ratio of Per Capita Dollars of Wholesale in SMSAs to Per Capita Sales in U.S. (in percent) by Type and Size of SMSA and by Type of Product, 1972

	SMSA Size	# of SMSAs	All Whole-sale	Motor Vehicle & Parts 501a	Metals & Minerals 505	Elect. Goods & Hard 506-7	Mach-inery 508	Apparel 513	Groce-ries 514	Farm 514	Chem & Petr. 516-7
Diversified Service Centers											
National Nodal	1	4	177.0	173.7	252.7	186.4	161.8	157.3	197.1	33.4	148.7
Regional Nodal	1	8	155.4	187.2	209.1	181.3	159.4	93.8	135.4	63.7	131.2
Subregional Nodal	2	11	149.0	200.5	124.0	186.5	179.2	50.0	139.9	82.8	120.6
Specialized Service Centers	3	10	166.8	332.2	86.4	185.9	168.9	31.0	155.0	169.6	119.0
Functional Nodal	1	3	127.7	150.7	258.2	146.0	142.1	28.3	122.4	3.3	152.4
	2	3	98.3	102.9	103.2	146.0	144.9	14.6	114.7	23.1	87.4
	3	12	98.7	61.1	75.6	78.9	98.7	20.8	69.6	20.2	130.3
Government	1	1	72.5	175.2	5.6	124.6	86.1	11.9	45.9	5.8	63.2
	3	2	71.9	39.5	8.6	78.2	116.6	29.9	91.6	21.0	86.9
Education-Manufacturing	3	2	83.6	42.9	74.3	121.4	78.5	31.3	71.4	1.5	156.2
Consumer-Oriented Centers											
Residential	1,2	2	75.0	94.2	31.8	100.7	68.0	52.9	88.4	7.0	66.4
Resort-Retirement	2,3	5	69.1	63.7	32.5	91.7	66.3	4.5	109.6	15.7	67.2
Production Centers											
Manufacturing	2	1	96.4	159.4	172.9	70.9	87.2	16.2	124.1	12.8	77.4
	3	8	77.1	49.5	64.3	76.1	119.2	97.7	129.8	20.8	107.1
Industrial-Military	2	1	41.6	55.4	7.6	50.9	38.6	n.a.	59.4	0.5	47.8
	3	2	67.5	61.8	41.8	70.9	58.2	9.2	99.2	57.9	78.8

aSIC code.
Note: Ratios are unweighted modified averages for major size-type groups. Since detailed data are available for the 74 leading wholesale centers only, averages are computed for size 1 through 3 only.
Source: Census of Wholesale Trade, 1972.

Table 8.8 Ten Leading Wholesaling Centers Ranked by Total
Dollar Volume of Sales (upper half of the table)
and Per Capita Sales (lower half of the table) for
All Wholesale and Eight Major Product Lines, 1972

Total Sales	All Wholesale	Motor Vehicle and Parts SIC 501	Metals and Minerals SIC 505
Rank			
1	New York(NN-1)	New York(NN-1)	New York(NN-1)
2	Chicago(NN-1)	Los Angeles(NN-1)	Chicago(NN-1)
3	Los Angeles(NN-1)	Chicago(NN-1)	Detroit(FN-1)
4	Detroit(FN-1)	Detroit(FN-1)	Dallas(RN-1)
5	Philadelphia(RN-1)	Dallas(RN-1)	Los Angeles(NN-1)
6	S. Francisco(NN-1)	Atlanta(RN-2)	Cleveland(RN-1)
7	Dallas(RN-1)	Philadelphia(RN-1)	Philadelphia(RN-1)
8	Boston(RN-1)	Boston(RN-1)	S. Francisco(NN-1)
9	Atlanta(RN-2)	S. Francisco(NN-1)	Pittsburgh(FN-1)
10	Houston(RN-1)	Washington(G-1)	St. Louis(RN-1)

Per Capita
Sales

Rank			
1	Charlotte(SR-3)	Charlotte(SR-3)	Houston(RN-1)
2	Memphis(SR-3)	Jacksonville(SR-3)	Cleveland(RN-1)
3	New York(NN-1)	Memphis(SR-3)	Detroit(FN-1)
4	Atlanta(RN-2)	Atlanta(RN-2)	Chicago(NN-1)
5	Kansas C.(RN-2)	Kansas C.(RN-2)	Birmingham(M-3)
6	Jacksonville(SR-3)	Dallas(RN-1)	New York(NN-1)
7	Portland((RN-2)	Cincinnati(RN-2)	Cincinnati(RN-2)
8	Patterson(FN-4)	Portland(RN-2)	Pittsburgh(FN-1)
9	Dallas(RN-1)	Richmond(SR-3)	Charlotte(SR-3)
10	Chicago(NN-1)	Patterson(FN-4)	Atlanta(RN-2)

Note: Places are shown with type and size indicated in
parentheses. NN: national nodal; RN: regional nodal;
SR: subregional nodal; FN: functional nodal; M: manufacturing; G: government; and 1,2,3,4 refer to
population size groups.

Electrical Goods and Hardware SIC 506-7	Machinery SIC 508	Apparel SIC 513
New York(NN-1)	Chicago(NN-1)	New York(NN-1)
Chicago(NN-1)	New York(NN-1).	Los Angeles(NN-1)
Los Angeles(NN-1)	Los Angeles(NN-1)	Chicago(NN-1)
Philadelphia(RN-1)	S. Francisco(NN-1)	Atlanta(RN-2)
Boston(RN-1)	Detroit(FN-1)	Dallas(RN-1)
S. Francisco(NN-1)	Philadelphia(RN-1)	Boston(RN-1)
Atlanta(RN-2)	Atlanta(RN-2)	St. Louis(RN-1)
Dallas(RN-1)	Houston(RN-1)	Philadelphia(RN-1)
Detroit(FN-1)	Dallas(NN-1)	Greensboro(FN-3)
Newark(FN-1)	Minneapolis(RN-1)	S. Francisco(NN-1)
Charlotte(SR-3)	Charlotte(SR-3)	New York(NN-1)
Indianapolis(RN-2)	Peoria(FN-4)	Greensboro(FN-3)
Atlanta(RN-2)	Atlanta(RN-2)	Atlanta(RN-2)
Syracuse(SR-3)	Memphis(SR-3)	Patterson(FN-4)
Kansas C.(RN-2)	Kansas C.(RN-2)	Dallas(RN-1)
Dallas(RN-1)	Des Moines(SR-4)	Greenville(M-3)
Nashville(SR-3)	Houston(RN-1)	St. Louis(RN-1)
Jacksonville(SR-3)	Hartford(FN-2)	Los Angeles(NN-1)
Cleveland(RN-1)	Denver(RN-2)	Miami(RN-2)
Newark(FN-1)	S. Francisco(NN-1)	Boston(RN-1)

(continued on next page)

Table 8.8 (continued)

Total Sales	Groceries SIC 514	Farms SIC 515	Chemical and Petroleum SIC 516-17
Rank			
1	New York(NN-1)	New York(NN-1)	New York(NN-1)
2	Chicago(NN-1)	Memphis(SR-3)	Chicago(NN-1)
3	Los Angeles(NN-1)	Kansas C.(RN-2)	Los Angeles(NN-1)
4	S. Francisco(NN-1)	Minneapolis(RN-1)	Philadelphia(RN-1)
5	Boston(RN-1)	Chicago(NN-1)	Houston(RN-1)
6	Minneapolis(RN-1)	Dallas(RN-1)	Newark(RN-1)
7	Dallas(RN-1)	Portland(RN-2)	S. Francisco(NN-1)
8	St. Louis(RN-1)	St. Louis(RN-1)	Atlanta(RN-2)
9	Newark(FN-1)	Omaha(SR-3)	Boston(RN-1)
10	Atlanta(RN-2)	Toledo(FN-3)	Charlotte(SR-3)
Per Capita Sales			
Rank			
1	Charlotte(SR-3)	Memphis(SR-3)	Charlotte(SR-3)
2	S. Francisco(NN-1)	Kansas C.(RN-2)	Akron(FN-3)
3	Grand Rapids(M-3)	Peoria(FN-4)	Houston(RN-1)
4	Patterson(FN-4)	Omaha(SR-3)	N. Brunswick(FN-3)
5	Spokane(SR-4)	New York(NN-1)	Newark(FN-1)
6	Boston(RN-1)	Portland(RN-2)	Atlanta(RN-2)
7	Jacksonville(SR-3)	Des Moines(SR-4)	Tulsa(FN-3)
8	New York(NN-1)	Toledo(FN-3)	New Haven(E-3)
9	Fresno(G-4)	Minneapolis(RN-1)	Cincinnati(RN-2)
10	Des Moines(SR-4)	Patterson(FN-4)	Greensboro(FN-3)

Source: U.S. Bureau of the Census, Census of Wholesale Trade, 1972.

Conclusion

Briefly then, this chapter indicates continuing strong concentration of distributive services in a restricted number of centers, especially in the largest diversified service centers and limited decentralization tendencies, particularly when measured in output terms. Indications of possible decentralization tendencies at work are found in the case of communications and wholesaling employment, with decentralization benefiting most the relatively smaller subregional nodal centers and the group of specialized service centers. In the case of the communications industry (mostly telephone), this would seem to suggest that some routine operations (account processing, billing, etc.) need no longer to be located in the most central places; in the case of wholesaling that, where there are needs for large and inexpensive tracts of land for new shipping and warehousing facilities, these are most likely to be found outside the largest and most central places, or that there may be an increasing need for proximity to centers of manufacturing operations.

Admittedly, we have excluded from our analysis some other industries that make up an important element of the distributive networks, such as trucking. This decision was based on the difficulty of finding data that could shed some new light on the industry. However, limited evidence disclosed in *Large Corporations and Urban Employment*[2] pertaining to major facilities of trucking companies would seem to indicate the existence of decentralization tendencies that are fairly similar to those identified in wholesaling.

In terms of the overall urban hierarchy, this analysis of the distributive service networks further emphasizes characteristics of centrality associated with the diversified and the specialized service centers, and shed new light on the special nature of subregional nodal places as centers of distribution in fairly restricted regional areas.

Notes

1. These are estimated on the basis of published data on business telephones per capita in exchange-areas.

2. U.S. House of Representatives Subcommittee on the City, op. cit.

CHAPTER NINE

Major Civilian and Military Government Facilities and the Research, Higher Educational and Medical Complex

This chapter touches on two rather distinct areas of economic activity each of which has grown substantially during much of the postwar era and has affected unevenly the economic base of major types of cities. The first relates to major facilities of the public sector: military installations, federal and state civilian bureaucracies, and the postal system; the second, to a set of private, nonprofit and public sector institutions and facilities, linked together in what we call the research, higher educational and medical complex.

There are a number of difficulties associated with the analysis of these major areas. The first is empirical in nature and is related to the lack of detailed employment data for most of the various subsectors involved in these areas. It is particularly critical in the case of public sector employment: except for government census years, the only consistent annual estimates of public sector employment in individual SMSAs are those compiled by the U.S. Bureau of Labor Statistics for its *Employment and Earnings Series*. These estimates, with the exception of a few of the largest SMSAs, are published only for combined government employment, with no breakdown among federal, state, and local government employees and no functional breakdown among government services (between civilian and military federal employees, among education, health, or other services, and so forth).

The second is conceptual and relates to the multiplicity of functions that these sectors perform in the economy. Here the most important problem is that of distinguishing between local sector and export oriented functions. Many such services are essentially local population-serving (grade school, sanitation, or public transportation); local business-serving (publicly owned industrial parks or harbor facilities); or both at once (police or highway maintenance). Many are also export oriented services and contribute to specialization of metropolitan economies (medical schools, universities, research laboratories, state or federal bureaucracies, military installations, and so forth). An additional problem is that of distinguishing between those services which fall within the range of short-term and daily economic transactions and those which represent important contributions to the enhancement of the economy's stock of capital, both physical and human, as with construction of roads, sewers or publicly owned facilities, or with flow of funds in R&D or higher education.

In this chapter, we simply seek to determine the extent to which the different private, nonprofit and public sector activities studied here have tended to concentrate unevenly in major types of SMSAs and thus to extend the economic specialization of metropolitan places. We first turn to an analysis of conventional employment data for nonprofit and public sectors for such light as they may shed on the locational trends at work.

Locational Tendencies of Employment in the Nonprofit and Public Sectors

Table 9.1 presents location quotients of employment in the nonprofit and public sectors in different sizes and types of SMSAs for both 1976 and 1959. Employment in the nonprofit sector is broken down in terms of its major components, health and education. Note, however, that employment in health and educational services provided by the public sector is included under government (municipal and VA hospitals, public schools or state universities).

Among nonprofit services, the two major subsectors display sharply distinct tendencies. Locational tendencies in health reflect a behavior typical of a residential activity—with most places scoring near 100. Employment in education (mostly private, higher education), however, is much more specialized, with some places—especially the largest diversified and specialized service centers—exhibiting relatively strong concentration of employment in the industry in both 1959 and 1976.

With respect to the government sector, locational tendencies of employment shown in Table 9.1 are straightforward. Government-education and industrial-military places display relatively high concentration of employment in the sector in both 1959 and 1976, consistent with their functional roles in the system of cities (see Chapter 4). As for other types of centers, government employment is much more evenly distributed—indicating once again the residential nature of most government services, although the smaller places (see in particular the data for size 5 SMSAs and non-metropolitan areas) show somewhat higher concentration of employment than the larger ones.

In short, in both the nonprofit and government sectors there is evidence of specialization with regard to location. In the paragraphs which follow we attempt to identify more clearly some of the trends involved through analysis of some specific indicators of specialization.

Federal and State Civilian Agencies, Military Installations and Post Office Facilities

The growing importance of the public sector during the postwar era in terms of both employment and GNP has been noted in Chapter 2. Table 9.2 presents a few simple additional data that help us to understand at which level (federal, state, or

Table 9.1 Location Quotients of Employment in the Nonprofit and Public Sectors by Type and Size of SMSA, 1976 and 1959

	SMSA Size	# of SMSAs	Nonprofit	
			1976	1959
Diversified Service Centers				
National Nodal	1	4	104.4	95.9
Regional Nodal	1	8	117.4	120.3
	2	11	95.8	98.9
Subregional Nodal	3	9	93.8	110.2
	4	4	105.8	122.6
Specialized Service Centers				
Functional Nodal	1	3	106.1	100.4
	2	3	112.1	103.5
	3	12	97.5	92.9
	4	6	103.4	98.7
Government-Education	1	1	96.3	101.5
	3	2	106.9	109.9
	4	12	98.1	99.3
Education-Manufacturing	1-4	5	140.4	145.5
Consumer-Oriented Centers				
Residential	1-4	3	114.5	99.7
Resort-Retirement	1-4	9	98.8	99.3
Production Centers				
Manufacturing	2	1	106.4	103.5
	3	9	104.9	99.5
	4	19	93.6	92.3
Industrial-Military	2	1	91.4	91.3
	3	2	96.6	83.3
	4	10	83.2	70.7
Mining-Industrial	4	7	98.2	118.0
Size 5 SMSAs and Non-metropolitan Areas			90.0	93.5

Note: Location quotients are unweighted modified averages for major size-type groups.

Column heads: Same as Table 2.2.

Source: County Business Patterns, 1959 and 1976; Employment and Earnings in State and Local Areas, 1959 and 1976.

	(Health)		(Education)		Government	
	1976	1959	1976	1959	1976	1959
	99.0	95.2	126.9	98.6	80.9	76.6
	108.9	108.2	152.7	165.5	79.2	77.5
	96.2	98.7	94.3	99.6	88.7	91.8
	90.8	101.9	106.2	141.2	101.6	106.6
	109.1	129.3	91.9	97.5	99.8	108.1
	113.2	105.7	76.5	80.5	79.0	67.8
	106.7	107.7	134.5	88.1	69.2	63.8
	96.2	95.4	103.2	83.5	77.3	72.5
	114.3	111.8	57.8	49.9	74.6	68.5
	76.7	62.8	177.8	245.6	194.0	247.1
	107.8	110.6	103.1	107.3	182.1	186.4
	90.6	89.5	129.1	135.8	156.3	168.4
	121.0	115.2	221.1	258.3	99.3	88.8
	114.3	101.0	114.9	95.0	97.8	116.0
	103.9	97.6	77.5	105.5	102.2	126.8
	109.5	104.3	93.7	100.5	95.6	73.4
	106.2	100.0	99.3	97.6	71.5	63.8
	98.2	99.4	74.2	65.9	77.0	76.0
	95.6	102.4	74.2	49.9	134.9	129.5
	101.2	85.8	77.4	73.9	142.9	184.3
	86.4	86.6	69.7	54.3	153.4	186.7
	109.6	131.2	50.5	68.8	108.9	104.7
	95.9	99.3	65.6	70.2	118.6	125.1

Table 9.2 Employment and Expenditures of Federal, State and
        Local Governments, 1960, 1970 and 1978

	EMPLOYMENT				
	Empl. in Thousands			Percentage Change	
	1960	1970	1978	1960-70	1970-78
Federal (civilian)	2,421	2,881	2,888	19.0	0
State	1,527	2,755	3,539	80.6	28.5
Local	4,860	7,392	9,204	52.1	24.5

	EXPENDITURES				
	Exp. in $ Billions			Percentage Change	
	1960	1970	1978	1960-70	1970-78
Federal (including transfers to state/local)	90	195	412	116.6	111.3
Transfers to State/Local Gov.	(7)	(23)	(66)	228.6	187.0
State	22	56	129	154.5	130.3
Local	39	92	193	135.9	109.8

Source: U.S. Statistical Abstract, 1981.

local) the growth of the government sector has been felt most strongly.

Both halves of the table (upper half: employment; lower half: expenditures) emphasize a point that is easily lost in the current controversy on the growth of the public sector: that it is at the state level that growth has been the strongest since the early 1960s, although admittedly, employment and output were typically much smaller there to begin with. Obviously, as the second line of the lower half of the table indicates, federal transfers state and local governments (grants-in-aid) have played a major role in fueling the growth of state and local government sectors: by 1978, federal transfers represented over 20 percent of state and local financial resources.

To clarify somewhat the impact of public sector employment on the system of cities, we have developed in Table 9.3 location quotients of employment for federal civilian employees by type and size of SMSAs for both 1966 and 1976 (left side of the table: all federal civilian employees excluding postal workers; right side of the table: postal workers). When Table 9.3 and Table 9.1, in which location quotients of employment are shown for all government employees combined (i.e., military personnel and civilian federal, state and local employees), are analyzed simultaneously, certain basic tendencies become explicit.

Table 9.3 shows that the location of federal civilian employees (less postal workers) has, for the most part, remained highly concentrated in government-education and industrial-military centers (with the additional exception of the subregional nodal centers). The high concentration of federal civilian employees in the government-education SMSAs simply indicates that the federal government must maintain an active presence in state capitals if only because of necessary close interaction with state level bureaucracies. The lower location quotients of federal employees in size 3 and 4 government SMSAs than those shown in Table 9.1 for all government employees simply point to the fact that overconcentration of public sector employees in state capitals in both actual and relative terms is due primarily to state government employees.

A surprising finding is that the designation of a city as a federal regional center does not lead automatically to an overconcentration of federal employees in that SMSA. As shown in the text table presented below, three federal regional centers display a clear overconcentration of federal employment in 1977 (Denver, Kansas City, and San Francisco) and three an underconcentration (New York, Chicago, and Dallas) while the other four are near average.

1977 Location Quotients of Federal
Employment
in the Ten Federal Regional Centers

New York	42.9
Chicago	47.1
San Francisco	131.2
Philadelphia	111.8
Boston	92.3
Dallas	62.3
Atlanta	114.6
Kansas City	130.0
Denver	165.3
Seattle	88.6

The high concentration of federal civilian employees in industrial-military places indicates that, in addition to sizable military personnel (included in the data in Table 9.1), the presence of bases and other military facilities tends to generate sizable concentration of federal civilian employees. Likewise, subregional nodal places as a group have fared relatively better than other places in attracting federal civilian employees in part because several among them have important military installations (e.g., Omaha, Jacksonville, or Salt Lake City).

The decline in the number of postal workers between 1966 and 1976 (−6.8 percent change) at a time when the volume of mail increased very rapidly is a strong indication of a public service in which major productivity increases have

Table 9.3 Location Quotients of Employment of Federal Civilian Employees (less postal workers) and Postal Employees by Size and Type of SMSA, 1976 and 1966, Percentage Change of Employment, 1966-1976

	SMSA Size	# of SMSAs	All Fed. Civ. Empl. (less postal workers)			Postal Employees		
			LQ 1976	LQ 1966	%Change 1966-76	LQ 1976	LQ 1966	%Change 1966-76
Diversified Service Centers								
National	1	4	49.7	46.0	5.7	129.1	271.5	-19.0
Regional	1	8	78.6	80.7	9.7	105.6	100.9	-0.3
	2	11	93.6	86.6	20.8	97.2	102.8	3.2
Subregional	3	9	128.4	155.7	15.6	91.6	101.6	3.9
	4	4	100.8	86.6	44.5	93.6	113.0	9.8
Specialized Service Centers								
Functional Nodal	1	3	48.7	46.5	3.9	103.9	98.7	-11.5
	2	3	39.6	40.4	25.5	88.8	95.6	0.2
	3	12	31.4	29.4	10.5	83.6	81.8	-0.9
	4	6	30.9	25.4	47.0	81.3	80.1	-3.4
Government-Education	1	1	873.9	939.0	12.9	153.8	178.1	-8.1
	3	2	178.5	232.9	-10.6	102.7	101.4	-6.8
	4	12	117.1	146.9	41.1	86.6	89.6	5.5
Education-Manufacturing	3,4	5	49.6	55.2	17.4	97.5	158.7	-2.8

Consumer-Oriented Centers

Residential	1,2,4	3	110.0	33.4	27.3	105.5	105.7	8.8
Resort-Retirement	2,3,4	9	98.4	123.9	32.6	85.1	96.0	14.9

Production Centers

Manufacturing	2	1	46.6	31.9	25.1	108.3	92.7	-12.1
	3	9	24.8	19.0	28.3	80.8	83.3	-5.5
	4	19	46.0	76.2	16.4	76.3	80.2	-3.7
Industrial-Military	2	1	228.6	262.0	28.7	94.5	109.5	11.6
	3	2	436.0	522.8	1.4	86.9	86.9	2.1
	4	9	360.8	440.8	12.2	71.1	81.8	0.6
Mining-Industrial	4	7	66.5	110.4	40.3	88.3	97.9	2.1

Size 5 SMSAs and Non-metropolitan Areas			83.7	66.7	12.8	90.9	75.6	-5.0

United States					6.2			-6.8

Note: Location quotients are unweighted modified averages for major size-type groups.

Source: Federal Civilian Workforce Statistics, Annual Report of Employment by Geographic Areas, U.S. Civil Service Commission 1966 and 1976.

been achieved, largely by way of a sizable investments in new and heavily mech-anized distribution centers. The tendency towards decentralization of postal worker employment during the period indicated by Table 9.3 appears due not only to the decentralization of residential population but also to the construction of these more modern distribution centers away from the CBDs of the largest cities.

The Research, Higher Educational, and Medical Complex

Chapter 2 pointed to the growing importance of R&D functions and of engineer-ing, technical, and related professional skills in today's economy. Casual obser-vation alone suggests that the past 20 years or so have been characterized by powerful forces of agglomeration among firms with a strong technological orien-tation, R&D laboratories and pools of highly skilled personnel—including other technology oriented firms that are themselves large employers of skilled person-nel, or universities that are training grounds for such a labor force. For example, research and training efforts that went on during the 1950s and 1960s in and around Stanford University or the Massachusetts Institute of Technology are rec-ognized as having played major incubating roles in the development of both the Silicon Valley in the San Jose area and Route 128 around Boston. But beyond these two well known examples, these seem to be evidence of other places where similar agglomerations have taken hold, sparking the growth of new activities in both old and new firms: Rochester has become a major center of research and development in the areas of photography and photocopying office equipment largely by succeeding in promoting the development of a similar mix of private firms, R&D labs, universities and technical colleges; the Raleigh-Durham-Chapel Hill area has tried to use the campuses of Duke University and the Uni-versity of North Carolina to attract research institutions and high technology firms; Philadelphia and Boston have sparked new activity in the medical field by the presence of strong teaching and research hospital facilities; and other metro-politan areas around the country are now trying to follow similar directions (e.g., Ann Arbor, Albany-Troy-Schenectady, or Nassau-Suffolk).

What is less clear, however, is the extent to which these special agglomera-tions of private sector firms, nonprofit, or even public sector institutions (or the potentials for their development) have remained confined to certain metropolitan areas. This section is an attempt to shed light on this question through an analysis of the tendencies for R&D facilities, major universities, and medical institutions to agglomerate in certain types of metropolitan economies.

R&D FACILITIES

Between 1960 and 1976, total funds devoted to R&D by both the public and the private sectors rose from $13.5 billion to $37.4 billion in current dollars (Table 9.4). These numbers fail to reflect, however, the relative decline of the nation's R&D bill during the most recent decade when measured as a share of GNP. This development is well known and has been identified in many policy circles as one of the reasons for the loss of U.S. competitiveness in many major markets.

It is interesting to note from Table 9.4 that while the share of R&D expendi-

Table 9.4 R&D Funds (current dollars) by Source and by User Sector, 1960, 1970 and 1976

	1960		1970		1976	
	$ Millions	Share (%) of Total	$ Millions	Share (%) of Total	$ Millions	Share (%) of Total
Total R & D Funds	13,523	100.0	25,905	100.0	37,363	100.0
Source						
Private Source	8,735	64.6	15,157	58.5	20,233	54.1
Federal Funds	4,788	35.4	10,748	41.5	17,130	45.9
User Sector						
Industry	10,509	77.7	18,062	69.7	25,500	68.3
Fed. Funds	(6,081)		(7,779)		(9,500)	
Ind. Funds	(4,428)		(10,283)		(16,000)	
Federal Government	1,726	12.8	3,855	14.9	5,800	15.5
All Universities & Colleges	1,006	7.4	3,072	11.9	4,740	12.7
Other Non Profit Institutions	282	2.1	916	3.5	1,323	3.5

Source: Statistical Abstract, 1977, p. 612-613.

tures financed by federal funds grew from 35 percent in 1960 to 46 percent in 1976, the conduct of R&D has remained largely in the hands of the private sector. Thus, over 68 percent of all R&D funds were spent in private sector R&D laboratories in 1976 (as against 78 percent in 1960). Another 15.5 percent were spent in federal research facilities, followed by universities and colleges (12.7 percent) and other nonprofit institutions (3.5 percent). A major implication for what follows is that measures of R&D activity that emphasize the role of private sector laboratories are likely to be the most meaningful.

Data sources.   To carry out the following analysis we developed measures of R&D activity based on three sources of data:

1. a measure of concentration of R&D establishments of corporations and of independent private and nonprofit laboratories in SMSAs based on the 1956 and 1975 editions of the Directory of *Industrial Research Laboratories in the United States*,[1]
2. measures of concentration of employment of scientists and engineers in product testing, R&D, and consulting in SMSAs based on the 1974 National Science Foundation (NSF) *Characteristics of the National Sample of Scientists and Engineers*,[2] and
3. measures of concentration of employment in the R&D establishments of manufacturing firms in SMSAs based on special studies of Central Administrative Offices and Auxiliary Establishments of the 1972 and 1963 *Enterprise Statistics*.[3]

The 1956 and 1975 directories of *Industrial Research Laboratories* lists: "non-governmental laboratories devoted to fundamental and applied research, including development of products and processes. Most of the laboratories are owned and operated by industrial firms, but also included are some university, foundation and cooperative laboratories having separate research facilities."[4] In the case of industrial firms with various research establishments, each establishment is listed according to its parent division (or subsidiary).

In 1975, the directory reported 6,661 laboratories belonging to 3,241 organizations; in 1956, 4,834 labs belonging to 4,060 organizations. While the increase in the number of laboratories seems logical, the decrease in the number of organizations would require some explanation: Is the decline in organizations due to changes in reporting procedures, or is it the result of mergers among industrial firms during the period? Unfortunately, the directory remains silent on this question.

The 1974 NSF survey accounts for all U.S. scientists and engineers or consulting by either private, nonprofit or public sector establishments. This is the earliest NSF study available with a geographical breakdown of the employment data. Comparison with an earlier period is thus impossible.

Finally, the special studies of the *Enterprise Statistics*, which have been published for several census years, are different in scope than the NSF study since they cover all employees (engineers, scientists and others) in R&D establishments of private sector firms—mostly manufacturing firms. The strong emphasis of these special studies on the facilities of the manufacturing sector is not a serious limitation since, as was suggested earlier, these form the main locus for the nation's R&D effort.

Despite differences, the tendencies indicated by these three sources are quite consistent with one another, and provide solid information regarding basic characteristics of R&D activities among various sizes and types of SMSAs.

The main trends and locational characteristics. Table 9.5 makes use of the first set of measures and presents the distribution (number and percentages) of industrial research laboratories among diversified service centers, specialized service centers, and residential centers for both 1956 and 1976. This table shows, at once, high concentration of R&D facilities among most nodal and functional nodal centers in both 1956 and 1975, and some tendencies toward decentralization away from these centers during the 20-year period. Thus, while only the national nodal centers and the much smaller group of size 3 education-manufacturing places (New Haven and Springfield, Mass.) exhibit a net decline in the *number* of laboratories they host, there is a significant decline in the *share* of laboratories hosted by all diversified and specialized service centers between 1956 and 1975: from roughly 70 percent of all U.S. labs down to 56 percent. (Government places and the two largest residential centers do show a noticeable increase in their relative share of U.S. labs over the period: from less than 5 percent to 8 percent, with Washington, D.C.'s share growing from 1.2 percent to 3.2 percent.) The combined share of the remaining SMSAs and non-metropolitan areas (shown as "residual") increased from 23 to 34 percent.

Table 9.6 presents locational characteristics and historical trends among research facilities (based on 1975 and 1956 Directories of *Industrial Research Laboratories*), scientists and engineers employed in product inspection, R&D per se, management of R&D, and consulting (based on the NSF, *1974 Survey*), and employees of R&D establishments surveyed in the *Enterprises Statistics* (1972 and 1963). Like other tabulations presented in this chapter, these data are normalized to the population share of each SMSA group, using, respectively, 1976 population shares for the most recent data (1975, 1974, and 1972) and 1960 shares for the earlier data (1962 and 1956). Wherever possible, these tabulations are extended to each major size-type SMSA grouping and to the residual metropolitan and non-metropolitan areas.

In general, the location measures of R&D facilities (first two major columns of the table) show high—though selective—concentration of such establishments in diversified and specialized service centers, and low concentration everywhere else. More specifically, the table indicates that research labs have remained strongly concentrated in national nodal centers, size 1 regional nodal and size 1 through 3 functional nodal places during the 1956–75 period despite some relative decline, and have improved their concentration in government-education and education-manufacturing centers over the same period, although typically from a lower initial base. Noticeably, however, concentration remains rather weak in size 2 regional nodal and size 3 and 4 subregional nodal centers (mostly, Sunbelt places).

The 1974 NSF employment measures of scientists and engineers in product inspection, R&D and consulting (next four major columns of Table 9.6) show

Table 9.5 Distribution (number and percentage) of Industrial Research Laboratories among Diversified Service Centers, Specialized Service Centers and Residential Centers, 1975 and 1956

	SMSA Size	# of SMSAs	1975 # of Labs	1975 Share of All	1956 # of Labs	1956 Share of All
Diversified Service Centers				40.2		50.8
National	1	4	1,327	19.9	1,377	28.5
Regional	1	8	885	13.3	753	15.6
	2	11	348	5.2	216	4.5
Subregional	3	10	104	1.6	93	1.9
	4	6	15	0.2	15	0.3
Specialized Service Centers						
Functional Nodal				15.9		19.0
	1	3	375	5.6	376	7.8
	2	3	210	3.2	127	2.6
	3	12	396	6.0	357	7.4
	4	6	76	1.1	60	1.2
Government-Education				5.6		3.0
	1	1	212	3.2	60	1.2
	3	2	29	0.4	25	0.5
	4	12	132	2.0	62	1.3
Education-Manufacturing				1.2		1.9
	3	2	42	0.6	66	1.4
	4	3	43	0.6	24	0.5
Consumer-Oriented Centers				2.6		1.9
Residential	1	1	103	1.5	65	1.3
	2	1	60	0.9	17	0.4
	3	1	13	0.2	10	0.2
All Type and Size Shown			4,370	65.6	3,703	76.6
United States			6,661	100.0	4,834	100.0

Source: Industrial Research Laboratories of the United States, 1956 and 1975.

strong concentrations of employment in the specialized service centers and in the national nodal and size 2 regional nodal centers; weak concentration everywhere else, with the exception of industrial-military centers.

The *Census of Enterprises* measures (the last two columns) show not only a *very high* concentration of corporate-based R&D employment in functional nodal centers, but also a relative strengthening of that concentration between 1963 and 1972. Government-education and education-manufacturing centers show weak concentration, indicating (when compared with the NSF data) that R&D in such centers tends to be based in universities, consulting firms, or federal government facilities. As for national nodals and size 1 regional nodals, the results are mixed.

Examined jointly, the three sets of measures seem to indicate strong R&D activity in the specialized service centers, as well as in the national nodal and, though more selectively, regional nodal centers; weak R&D almost everywhere else. In the latter case, the noticeable exception is that of industrial military centers, likely because of the importance of R&D in military-related industries. In the case of regional nodal centers there are differences between the NSF data and the *Enterprise Statistics* data. The NSF data show relatively weak employment measures among size 1 regional nodal centers and relatively strong ones among size 2 regional nodal centers; the *Enterprise Statistics* show the reverse. A likely explanation is that R&D tends to be corporate-based in size 1 regional nodals (mostly Snowbelt) whereas it is based in government, consulting firms, and non-profit facilities (not unlike what was found for government places) among size 2 regional nodal centers (mostly Sunbelt).

HIGHER EDUCATION

The explosion of the field of higher education in the postwar era, and particularly during the 1960s and early 1970s, needs little emphasis. Between 1960 and 1977, college enrollment more than tripled, from 3,570,000 to 10,217,000 enrollees. This was followed by a slight decline in the latter years of the 1970s, reflecting largely the end of the passage of the postwar baby boom generation through the educational system. Of those who went to college during the period, over two-thirds went to colleges offering 4-year-or-more degrees, with the rest going to junior and community colleges offering two-year degrees. In general, the very rapid growth of college enrollment has reflected the increasing importance of college training in the American society: although only slightly over a tenth (11.0 percent) of those in the 25 to 29-year age bracket had received 4 years or more of college education in 1960, by 1980 their share had risen to 23.3 percent, well over a fifth.[5]

Which cities have benefited the most from this explosion of the higher educational field? To get a partial answer to this question, we have analyzed enrollment in the 100 largest university campuses (offering programs of 4 years or more) on the assumption that the larger the campus, the greater its impact on the surrounding community in terms of services and goods purchased by the institution, and salaries and wages paid out to faculty, administrators, and other employees. This procedure has the advantage of including the most prestigious private and state universities, which traditionally attract students from many areas

Table 9.6 Normalized Shares of R&D Laboratories (1965 and 1975), Scientists and Engineers Employed in R&D Activity (1974), and R&D Employees in CAO&A Establishments (1972 and 1963) by Type and Size of SMSA

	SMSA Size	# of SMSAs	Research Labs		Scientists and Engineers in R&D, 1974				R&D Employees in CAO&A Establishments	
			1975	1956	Product Inspection	R&D Per Se	R&D Management	Con-sulting	1972	1963
Diversified Service Centers										
National	1	4	160.5	209.7	144.7	127.1	122.4	114.3	102.2	91.0
Regional	1	8	126.9	152.2	93.4	92.4	93.4	89.8	104.8	149.9
	2	11	77.1	121.0	111.3	123.6	118.0	135.6	61.8	46.7
Subregional	3	10	47.6	63.5	85.2	74.3	50.5	89.3	52.5	n.a.
	4	6	31.9	42.2	57.4	38.1	82.8	76.0	n.a.	n.a.
Specialized Service Centers										
Functional Nodal	1	3	139.0	171.0	118.4	151.2	158.3	131.2	715.0	618.1
	2	3	186.0	170.5	117.5	214.9	188.8	167.4	118.9	109.0
	3	12	149.2	181.2	85.1	138.9	110.9	128.1	241.3	182.4
	4	6	93.5	104.3	188.2	189.0	186.4	163.8	n.a.	n.a.
Government-Education	1	1	225.0	105.9	382.1	255.7	639.3	123.9	17.9	77.2
	3	2	50.0	69.5	187.7	150.1	116.4	115.3	n.a.	n.a.
	4	12	101.3	69.5	122.3	126.4	163.3	95.9	n.a.	n.a.
Education-Manufacturing	3	2	93.7	205.9	48.4	87.1	82.5	45.5	75.4	54.1
	4	3	148.8	116.5	181.7	126.4	128.6	89.2	n.a.	n.a.

	Size	n								
Consumer-Oriented Centers										
Residential	1,3,4	3	113.0	114.0	n.a.	n.a.	n.a.	n.a.	n.a.	n.a.
Resort-Retirement	2	2	22.8	6.9	47.1	37.0	59.0	79.2	14.5	n.a.
	3	3	42.1	19.1	107.8	83.1	112.7	107.9	n.a.	n.a.
	4	4	67.6	44.3	111.6	172.6	121.2	76.9	n.a.	n.a.
Production Centers										
Manufacturing	2	1	123.8	207.9	66.7	123.2	77.2	99.3	38.1	121.6
	3	8	65.7	69.9	41.6	46.9	29.4	84.5	31.9	n.a.
	4	16	n.a.	n.a.	86.9	84.8	83.8	102.6	n.a.	n.a.
Industrial-Military	2	1	103.2	64.9	136.8	162.7	155.8	69.0	4.0	n.a.
	3	2	23.6	27.9	61.3	28.4	35.7	36.4	n.a.	n.a.
	4	11	n.a.	n.a.	167.6	151.6	236.1	130.2	n.a.	n.a.
Mining-Industrial	4	7	n.a.	n.a.	90.8	109.8	61.6	100.0	n.a.	n.a.
All Size 5 SMSA and Non-metropolitan Areas			85.4	45.8	70.8	66.8	55.5	84.0	50.9	52.9

n.a.: not available.

Note: Shares are unweighted modified averages for major size-type groups of SMSAs. Shares are normal-ized against population of SMSAs, using 1976 population shares for 1975, 1974 and 1972 data and 1960 population shares for 1962 and 1956 data.

Source: Industrial Research Laboratories of the United States, 1975 and 1956. U.S. Scientists and Engineers in 1974, Part 3: Geographic, NSF Publication #76330. Enterprise Statistics, Part 2: Central Administrative Offices and Auxiliary Establishments, 1972 and 1963.

of the country, and of excluding smaller ones, which are typically locally oriented institutions. As of 1977, these 100 largest campuses accounted for less than 6 percent of the total number of institutions but included 35 percent of the population of college enrollees (a slight decline from 1959, when they attracted 41 percent of the college population).[6]

In Table 9.7, we have distributed enrollment in these 100 largest campuses on the basis of a type and size of SMSAs and normalized each SMSA group's share of its enrollment to the SMSA group's population base. As of 1977, with only a few exceptions, there was a clear overconcentration of these largest and usually most prestigious institutions in diversified and specialized service centers; a clear underconcentration in the consumer-oriented and production centers.

As regards centers with a relatively high concentration of these 100 largest higher educational institutions, one must note the marked decline in the relative importance of such institutions in the four national nodal and the three largest (size 1) functional nodal centers. The explanation revealed by an analysis of the shifts in the ranking among the 100 largest institutions (not shown here) seems to be twofold. On one hand, enrollment in the large private universities, which have historically tended to be highly concentrated in these largest centers, did not grow as rapidly as in state universities. On the other hand, there seems to have been a tendency for the largest state universities to avoid expanding rapidly in the largest and most central centers, and to prefer a growth strategy centered on both smaller and more off-centered places: primarily in government-education, education-manufacturing, medium-size functional nodal and very small urban centers (for example, University of Massachusetts in Amherst, University of Illinois in Urbana-Champaign, or Pennsylvania State in University Park). This is reflected in Table 9.7 in the sharp gains registered in most of these groups, including in a number of the smaller (size 4 and residual) centers.

To conclude, this analysis of enrollment in the largest universities indicates strong tendencies for this highly specialized service to concentrate in the most service-oriented centers of the urban hierarchy, with some (but limited) spin-off to small, off-centered places. The finding that the specialized service centers are the most specialized in terms of higher education, as they are in research, is strongly suggestive of the importance taken by educational-research complexes in the economic base of most of these centers. Indeed, there is at least indirect evidence that it is in these centers that much of the new, high-technology entrepreneurship is taking place largely because of the strong agglomeration of universities, research laboratories and large, often technology-oriented firms and the resulting availability of large numbers of highly trained professionals, scientists and engineers.

HEALTH

Like that of the higher educational field, the growth of the health care sector in the postwar era has been astounding. Between 1960 and 1978, national health expenditure grew almost eight times, from $27 billion to $193 billion, nearly doubling its share of GNP (from 5.2 percent to 9.1 percent). While much of the activity of the health care sector is local population-saving in orientation, areas

Table 9.7 Normalized Shares of Student Enrollment in 100
Largest Campuses by Size and Type of SMSA, 1977
and 1959

	SMSA Size	# of SMSAs	1959	1977
Diversified Service Centers				
National	1	4	171.5	106.3
Regional	1	8	149.4	131.5
	2	11	136.2	142.9
Subregional	3	9	98.7	132.5
	4	4	0.0	0.0
Specialized Service Centers				
Functional Nodal	1	3	96.7	59.2
	2	3	208.1	175.1
	3	12	83.4	144.4
	4	6	125.9	196.4
Government-Education	1	1	196.2	169.6
	3	2	80.6	188.9
	4	12	379.2	431.2
Education-Manufacturing	3,4	5	238.8	285.7
Consumer-Oriented Centers				
Residential	1,2,4	3	41.9	39.2
Resort-Retirement	2,3,4	9	25.0	85.6
Production Centers				
Manufacturing	2	1	110.2	129.4
	3	9	0.0	0.0
	4	19	22.4	30.0
Industrial-Military	2	1	139.4	158.5
	3	2	0.0	0.0
	4	10	0.0	0.0
Mining-Industrial	4	7	87.4	108.6
Size 5 SMSAs and				
Non-metropolitan Areas			55.6	72.9

Note: Campuses of colleges offering four-year or more degrees. Shares are unweighted modified averages for
major size-type groups of SMSAs. Shares are normalized
against the population share of SMSAs.

Source: U.S. National Center for Education Statistics,
Education Statistics, 1959 and 1977.

Table 9.8 Normalized Shares of Medical Students, and Interns and Residents by Type and Size of SMSA, 1974 and 1959

	SMSA Size	# of SMSAs	1974		1959		# of Med. Schools	
			Med. Std'ts	Int's & Resd'ts	Med. Std'ts	Int's & Resd'ts	1974	1959
Diversified Service Centers								
National	1	4	138.9	205.2	154.4	202.4	16	15
Regional	1	8	182.0	165.7	216.1	234.2	17	16
	2	11	187.6	172.4	248.0	248.3	12	11
Subregional	3	9	282.2	214.8	380.1	279.2	9	9
	4	4	292.9	112.0	360.6	230.4	2	2
Specialized Service Centers								
Functional Nodal	1	3	89.2	87.5	56.9	52.6	3	2
	2	3	118.9	140.7	140.2	149.4	3	2
	3	12	131.8	72.5	72.4	71.9	5	3
	4	6	0.0	0.0	0.0	0.0	0	0
Government-Education	1	1	245.6	163.9	334.6	219.4	3	3
	3	2	193.2	246.5	109.5	129.8	2	1
	4	12	241.7	187.3	105.7	201.7	6	4
Education-Manufacturing	3,4	5	234.0	229.6	321.0	308.7	2	2

Consumer-Oriented Centers								
Residential	1,2,4	3	32.5	80.5	0.0	0.0	2	0
Resort-Retirement	2,3,4	9	82.9	57.8	0.0	0.0	4	0
Production Centers								
Manufacturing	2	1	161.4	146.3	139.6	177.1	1	1
	3	9	61.5	89.0	36.0	31.3	4	1
	4	19	45.2	40.6	0.0	0.0	2	0
Industrial-Military	2	1	67.1	127.5	0.0	0.0	1	0
	3	2	118.9	133.2	0.0	0.0	2	0
Mining-Industrial	4	10	90.8	47.4	201.6	115.8	2	1
	4	7	61.8	55.4	0.0	0.0	2	0
Size 5 SMSAs and Non-metropolitan Areas							15	10
United States							113	84

Note: Shares are unweighted modified averages for major size-type groups of SMSAs. Shares are normalized against the population share of SMSAs.

Source: American Medical Association, Directory of Residency Training Programs, 1974-75 and 1959-60, and Journal of American Medical Association, November issues, 1960 and 1975.

dealing with education, training, research and delivery of highly specialized medical services are essentially export-based in nature. Only selected metropolitan places succeed in developing sufficient resources to provide for such services. To get some sense as to where such specialization has occurred, we have developed two measures for each group of SMSAs: a normalized share of students registered in local medical schools and a normalized share of interns and residents undergoing training in local medical institutions. These measures are presented in Table 9.8.

Before examining the findings of the table, some understanding of the differences between these two measures is necessary. In 1975, there were 54,074 students registered in 113 medical schools throughout the country, as against 29,891 students in 84 schools in 1959. Most of the medical schools added to the list between 1959 and 1975 were in centers that did not have such institutions in 1959: usually in some of the most off-centered places of the urban hierarchy (the last two columns in Table 9.8). As for interns and residents, their number grew from 16,177 in 1959 to 36,085 in 1976.

At the local level, the resources necessary to handle these populations of students and medical trainees differ in ways that reflect the medical resources available in each locale. Whereas medical education requires a capacity to assemble a team of local practitioner-teachers to conduct a curriculum of courses, internship and residentship requires not only practitioner-supervisors but also resources in local hospitals to handle the flow of trainees. In that sense, internship and residentship reflect more fully the entire medical resources of a given community. Thus, local hospitals in the smaller SMSAs with a medical school usually cannot offer the number of internship openings necessary to absorb all of the school's graduates, whereas larger metropolitan centers, with numerous hospital institutions, can provide intership positions in excess of the number of local graduates. Thus, there tends to be a high locational turnover among medical school graduates between the end of school and the beginning of internship, one that is accentuated by the fact that the best graduates from every school try to go to the most prestigious medical institutions.

Table 9.8 shows that in 1959 both medical education and internships were heavily concentrated in the diversified and specialized service centers, with national nodal, size 1 regional nodal, size 2 functional nodal, size 3 and 4 government centers tending to offer a surplus of internship positions. (Location quotient for interns in excess of that for medical students.) By 1976, there had been a substantial decentralization with medical education and internship program taking hold in more off-centered places, although those centers that were prominent in 1959 were still maintaining their lead in the field in 1976.

The significance of the tendencies just described is similar to that which has been suggested in the case of higher education. Medical educational and training facilities are known to both necessitate the presence and promote the growth of a wide range of related service and manufacturing activities (from research to medical supplies or medical equipment) to contribute significantly to a kind of economic base transformation characterized by the development of technology-oriented firms and highly trained personnel. That these are found to have remained heavily concentrated in the diversified and specialized service centers is one additional indication of the headstart which these places have enjoyed in effecting their transition to the service economy.

Conclusion

The short analyses presented in this chapter have highlighted the ways in which major civilian and military government facilities as well as institutions of the research, higher educational, and medical complex have contributed to economic specialization of places.

In the case of government, this chapter has shown that state capitals and industrial-military places, for reasons that differ in both types of places, are well entrenched and unlikely to be dislodged from their position as leading recipients of public sector employment. In the case of the U.S. postal service, however, we found evidence of decentralization tendencies away from the largest urban centers.

A quite different, but highly significant finding, has been that indicating that it is in the specialized service centers and in the largest diversified service centers that the strongest complexes of research and education (involving various types of private, nonprofit, and public research and higher educational institutions, and some of the most advanced medical institutions) have developed, since there is strong evidence that these complexes provide for the kind of environment in which the newest and the most technologically advanced industries grow best. This development is important in and of itself, but needs also to be compared with that found in the case of the complexes of corporate activities. This is done in the next and final chapter.

Notes

1. Op. cit., New York: R.R. Bowker Co., 1975; Op. cit., Washington: National Academy of Sciences, 1956. While published nowadays by commercial publishers, these directories have been developed over the years under the supervision of the National Academy of Sciences/National Research Council.

2. Op. cit., Part 3. Geographic, NSF Publication 76-330, Washington, D.C.: U.S. Government Printing Office.

3. Op. cit., Part II, U.S. Department of Commerce, Bureau of the Census, Washington, D.C.: U.S. Government Printing Office.

4. Quoted from the introduction to the 1975 Directory.

5. All data from *U.S. Statistical Abstract*, 1981.

6. U.S. National Center for Education Statistics, *Education Statistics*, 1959 and 1977.

CHAPTER TEN

Major Findings and Their Implications for Economic Development of Metropolitan Places

A basic thesis of this study has been that the postwar U.S. economy has been characterized by a dramatic shift in employment and value added towards services, with major implications for metropolitan economic development. This shift has resulted from a complex set of transformations, including changes in the scope of markets, in transportation and in technology, and the growing importance of producer service firms, government, nonprofit institutions and the large corporation.

The period of the 1960s and 1970s has been one during which production in plants has tended to require increasingly less direct labor input and less managerial attention, largely because of major advances in technology, at the same time that corporations have had to devote greater resources to the service inputs associated with product engineering and marketing, research and development, and corporate strategy and planning.

Hence, the significance of the transformation which has unfolded resides not so much in the rise of services as free standing final outputs as it does in the changing emphasis on functions performed and in *how* society produces. In large part this is what the service transformation is about: new ways of producing and marketing final commodities, involving an increase in service or service-like inputs, involving a move towards operating production facilities and penetrating consumer markets largely on a national, if not on a world scale, and resulting in a significant reorganization of the geography of goods and services production.

The implications for the system of cities have been dramatic. Traditional manufacturing activities have increasingly been "shaken loose" at least from the largest metropolitan centers, where they once used to concentrate, with these cities becoming more and more specialized in the production and export of high level services. The result has been a profound transformation of both the economic base of most cities and the whole structure of institutional and economic relationships which links cities to one another, and has involved not simply the so called "rise of the Sunbelt cities" but a much more complicated process of change in which many Snowbelt cities have clearly held their own.

In this final chapter, we summarize some of the major findings of the study and suggest their implications for policymakers, focusing in particular, on *structure* and *development*. Under ''structure,'' we review what has been learned about the transformation of the economic base of major types of cities and what has been learned about the changing nature of intermetropolitan linkages; under ''development,'' we examine which industries are likely to continue to grow, what kinds of jobs are being opened up and where.

Structure

KEY CHARACTERISTICS OF ECONOMIC STRUCTURE OF MAJOR TYPES OF CITIES

The Diversified Service Centers. This first major group of cities includes 39 metropolitan centers characterized by large shares of their employment in the distributive services, in the complex of corporate activities, and somewhat more selectively in universities, hospitals, and public sector services. In other words, they are both centers of distribution for hinterland markets and strong centers of high level services, with size of places an important determinant of diversification.

At the apex of the group stand the national nodal centers: New York, Chicago, Los Angeles and San Francisco. As of the late 1970s nearly a third of the nation's 1150 largest corporations were headquartered in one of these four centers; nearly a fourth of the industrial divisions of the 650 largest American corporations were headquartered there; and about one out of every two large U.S. corporations maintained regional sales headquarters in each of these four places. New York, obviously, has a special place as the dominant American urban center. As of 1976, nearly two-thirds of the area's labor force was employed in the complex of corporate activities, in nonprofit institutions or in the public sector. One out of every five Fortune 1000 firms were headquartered in the New York SMSA. Close to 30 percent of the nation's commercial banking deposits were controlled by New York banks. This was where the very large investment banks were headquartered, where most of the nation's advertising industry operated, and so forth.

More generally speaking, the national centers are places characterized by enormous banking resources, great depth in many business service areas such as accounting, advertising, legal counsel, or investment banking, and a capacity to provide specialized expertise to firms engaged in international operations unmatched anywhere else. As a result, over the years, most large U.S. corporations not already headquartered in one of these four cities have found it necessary to open financial offices or foreign trade/investment facilities in one of them because of the very special resources these offer. Likewise, it is there that foreign multinational corporations and transnational banks located their North American headquarters as they moved forcefully into U.S. markets during the late 1970s.[1]

The next group of cities, the regional centers, includes places ranging from Philadelphia, Boston, and Dallas to New Orleans, Portland, and Columbus. As of 1976, these 19 places accounted for another fourth of the headquarters of the nation's 1150 largest firms, and a roughly similar percentage of the headquarters of the industrial divisions of the 650 largest firms. Large corporations headquartered in those centers tended to be somewhat smaller and less international in orientation than those found in the very large national centers, and to have retained closer ties to their surrounding regional markets. For example, many large food, retail, transportation, and utilities companies were headquartered in such centers.

The producer service base of the regional centers remains extensive, but somewhat less sophisticated than that found in the national centers. With almost one out of every two large U.S. corporations locating regional sales headquarters in each of these regional centers, one of their key functional roles clearly has become that of providing a base from which large corporations can oversee their commercial operations in the major regional markets of the U.S. economy. This is also reflected in the fact that most of these places tend to have well-developed warehousing and shipping facilities, and airports with extensive air connections.

The subregional centers—e.g., Memphis, Omaha, or Charlotte—clearly have a less diversified base of high level services than their larger counterparts, but they do stand out by their strong involvement in the distributive services (wholesaling and trucking, in particular).

National and regional nodal centers have usually been characterized both by strong losses in their once important manufacturing sector and considerable rebuilding of their economic base in the advanced service sectors. In terms of overall growth, Sunbelt centers have typically performed better than their northern counterparts, if only because they had smaller manufacturing sectors to begin with, or because their manufacturing base has not yet been subject to the wrenching adjustments that have occurred in many older cities. Subregional centers have typically grown rapidly, although they appear to have been somewhat restricted in their development of high level service activities both by their size and function in the overall urban hierarchy. For example, few have been successful in bringing about the development of strong educational or research complexes, or in attracting large numbers of headquarters and divisional offices of major firms.[2]

The Specialized Service Centers.   This second major class includes 44 metropolitan centers distributed among three groups. The first group (the functional nodal centers) is exemplified by places like Detroit, San Jose, Rochester, or Akron, which are characterized by large numbers of central offices of large industrial corporations (primarily national headquarters and divisional head offices) and by strong concentrations of production establishments, usually in highly specialized complexes of industries: Detroit in automobile, San Jose in electronics, Rochester in scientific and office equipment, Akron in tires, and so forth. The second and third groups (government-education and education-manufacturing centers) are characterized by cities with strong concentrations of public sector facilities (e.g., state capitals), universities and other nonprofit institutions.

Specialized service centers tend to have in common that they are highly specialized in the range of advanced services that they offer, that they tend to be weak financial or business service centers, that they have limited involvement in regional consumer markets outside their immediate hinterland, but that they tend also to be well-oriented towards higher education and research. Two consequences follow: that corporations headquartered in such places often need to get the financial and business service assistance lacking in their locale from organizations located in the diversified advanced service centers and that, because of their orientation toward R&D and higher education, such places are likely to be good breeding grounds for new firms and new industries.[3]

Among this class of cities, the functional nodal and the education-manufacturing centers have usually experienced low growth, due to large losses of production jobs (depending, of course, on their industry of specialization) which they have only partially offset by employment gains in central offices of industrial firms or in other high level services. Their more restricted economic base has obviously made for a more difficult process of transition. Government-education centers have usually fared better, if only because of the lesser weight of manufacturing in their economic base and the surge of employment in the public and nonprofit sectors during the 1960s and 1970s.

The Production Centers. This third major class (45 centers) includes three groups of places—the manufacturing, industrial-military and mining-industrial centers—characterized respectively by an overconcentration of employment in manufacturing, in government (mostly military related installations, e.g., navy, army, or air force bases, arsenals, shipyards, etc.) or in mining.

Industrial-military places (e.g., San Diego, Norfolk, or Newport News) enjoyed fairly rapid development from the 1940s through the 1960s because of their direct linkage to the various war efforts (ordnance, shipbuilding, aerospace). Although the largest ones, particularly San Diego and San Antonio, seem to have succeeded in bringing about some diversity to their economic base, most remain highly dependent upon the flow of federal funds for military or related (e.g., space) projects.

Mining-industrial centers (e.g., Bakersfield or Charleston, West Virginia) enjoyed a certain vitality in the late 1970s, if only because of the nation's growing attention for domestic energy and mineral resources at that time. Their short term future does not appear as bright as it then did, however.[4]

Among manufacturing centers (e.g., Buffalo, Youngstown, Reading, etc.), the record has been, for the most part, dismal. This has been so not only because many are specialized in older manufacturing industries, but because of a key feature of their structure. By comparison to the functional nodal centers, manufacturing centers (and to a somewhat similar extent, military-industrial and mining-industrial places) have traditionally been more likely to be engaged in standardized production work (mostly assembly work). Furthermore, as a result of the accelerated process of corporate concentration characteristic of the 1960s and 1970s, they have often tended to lose whatever little involvement they may have had in the planning, administration, or research and development functions of their industry. As a result, they have tended to be the most vulnerable to adverse development affecting their particular industry and to the widespread shrinking of blue-collar jobs.[5] These centers have demonstrated very limited ability to dissociate themselves from their blue-collar image and have found very little relief other than through developing local public sector jobs or consumer-oriented services to fill the gap of plant shutdowns.[6]

The Consumer-Oriented Centers.   The last and smallest group of places (12 places only) includes two sets of cities: residential centers which are metropolitan areas outlying the national nodal metropolises (Nassau-Suffolk and Long Branch-Asbury Park near New York, Anaheim near Los Angeles) and resort-retirement cities (e.g., Orlando, West Palm Beach, or Las Vegas) that have sprung up in the postwar era under the combined effects of residential suburbanization, rising consumerism and widespread retirement benefits.

In general, these places have been characterized by trends in population settlement that have made for substantial growth. But with the exception of the few largest ones (Nassau-Suffolk, Anaheim, Orlando, and possibly Tampa), the orientation of their economic growth and employment expansion toward provision of consumer services has tended to work against agglomerations of activities which draw upon high level corporate, public and nonprofit services. The only consistent departure in their pattern of development we found has come through some (if limited) growth in the area of manufacturing assembly.

INTERMETROPOLITAN LINKAGES IN THE NEW URBAN SYSTEM

In light of the above, it is clear that the postwar transformation of the urban system has resulted in the emergence of a functional dichotomy between urban centers that are by now well positioned in terms of the production and export of high level services—the diversified and specialized service centers, and those which are not—the production and consumer-oriented centers. The implications of this dichotomy are important to assess.

Until recently, manufacturing had been a principal component of the export base of many of the current diversified and specialized service centers. Increasingly, however, it is high-level services that constitute the vital sector of their economies. Obviously, this development does not mean that goods producing activities are altogether losing their place in urban economies. Many diversified or specialized service centers will continue to carry out some form of goods production, whether it be for local markets or even for export (see in particular, the case of the functional nodal centers among the specialized service centers). More importantly, manufacturing is likely to remain a major, if not the principal component, of the economic base of many production centers, and possibly even grow in importance in some of the consumer-oriented centers. Still, the current concentration of high-level services in the economies of the diversified and specialized service centers does reflect changes in the nature of intermetropolitan linkages, and, ultimately, changes in the way in which growth impulses are being diffused throughout the entire urban system.

Since final outputs (whether manufactured goods or consumer services) and high-level services remain highly interdependent, growth of places specialized in high-level services remains fundamentally linked to growth of places specialized in the production of final goods and consumer services. In an economy which is more and more dominated by large multilocational organizations, growth increments are increasingly being transmitted from these lower ranking cities to the diversified or specialized service centers either through direct intra-firm linkages between remote plants or consumer-serving outlets and central offices, or because growth of activity in these remote facilities may necessitate the purchase of expertise from other high-level service institutions by the firm's central office.[7] Likewise demand generated in service cities flows back to production or consumer-oriented centers, for example, in the form of demand for the goods that they produce or in income spent by commuters, vacationers, or retirees.

But these processes of growth transmission are biased in two fundamental ways. First, if the past is any indication of the future, it is reasonable to assume that, on balance, diversified and specialized service centers enjoy the most favorable prospect since, as we have shown in Chapter 2, economic growth creates increasingly smaller shares of jobs and GNP in production establishments or consumer-services, and increasingly larger ones in the high-level services. Second, this tendency is aggravated by the fact that, directly through the headquarters of large firms and more indirectly through the community of business service firms which assist corporations in decision-making, the diversified and specialized service centers hold increasingly greater control over the diffusion of innovation, the flows of investment, and the creation of jobs in the lower ranking production and consumer-oriented centers.[8]

While the above remains a highly simplified set of propositions that cannot account for all of the ways in which the fortunes of cities are linked, the implications are important to recognize. Production centers have been and are likely to remain under considerable stress because the trend towards relative reduction of employment in production and increased international competition are bound to impact negatively in places in which large numbers of workers remain employed in goods producing activities. Of course, patterns are likely to differ depending on the industry in which such places tend to specialize, and some places may even grow as others stagnate or decline.

By comparison, diversified and specialized service centers are likely to be best positioned to benefit from the continuing shift to high level services, if present patterns continue, although different centers may benefit differently depending on the particular emphasis of the economic cycle. For example, if a particular period of cyclical expansion emphasizes the rebuilding of the nation's technological capacity, specialized service centers might benefit most from the flow of dollars into research, development, higher education and so forth because of the special role they play in the network of development functions (using Dunn's terminology).

On the other hand, if the emphasis is less on technology and more on reopening consumer markets, diversified service centers might reap a greater share of the benefits because of their function as distribution and control centers.

This is not to argue, of course, that diversified or specialized service centers will be problem free. Many will continue to be affected by the loss of traditional blue-collar jobs. Specialized service centers have against them that their fortune remains tied to that of a narrow range of industrial activity and the diversified service centers, to that of the markets they serve. Structural difficulties in one industry may thus affect particularly harshly the well being of certain specialized service centers, while diversified service centers may be hurt by the trend toward increased protectionism on world markets, in the case of the largest, and by adverse regional trends in the case of the smaller.

Development

In light of what has just been said, it is clear that the route to successful development is likely to vary considerably from place to place, that urban developmental strategies must differ, and that no single urban policy is likely to help unless it can recognize the diversity implicit in the structure of the urban system which is developing. In light of the analyses carried out in our study, one issue that must be raised is the extent to which "filtering down" of high level services is likely to occur, altering developmental patterns currently biased against the lower ranking production and consumer oriented centers.

IS DECENTRALIZATION OF HIGH LEVEL SERVICES IN THE OFFING?

In answer to this question, the evidence suggests that while there is no straightforward answer—our study shows instances where strong centralizing tendencies are at work, where strong decentralizing tendencies are at work, and instances where the record is ambivalent—it is likely that, if left to market forces alone, services will continue to concentrate most vigorously in the upper tiers of the urban system. The following examples illustrate some of the various trends at work.

Centralization. Among producer services, most often trends are favoring strong centralization. In banking, for example, centralization of assets in the few largest banking centers has been hefty throughout the postwar period and it appears that deregulation is bringing about even further centralization rather than decentralization of high level financial resources. Between the early 1960s and the early 1980s, the share of deposits in the 40 "top 250" commercial banks headquartered in the nation's money centers (New York, Chicago, Los Angeles, and San Francisco) has grown from roughly 30 percent to over 50 percent!

In advertising, we find little evidence of movement out of New York City. Among high level financial and corporate services aimed at assisting corporations in their conduct of foreign business, it appears that the four national nodal centers occupy a very special role with, thus far, only Miami and Houston having succeeded in finding a niche in this highly restricted network.

In air transportation, we find that the smallest diversified service centers and many among the specialized service centers have lost rather than gained air connections and traffic as a result of higher fuel costs and industry deregulation, while the largest diversified service centers consolidated their leadership.

Ambivalence. Among national headquarters and divisional offices of large firms, the trends have been somewhat ambivalent. During the 1960s and early 1970s, a number of large corporations did display some tendencies towards decentralizing their national headquarters. However, the great majority of the changes that took place amounted (1) to New York based corporations relocating to the Stamford-Greenwich-Bridgeport area or to some of the large regional diversified centers, namely Dallas, Houston, Atlanta, and Minneapolis; (2) to a few large corporations reshuffling their headquarters from one regional nodal center to another; or (3) to some local gains and losses associated with rank upgrading or downgrading of local corporations—a phenomenon which has always been going on and will continue to go on. Overall, there was practically no change between 1959 and 1976 in the total number of the nation's largest corporations (Fortune 500) headquartered in the diversified and specialized service center (roughly 85 percent).

Another ambivalent case is that of the divisional headquarters of large firms. On the one hand, we find strong evidence of an increasingly tighter relationship among divisional headquarters of firms, specialized production establishments (batch or short run production as opposed to assembly work) and research and higher educational facilities, if only because divisional offices and high level production establishments require the employment of increasingly larger numbers of highly skilled and highly trained personnel (engineers, draftsmen, technicians, computer specialists, etc.). On the other hand, we find that some decentralization in the location of research and higher educational facilities has occurred over the past two decades or so, which has permitted the development of new technology-oriented firms and has resulted in attracting key divisional offices or production facilities of established firms in places previously marginally affected by industrial development.[9] San Jose in the fifties or Raleigh-Durham-Chapel Hill in the seventies seem good examples of such a process of development. But research and higher education still have a lot to do with federal dollars and in the face of recent retrenchment, there may not be much room for change in the near future.

Decentralization. There are a few clear examples of decentralization, however. Data processing facilities of large businesses (insurance, banks, etc.) are being attracted to relatively off-centered locations largely because advances in communications permits such facilities to operate from a distance and because advances in EDP technology permits the employment of a relatively low skilled clerical labor force—by now plentiful almost anywhere.

Likewise, warehousing and trucking have been moving away from the largest centers, largely because the completion of the interstate highway system and the rise of large-scale containerization has made it increasingly profitable to operate large warehousing and shipping facilities in locations at a distance from the largest, often more congested, places.

Finally, the case can probably be made that small or medium sized regional corporations, which do not necessarily need highly centralized locations for their headquarters, are increasingly able to gain access to many of the producer services they need in relatively more decentralized locations as communications technology improves and as some of the producer service firms reach further out to their hinterland markets. Large accounting firms, for example, show a propensity to open offices offering basic audit and tax services in a large number of locations, provided they can gather enough business.

On balance, decentralization of high level services is likely to remain limited in the immediate future. Thus far, such decentralization has remained restricted mostly to a shift of services away from the largest diversified service centers towards smaller nodal centers and/or towards some of the specialized service centers.

THE QUALITY OF EMPLOYMENT

There is another area of concern, related to the broad economic shifts described in this study, which involves the kind of jobs likely to become available as economic growth and development proceed.

Our investigation elsewhere[10] indicates that there are sharp differences in skill, pay, and opportunity levels among workers engaged in service or service-like activities with a strong tendency for jobs to fall into a "good job" (full-time, rewarding work, which is typically secure in tenure and well paid) or "bad job" (work which is often part-time, unrewarding and poorly paid, and typically insecure) category, with opportunity for upward mobility unpromising and ill-defined in the latter. In part, these important differences are inherent in the service industries, themselves. Some industries, particularly retailing and consumer services, tend to be characterized by an overwhelming concentration of mostly "bad jobs" and to pay quite poorly across their entire range of occupations while others, especially distributive services and government, tend to offer predominantly desirable employment and to pay relatively well across the range of occupations they offer. Producer and nonprofit services tend to fall in between, offering mixes of good jobs and bad jobs, with more employment stability and relatively stronger pay than in the most unfavorable service industries—retailing and consumer services.

Still, this development toward a more dichotomized labor market structure is not simply the result of the expansion of services and of the low growth or decline of those industries, especially manufacturing, which have traditionally offered, for the most part, large numbers of relatively well paying blue-collar jobs; it is also the result of the strong tendency toward a "white-collarization" of the labor force, a tendency which is cutting across all industries and bringing about a greater differentiation between managerial, professional and technical jobs on the one hand, and blue-collar, clerical, and service worker[11] jobs on the other.

The present analysis of locational characteristics of corporate offices, producer and distributive services, as well as nonprofit and public sector establishments suggest that employment opportunities and the resulting structure of local labor markets are likely to vary considerably from place to place. While it is not easy to predict the final outcome, our earlier investigation of the labor markets of seven medium size SMSAs has led us to observe that where metropolitan economies are characterized by an overconcentration of employment in consumer services, retailing, or assembly type production, there is likely to be an overabundance of poor jobs; and where metropolitan economies are strongly specialized in the complex of corporate activities, in nonprofit services or in the public sector, there is likely to be a more balanced distribution between good jobs and bad jobs.[12] The two types of labor market may be expected to function somewhat differently, with particularly high employment turnover ratios occurring in places characterized by high concentration of "bad" jobs by virtue of the very instability of such jobs and the necessity for large numbers of workers to change jobs more frequently, seeking out (often with little success) opportunities to improve their position in the labor market.

Concluding Thoughts and Unanswered Issues

Clearly, the economic transformations analyzed in this book have had a dramatic impact upon employment. Under conditions of both stagnating employment in goods production and dramatic changes in the geography of production, services have been hard pressed to supply the kinds and numbers of jobs demanded by a rapidly expanding labor force, particularly in those places where production employment has declined dramatically.

But the problem is not simply that of the shift from "goods to services." While future employment expansion will most likely continue to come primarily from key service sectors—especially from those sectors which are direct, intermediate inputs to the production of final goods and service outputs—it also seems likely that sustained growth will come about only when the U.S. economy has found a new sense of direction. For, to a large extent, the 1970s have been a period of reaction to externally induced changes for the U.S. economy (oil crises, Western European and Japanese competition), not one of rejuvenated technological or economic leadership.

What role cities must play in the mapping out of a new economy is a question that is only very partially answered by this research. It is clear, however, that urbanization has left one era to enter a new one, and that we still know very little about the specifics of that which is unfolding. It is within this framework that urban theoreticians and policy makers must evaluate and monitor the ongoing tranformation of the U.S. urban system. The following areas, we feel, deserve further critical evaluation:

First, we know very little about the distribution of jobs and income in specific places, very little about developing trends and very little about how educational and other training resources should be focused in order to meet manpower demands. It is clear, however, that mental labor is fast replacing physical labor as the major form of work in our society and that public sector policies must be strongly attuned to the increasingly critical need for appropriate training and education.

Second, we know very little about the probable impact of emerging technologies. If changing technology has been a principal factor in changing the nature and location of goods production in years just passed, it may also become a major factor altering the nature and location of service activities in the years ahead. A principal issue is the extent to which new centrifugal tendencies may be in the offing as new computer and communications technologies make it increasingly feasible for more routine service activities to be relocated away from large cities in smaller places or in places previously regarded as unsuited for service specialization.

Third, we do not know much about the impact of the process of internationalization on the emerging urban structure. In a sense, much of what has been uncovered in this study applies to a period (the 1960s and first half of the 1970s) which preceded the massive opening of the U.S. markets to foreign competition. There are reasons to believe, however, that both the increasing opening of the U.S. economy to international trade and the resulting trend towards the relocation of production establishments of the large firms on a world scale are reinforcing the dichotomy that is emerging in the U.S. urban structure. On the one hand, the opening of the U.S. economy to world competition is acting to accelerate development in service oriented centers as more high level service inputs are required to handle growing international trade. On the other hand, the increasing footlooseness of production establishments raises the troublesome question of the extent to which manufacturing urban centers in the U.S. are engaged in more intensive competition with cities and areas of other nations.

Fourth, there is the question—not new, but taking on a new meaning—as to the extent to which the issues of economic development are a common concern of an entire metropolitan area or independent concerns of the central city and the other municipal entities which make up what is commonly accepted to be the metropolitan area. Clearly, the new environment raises new questions and poses new challenges in this regard.

Fifth, there is the short term, but no less critical issue of how a metropolitan economy adjusts to a rapidly changing economic environment and minimizes the costs of adjustment, whether they be fiscal or social costs. For example, most cities have yet to find the way by which to change their fiscal system from one that was designed to muster resources from highly capitalized manufacturing to one capable of dealing with a human intensive service society. Likewise, most cities are still faced with the difficult issue of smoothing the transition for workers displaced from obsolete, usually manufacturing-based occupations to service-oriented employment.

Last is the issue of what falls within the purview of policy makers and what does not. On the one hand, public sector intervention may be highly desirable if we are to promote a faster and more equitable transformation of metropolitan economies, although the level at which such intervention should take place remains at issue. On the other hand, not all may be within the reach of policy makers. To a large extent, the transformation which has been discussed is a long-term process involving intergenerational changes in the socioeconomic status of various population strata. Whether such changes can be controlled, guided, or altered within the framework of short or medium term policy efforts remain at issue.

Notes

1. Robert Cohen, *The Impact of Foreign Direct Investment on U.S. Cities and Regions*, research commissioned by the U.S. Department of Housing and Urban Development, Washington, D.C.: U.S.G.O.P., 1979, and Carl Sears and Robert G. Hawkins, *Foreign Firms in New York City: A*

Survey Study, Occasional Papers in Metropolitan Business and Finance, 1, New York University, Solomon Brothers Center for the Study of Financial Institutions, 1979.

2. See also Stanback and Noyelle, op. cit., 1982, discussion of some of the limits to development in Charlotte.

3. See Chapter 9; also Joint Economic Committee, *Location of High Technology Firms and Regional Economic Development*, 97th Congress, Washington, D.C.: U.S. Government Printing Office, 1982.

4. Data published by the U.S. Bureau of Labor Statistics for early 1983 indicates some of the nation's highest unemployment rates in many of these centers.

5. Barry Bluestone and Bennett Harrison, op. cit., 1982; and U.S. House of Representatives, Committee on Small Business, *Conglomerate Mergers: Their Effect on Small Business and Local Communities*, Washington, D.C.: U.S. Government Printing Office, 1980.

6. See Stanback and Noyelle , op. cit. 1982, discussion of Buffalo.

7. See especially Chapters 6 and 7 for concrete examples; see also Pred, op. cit., 1977.

8. Bluestone and Harrison, op. cit., 1980; Pred, op. cit., 1977; Committee on Small Business, op. cit., 1980.

9. See also Joint Economic Committee, op. cit., 1982.

10. Thomas M. Stanback, Jr. and Thierry J. Noyelle, op. cit., 1982.

11. Here we are referring to the *occupational category* labeled "service worker" which comprises a number of low level occupations such as cooks, orderly, laundry workers, guards, etc.

12. Based on Thomas M. Stanback, Jr. and Thierry J. Noyelle, op. cit., 1982. This formulation remains tentative since six of the seven places studied qualify as nodal centers, but only one (Buffalo) as a manufacturing center. Furthermore, Buffalo, like a number of older manufacturing centers, does not yet fit well the model of assembly-type production centers suggested above as the influence of unions on labor markets continue to be felt in the locale, resulting in large numbers of workers holding medium-paying jobs. However, our evaluation of the future of a place such as Buffalo is that of an economy that will either rebuild its manufacturing export sector by lowering wages (so as to become competitive with newer but cheaper manufacturing centers) or it will continue to decline. In the latter case, it is likely that mostly only low paying jobs in the retailing and consumer serving sectors will pick up any part of the slack created by a rapidly shrinking manufacturing base.

APPENDIX A

Clustering of the 140 Largest SMSAs by Major Types

Clustering Method

To classify the 140 largest SMSAs by major types, we used a simple hierarchical clustering algorithm[1] to group places on the basis of similarities in their industrial composition of employment.

The statistical information processed consists of the Z scores of the location quotients of employment in eleven sectors in each of the 140 SMSAs.[2] The clustering algorithm proceeds by measuring the Euclidian distance[3] between pairs of SMSAs in an iterative process which results in breaking out groups of most similar SMSAs.[4]

The results of the procedure is a clustering tree. A simple analysis of the tree permitted ready identification of 19 clear-cut clusters of places characterized by a maximum internal Euclidian distance of less than one-fourth of the total distance necessary to cluster the 140 places into a single cluster (except for three clusters with a maximum internal distance slightly above one fourth). These 19 clusters accounted for a total of 118 places, leaving 22 unclassified places. The classification process was then completed in three steps:

First, the 19 clusters were reduced to seven clusters (Appendix Table A.1) by observing similarities among those industrial classes in which Z scores were positive (i.e., location quotients of employment above the national average), indicating export specialization.

Second, 19 of the 22 remaining places were allocated to the best possible cluster on the basis of patterns of positive Z scores characteristic of each place, and a new group was created for the remaining three places: the group of residential centers.

Finally, we disaggregated two of the major clusters. First we separated out the group of nodal centers into three subgroups—national, regional and subregional nodal centers—on the basis of population size, except for the four national nodal centers which were grouped on the basis of other evidence as regards their uniqueness in terms of activities carried out in their corporate complex (see Chapters 6 and 7). Second, we disaggregated the government-military cluster into government-education and military-industrial places using a single

Table A.1 Seven Basic Clusters of SMSAs

Clusters	Maximum Euclidian Distance Within Each Cluster
Education-Manufacturing	1.729
Manufacturing	2.721
Resort-Retirement	3.044
Nodal	3.711
Government-Education and Industrial-Military	4.060
Mining-Industrial	4.354
Functional Nodal	4.361

measure—1975 federal civilian and military wage and salaries as a share of all wage and salaries paid out in the SMSA.[5] Such measure is surprisingly clean-cut. While both types of places have an abnormally high share of local wages and earnings originating from the government sector, in one, government-education places, it is due mostly to state and local government wages, while in the other, industrial-military places, it is due to federal civilian and military wages.

The reader will note in Appendix Table A.1, that the 7 basic clusters exhibit maximum internal Euclidian distance of about a third or less of the total distance for complete clustering, with the least homogeneous groups characterized by the largest Euclidian distances.

Borderline Cases

While on the whole the procedure which is described above and which rests largely on the results of the clustering algorithm analysis led to reasonably well-defined groupings, there were a number of cases in which SMSAs seemed to be eligible for more than one classification. These cases are shown with final and alternative classifications in Appendix Table A.2. The final decision as to the best possible type was based in most cases on the direction of the transformation undergone by these places during the 1959–76 period. For example, Oklahoma City shows characteristics of both a nodal and government place, but changes during the 1959–76 period suggest that it is being transformed into a nodal place.

Table A.2 Nineteen Borderline Cases: Final and Alternative Classifications

City	Final Classification	Alternative Classification
Phoenix	nodal (regional)	gov't-educ. or resort
Oklahoma City	nodal (subregional)	government-educ.
Salt Lake City	nodal (subregional)	government-educ.
Newark	functional nodal	nodal (regional)
Milwaukee	functional nodal	nodal (regional)
Louisville	functional nodal	nodal (subregional)
Wichita	functional nodal	nodal (subregional)
Harrisburg	government-educ.	nodal (subregional)
Tacoma	education-mfg	industrial-military
Tampa	resort-retirement	nodal (regional)
Riverside	resort-retirement	industrial-military
Albuquerque	resort-retirement	government-education
Buffalo	manufacturing	nodal (regional) or functional nodal
Davenport	manufacturing	nodal (subregional)
El Paso	industrial-military	manufacturing
Lexington	industrial-military	manufacturing
Tucson	mining-industrial	government-educ.
Lakeland	mining-industrial	resort-retirement
Johnstown	mining-industrial	manufacturing

Notes

1. Bio Medical Computer Program.

2. The eleven employment sectors are as follows: manufacturing, TCU, wholesale, CAO&A, FIRE, Corporate Services (producer services excluding FIRE), retailing, mostly consumer services, government and mining (see Table 1.1 for definitions).

3. $d_{i,j} = \sqrt{\sum_k (Z_i^k - Z_j^k)^2}$ is the distance between each possible pair of city i and city j where Z_i^k and Z_j^k represent the Z scores of city i and city j respectively for each of the 11 variables (described by superscript k).

4. For reference, the first pair of cities clustered at a distance of d = 0.523, and the final clustering of the 140 places into a single group was achieved at a distance of d = 11.114.

5. U.S. Department of Commerce, Bureau of Economic Analysis, *Personal Income in State and Local Areas 1970–1975*, Washington. D.C.: U.S. Government Printing Office, 1976.

APPENDIX B

Coefficients of Correlation Among Rates of Employment Change in Major Industry Groupings for Major Types of SMSAs, 1959–1969

Table B.1 Coefficients of Correlation among Rates of Employment Change in Major Industry Groupings for Major Types of SMSAs, 1959-1969

DIVERSIFIED SERVICE CENTERS
National Nodal and Regional Nodal (23 Places)

TCU	Whl	CAO	FIRE	CS	Ret	MCS	Hlth	Educ	Gov	
.53	.70	.56	.78	.63	.81	.60	.87	-	.71	Mfg
	.67	-	.75	.42	.59	.40*	.51	-	.57	TCU
		.39*	.76	.56	.62	.49	.72	-	.58	Whl
			.37	.66	-	-	.60	.39*	.51	CAO
				.65	.85	.73	.69	.38*	.73	FIRE
					.62	.65	.63	.55	.77	CS
						.85	.65	-	.76	Ret
							.48	.39*	.64	MCS
								.45	.72	Hlth
									.47	Educ

Subregional Nodal (16 Places)

TCU	Whl	CAO	FIRE	CS	Ret	MCS	Hlth	Educ	Gov	
-	-	-	.50	-	-	-	-	-	-	Mfg
	.53	-	.46*	.55	-	-	-	.52	-	TCU
		-	.60	.75	.49	-	-	-	-	Whl
			.62	-	-	.72	-	-	.46*	CAO
				.47*	.48*	.76	-	-	.59	FIRE
					.43*	-	-	-	.56	CS
						-	-	-	.45*	Ret
							-	-	.67	MCS
								-	-	Hlth
									-	Educ

SPECIALIZED SERVICE CENTERS

Functional Nodal (24 Places)

TCU	Whl	CAO	FIRE	CS	Ret	MCS	Hlth	Educ	Gov	
.78	.75	-	.83	.63	.80	.58	.78	.77	.67	Mfg
	.80	-	.88	.67	.78	.64	.70	.61	.75	TCU
		-	.86	.65	.80	.58	.67	.74	.83	Whl
			-	-	-	-	-	-	-	CAO
				.74	.87	.60	.67	.71	.83	FIRE
					.81	.78	.57	.65	.66	CS
						.68	.66	.76	.79	Ret
							.61	.67	.36*	MCS
								.70	.65	Hlth
									.60	Educ

Government-Education (15 Places)

TCU	Whl	CAO	FIRE	CS	Ret	MCS	Hlth	Educ	Gov	
.43*	.43*	-	.65	.63	.55	-	.70	-	-	Mfg
	.50	-	.69	.59	.84	-	.64	-	.42	TCU
		-	-	.78	-	-	.52	-	-	Whl
			-	-	-	-	-	-	-	CAO
				.52	.91	.53	.92	-	.57	FIRE
					.43*	-	.66	-	-	CS
						.50	.83	-	.57	Ret
							-	.47	-	MCS
								-	.52	Hlth
									-	Educ

(continued on next page)

Table B.1 (continued)

PRODUCTION CENTERS

Manufacturing (25 Places)

TCU	Whl	CAO	FIRE	CS	Ret	MCS	Hlth	Educ	Gov	
.66	.46	-	.36*	.36*	.40	-	-	-	.35*	Mfg
	.44	-	-	.43	.36*	-	.41	-	.60	TCU
		-	.38*	.45	.62	-	.41	-	.38*	Whl
			-	-	-	-	-	-	-	CAO
				.39	.44	-	-	-	-	FIRE
					-	-	-	-	.33*	CS
						.52	.35*	-	-	Ret
							-	-	-	MCS
								-	-	Hlth
									-	Educ

Industrial-Military (13 Places)

TCU	Whl	CAO	FIRE	CS	Ret	MCS	Hlth	Educ	Gov	
-	-	-	.52*	-	-	-	-	-	.49*	Mfg
	.75	-	-	-	.75	-	-	-	-	TCU
		-	.51*	.81	.60	-	-	.72	-	Whl
			-	-	-	-	-	-	-	CAO
				.73	.48*	.44*	-	.49*	-	FIRE
					.45*	-	-	.85	-	CS
						.44*	-	-	-	Ret
							-	-	-	MCS
								.48*	-	Hlth
									-	Educ

CONSUMER-ORIENTED CENTERS

Residential and Resort-Retirement (12 Places)

TCU	Whl	CAO	FIRE	CS	Ret	MCS	Hlth	Educ	Gov	
.62	-	-	-	-	.48*	-	-	.51	.86	Mfg
	-	-	-	-	-	-	-	-	.74	TCU
		-	.81	.70	.86	.90	.78	.67	.61	Whl
			-	-	-	-	-	-	-	CAO
				.80	.94	.90	.55*	.59	.55*	FIRE
					.86	.76	.63	-	-	CS
						.92	.72	.60	.66	Ret
							.65	.53*	.54	MCS
								.63	.54*	Hlth
									.62	Educ

Note: Only coefficients of correlation of .20 or above with a statistical reliability of .90 or better are shown. Where reliability is between .90 and .95 the coefficient value is identified with an asterisk. There are 11 industry groups resulting in a total of 55 correlation coefficients in each matrix.

National nodal and regional nodal SMSAs are combined, as are residential and resort-retirement places. Education-manufacturing and mining-industrial places are omitted. They are too dissimilar from other groups to be combined and too small a group for separate analysis.

Column and row heads: Same as Table 2.2. Nonprofit is broken down between health and education.

Source: County Business Patterns, 1959 and 1969; Employment and Earnings in State and Local Areas, 1959 and 1969.

APPENDIX C

Four-Industry Analysis: Rankings of SMSAs in Terms of Their Importance as Centers of Administration, Research, and Production, 1976

General Procedure

To identify and rank SMSAs in terms of their importance as centers of administration and centers of research in each of the four industries studied, we first developed lists of the largest firms in each industry, using Fortune's 1000 industrial firms (1976). Fortune uses a 28-industry classification system of the 1000 largest industrial firms which can be interpreted easily in terms of the Standard Industrial Code (see text table below). This procedure yielded 32 Fortune 1000s in Motor Vehicle and Parts, ranging from General Motors (Fortune rank #2) to Safeguard Industries (#961); 65 Fortune 1000s in Electrical Appliances and Electronics, ranging from General Electric (#9) to Dynascan (#989); 15 Fortune 1000s in Aerospace and Ordnance, ranging from Rockwell International (#34) to Gear Learjet (#721); and 48 Fortune 1000s in Office, Scientific and Measuring Equipment, ranging from IBM (#8) to Telex (#965).

Major centers in terms of administration and management were identified and ranked for each industry separately on the basis of (1) the number of Fortune 1000s headquartered in the SMSA; (2) their volume of sales; and (3) the number of divisional head offices of both local and non-local Fortune firms located in the SMSA. The first two pieces of information were drawn from Fortune (1976); the third one from the *Directory of Corporate Affiliations* (1976). On the basis of this composite information, rankings of centers most important for the administration and management of the four industries were established (Appendix Tables C.1 to C.4).

Major centers in terms of research and development were identified and ranked for each industry separately on the basis of (1) the number of local and non-local Fortune firms with research laboratories located in the SMSA; (2) the number of local research laboratories; and (3) employment in these research laboratories. These three pieces of information were drawn from the *Directory of Industrial Research Laboratories in the United States* (1975).[1] On the basis of this composite information, rankings of the centers most important for research and development in the four industries were established (Appendix Tables C.5 to C.8).

Last, centers were ranked according to value added per production worker in their production establishments, using the 1977 *Census of Manufactures* (Appendix Table C.9). In theory, at least, the *Census of Manufactures* records employment and value added data at a three digit SIC industry level on an SMSA basis. In practice, however, because the Census Bureau must respect standards of confidentiality, 3-digit SIC industries are often not distinguished in large centers and are combined and shown in larger 2-digit SIC grouping so as not to disclose information on very large establishments, or are altogether withheld in many of the small SMSAs.

Such restrictions placed serious limitations on our analysis. A number of SMSAs engaged in several of the 3-digit SIC industries studied here had to be excluded because of a lack of proper data. On average, value added data on an SMSA basis was available for roughly two-thirds of the nation's employment in each industry. We made certain, however, that the largest production centers for each of the four industries were adequately covered.

In the end, two factors restricted the number of places for which comparable measures can be developed. First, as was just noted, the number of SMSAs for which characteristics of production, administration, and research could be identified was limited by the number of SMSAs for which full disclosure on value added was available. Second, the analysis of spatial concentration of administrative and research facilities in SMSAs included in the East and West Coast megalopolises (e.g., Greater New York or Greater Los Angeles) seemed to unduly underestimate the strength of these megalopolises, if carried out on an individual SMSA basis. Indeed, such facilities are now routinely dispersed by corporations among nearby SMSAs within these Greater Metropolitan areas. Accordingly, we made use of aggregate measures for the Greater New York metropolitan area (including New Brunswick, Long Branch-Asbury, Newark, Jersey City, Paterson-Passaic, New York, Nassau-Suffolk and Stanford-Greenwich-Bridgeport), the Greater Los Angeles area (including Los Angeles, Anaheim, Riverside), the Greater San Francisco area (including San Francisco and San Jose), and the Greater Washington, D.C. area (including Washington, D.C., and Baltimore) rather than restricting the analysis to SMSA boundaries. The numbers of metropolitan centers for which full disclosure was available thus was reduced to the following:

Fortune Code	Industry	SIC Code	Number of Metropolitan Centers with full disclosure
40	Motor Vehicle and Parts	371	30
36	Electrical Appliances	365-366,	20
	and Electronics*	367	17
41	Aerospace and Ordinance	372-376	22
38, 44	Office, Scientific and	381-387,	28
	Measuring Equipment**	357	10

*20 places in the case of SIC 365-366; 17 in the case of SIC 367 (see below–special cases)

**28 places in the case of SIC 381-387; 10 in the case of SIC 357 (see below–special cases)

Table C.1 Ten Most Important Centers of Administration and Management for the Motor Vehicle and Parts Industries, 1976

Rank[a]		Total Sales of Firms Headquartered in SMSA ($ billions) 1	# of Firms Headquartered in SMSA 2
1	Detroit	100.118	10
2	Cleveland	6.238	4
3	Chicago	2.193	2
4	Greater Los Angeles[b]	2.452	1
	Los Angeles	(2.452)	(1)
	Anaheim	(-)	(-)
	Riverside	(-)	(-)
5	Toledo	2.363	3
6	Greater New York[c]	0.532	2
	New York	(-)	(-)
	Bridgeport	(0.239)	1
	Nassau-Suffolk	(0.263)	(1)
	Newark	(-)	(-)
	Jersey City	(-)	(-)
	New Brunswick	(-)	(-)
7	Philadelphia	0.107	1
8	Dayton	-	-
9	Minneapolis	-	-
10	Greater San Francisco[d]	-	-
	San Francisco	(-)	(-)
	San Jose	(-)	(-)

[a]Rank as shown in first column of Table 5.7.

[b]Los Angeles, Anaheim and Riverside combined.

[c]New York, Bridgeport, Nassau-Suffolk, Newark, Jersey City and New Brunswick combined.

[d]San Francisco and San Jose combined.

# of Firms not Hdqtr'd Locally but with a Divisional Head Office in SMSA	Total # of Motor Vehicle Firms Present in SMSA (col. 2 + 3)	Total # of Divisional Head Offices Located in SMSA
3	4	5
8	18	116
2	6	23
13	15	68
13	14	83
(12)	(13)	(67)
(3)	(3)	(12)
(2)	(2)	(4)
3	6	28
9	11	27
(6)	(6)	(15)
1	(2)	(3)
(1)	(2)	(4)
(2)	(2)	(2)
(1)	(1)	(1)
(2)	(2)	(2)
6	7	15
6	6	10
6	6	7
6	6	7
(6)	(6)	(6)
(1)	(1)	(1)

Note: Based on survey of the 32 Fortune 1000 firms in the
motor vehicle and parts industry. Tire makers are
classified by Fortune under a different industrial
grouping (Rubber), which explains why Akron does not
show in this listing.

Source: Fortune 1000 industrial firms with largest volume of
sales in Motor Vehicle and Parts, 1976; Directory of
Corporate Affiliations, 1976.

Table C.2 Seven Most Important Centers of Administration
and Management for the Electrical Appliance and
Electronics Industries, 1976

Rank[a]		Total Sales of Firms Headquartered in SMSA ($ billions) 1	# of Firms Headquartered in SMSA 2
1	Greater New York[b]	58.366	18
	New York	(41.820)	(11)
	Nassau-Suffolk	(0.350)	(2)
	Bridgeport	(15.935)	(3)
	Newark	(-)	(0)
	New Brunswick	(-)	(0)
	Jersey City	(0.261)	(2)
2	Chicago	7.227	12
3	Greater Los Angeles[c]	2.913	4
	Los Angeles	(2.800)	(3)
	Anaheim	(-)	(0)
	Riverside	(0.113)	(1)
4	Greater San Francisco[d]	1.599	5
	San Jose	(1.336)	(4)
	San Francisco	(0.263)	(1)
5	Cleveland	1.865	3
6	Dallas	1.979	2
7	Boston	0.251	1

[a]Rank as shown in Table 5.8.

[b]New York, Nassau-Suffolk, Bridgeport, Newark, New Brunswick
and Jersey City combined.

[c]Los Angeles, Riverside and Anaheim combined.

[d]San Jose and San Francisco combined.

# of Firms Not Hdqtr'd Locally but with a Divisional Head Office in SMSA	Total # of Firms Present in SMSA (col. 2 + 3)	Total # of Divisional Head Offices Located in SMSA
3	4	5
17	35	150
(13)	(24)	(75)
(13)	(15)	(33)
(8)	(11)	(18)
(10)	(10)	(16)
(3)	(3)	(5)
(0)	(2)	(3)
21	33	108
28	32	76
(25)	(28)	(59)
(9)	(9)	(12)
(1)	(2)	(5)
10	15	53
(7)	(11)	(40)
(6)	(7)	(13)
12	15	28
7	9	16
13	14	32

Note: Based on survey of the 65 Fortune 1000 firms in the Electrical Appliance and Electronic Industry.

Source: Fortune 1000 industrial firms with largest volume of sales in Electrical Appliance and Electronics, 1976; Directory of Corporate Affiliations, 1976.

Table C.3   Seven Most Important Centers of Administration
and Management for the Aerospace and Ordnance
Industries, 1976

Rank[a]		Total Sales of Firms Headquartered in SMSA ($ billions) 1	# of Firms Headquartered in SMSA 2
1	Greater Los Angeles[b]	4.467	2
	Los Angeles	(4.467)	(2)
	Anaheim	(-)	(0)
	Riverside	(-)	(0)
2	Seattle	3.918	1
3	Greater New York[c]	2.131	2
	New York	(-)	(0)
	Newark	(-)	(0)
	Nassau-Suffolk	(1.502)	(1)
	Bridgeport	(0.629)	(1)
4	Pittsburgh[d]	5.222	1
5	Hartford[d]	5.166	1
6	St. Louis	3.543	1
7	Washington DC	1.476	2

[a]Rank as shown in Table 5.9.

[b]Los Angeles, Anaheim, Riverside combined.

[c]New York, Newark, Nassau-Suffolk and Bridgeport combined.

[d]Implicit adjustment is made in this ranking for the fact
that Rockwell International (Pittsburgh) and United Technology (Hartford) are also engaged in industries other
than aerospace and ordnance.

To investigate the relationship between value added per production worker in
manufacturing establishments of metropolitan centers and the importance these
centers play in either the administrative and managerial, or research and development functions of the industry, we then summarized, for each of the four industries, the rankings established for these three functions by listing in a single tabulation the metropolitan centers in the *upper tier of the array developed for each
function* (Tables 5.7 to 5.10 in Chapter 5). For example, in the case of the Motor

# of Firms not Hdqtr'd Locally but with a Divisional Head Office in SMSA 3	Total # of Firms Present in SMSA (col. 2 + 3) 4	Total # of Divisional Head Offices Located in SMSA 5
7	9	45
(6)	(8)	(30)
(3)	(3)	(14)
(1)	(1)	(1)
1	2	23
7	9	22
(3)	(3)	(3)
(3)	(3)	(3)
(1)	(2)	(10)
(2)	(3)	(6)
2	3	15
1	2	9
2	3	7
1	3	12

Note: Based on survey of the 15 Fortune 1000 firms in the aerospace and ordnance industry.

Source: Fortune 1000 industrial firms with largest volume of sales in Aerospace and Ordnance, 1976; Directory of Corporate Affiliations, 1976.

Vehicle and Parts industry, we listed in the same table the 10 (top third) most important centers in terms of administration, the 10 most important centers in terms of research and development, and the 10 centers with the highest value added per production worker, showing each with its respective rank order. Since many centers ranked high on more than one of these functions, the combined list numbered only 18 metropolitan centers.

Table C.4 Ten Most Important Centers of Administration and
Management for the Office, Scientific and Measuring
Equipment Industries, 1976

Rank[a]		Total Sales of Firms Headquartered in SMSA ($ billions) 1	# of Firms Headquartered in SMSA 2
1	Greater New York[b]	26.751	13
	New York	(22.004)	(9)
	Nassau-Suffolk	(-)	(0)
	Newark	(0.314)	(2)
	Bridgeport	(4.753)	(2)
2	Minneapolis	7.595	5
3	Rochester	5.787	2
4	Boston	2.221	4
5	Chicago	1.686	7
6	Greater Los Angeles[d]	0.364	2
	Los Angeles	(-)	(0)
	Anaheim	(0.364)	(2)
	Riverside	(-)	(0)
7	San Jose	1.112	1
8	Detroit[e]	1.871	1
9	Dayton[f]	2.313	1
10	Philadelphia	0.275	2

Note: Based on Survey of the 48 Fortune 1000 firms in the
office, scientific and measuring equipment industries.

[a]Rank as shown in Table 5.10.

[b]New York, Nassau Suffolk, Newark and Bridgeport combined.

[c]Mostly divisions and subsidiaries of 3 M, Honeywell and
Control Data.

[d]Los Angeles, Anaheim and Riverside combined.

# of Firms Not Hdqtr'd Locally but with a Divisional Head Office in SMSA	Total # of Firms Present in SMSA (col. 2 + 3)	Total # of Divisional Head Offices Located in SMSA
3	4	5
8	21	67
(6)	(15)	(43)
(6)	(6)	(6)
(4)	(6)	(9)
(3)	(5)	(9)
2	7	73[c]
4	6	14
10	14	28
5	12	26
15	17	47
(13)	(13)	(24)
(5)	(7)	(21)
(1)	(1)	(1)
8	9	22
2	3	9
0	1	0
5	7	16

[e]Home of a large firm, Burroughs, but not site for much activity by other, outside firms.

[f]Home of a large firm, NCR, but not site for much activity by other, outside firms.

Source: Fortune 1000 industrial firms with largest volume of sales in Office, Scientific and Measuring Equipment, 1976; Directory of Corporate Affiliations, 1976.

Table C.5 Ten Most Important Centers of Research and Development in the Motor Vehicle and Parts Industries, 1976

Rank[a]		# of Firms with Research Labs in SMSA	# of Research Labs	# of Research Labs with Employment Disclosed	Employment Disclosed Total
1	Detroit	14	59	35	10,737
2	Greater L.A.[b]	6	11	4	653
	Los Angeles	(5)	(10)	(3)	(597)
	Anaheim	(1)	(1)	(1)	(56)
3	Dayton	5	10	6	725
4	Chicago	4	10	7	837
5	Cleveland	4	13	9	398
6	Grand Rapids	4	5	4	206
7	Philadelphia	3	4	2	88
8	Milwaukee	2	5	4	351
9	Toledo	2	4	3	64
10	St. Louis	1	2	1	302
10	Akron	1	1	1	23

Note: Based on survey of the 32 Fortune 1000 firms in the motor vehicle and parts industry.

[a]Rank as shown in Table 5.7.
[b]Los Angeles and Anaheim combined.
[c]Since the tire companies are not included in the 32 firms surveyed, the role of Akron as a research center in automobile related industries may be underemphasized.

Source: Fortune 1000 industrial firms with largest sales in Motor Vehicles and Parts, 1976; Industrial Research Laboratories of the United States (14th Edition), 1975.

Table C.6 Seven Most Important Centers of Research and Development in the Electrical Appliances and Electronic Industries, 1976

Rank[a]	# of Firms with Research Labs in SMSA	# of Research Labs	# of Research Labs with Employment Disclosed	Employment Disclosed Total
1 Greater N.Y.[b]	18	28	5	5,276
New York	(7)	(12)	(1)	(191)
Bridgeport	(3)	(5)	(1)	(48)
Nassau Suffolk	(4)	(5)	(2)	(3,477)
Newark	(3)	(3)	(0)	n.a.[c]
New Brunswick	(2)	(3)	(1)	(1,560)
2 Chicago	15	22	5	399
3 Greater L.A.[d]	11	24	1	193
Los Angeles	(10)	(20)	(1)	(193)
Riverside	(1)	(4)	(0)	n.a.
4 Greater S.F.[e]	5	12	8	8,793
San Jose	(4)	(10)	(7)	(8,733)
San Francisco	(2)	(2)	(1)	(60)
5 Dallas	5	12	1	17
6 Greater D.C.[f]	8	13	3	149
Washington D.C.	(7)	(11)	(2)	(134)
Baltimore	(1)	(1)	(1)	(45)
7 Milwaukee	2	9	6	496

Note: Based on survey of the 65 Fortune 1000 firms in the Electrical Appliance and Electronic Industry.
[a]Rank as shown in Table 5.8.
[b]New York, Bridgeport, Nassau Suffolk, Newark, New Brunswick combined.
[c]Several thousand employees in several Bell Lab facilities.
[d]Los Angeles, Anaheim, Riverside combined.
[e]San Jose, San Francisco combined.
[f]Washington DC and Baltimore combined.

Source: Fortune 1000 industrial firms with largest sales in Electronics and Electrical Appliances, 1976; Industrial Research Laboratories of the United States (14th Edition), 1975.

Table C.7 Seven Most Important Centers of Research and Development for the Aerospace and Ordnance Industries, 1976

Rank[a]	# of Firms with Research Labs in SMSA	# of Research Labs	# of Research Labs with Employment Disclosed	Employment Disclosed Total
1 Greater L.A.[b]	11	28	9	4,251
Los Angeles	(11)	(26)	(8)	(3,939)
Anaheim	(2)	(2)	(1)	(312)
2 Boston	5	32	28	2,218
3 Greater S.F.[c]	5	7	2	598
San Francisco	(2)	(2)	(0)	not disc.
San Jose	(3)	(5)	(2)	(598)
4 Greater N.Y.[d]	5	7	4	293
Newark	(3)	(5)	(3)	(141)
Nassau-Suffolk	(2)	(2)	(1)	(152)
5 Philadelphia	3	12	(2)[e]	217
6 Greater D.C.[e]	3	6	1	81
Washington	(3)	(5)	(0)	(-)
Baltimore	(1)	(1)	(1)	(81)
7 Seattle	1	not disc.[g]	not disc.	not disc.

Note: Based on survey of the 15 Fortune 1000 firms in the aerospace and ordnance industry and the major aerospace and ordnance divisions of 6 other Fortune firms -- G.E., I.T.T., T.R.W., R.C.A., Signal Companies and Sperry Rand.
[a]Rank as shown in Table 5.9.
[b]Los Angeles and Anaheim combined.
[c]San Francisco and San Jose combined.
[d]Newark and Nassau-Suffolk combined.
[e]Although the number of employees is not disclosed, these are major (mostly G.E.) research installations.
[f]Washington and Baltimore combined.
[g]Boeing does not disclose the location of its research facilities.

Source: Fortune 1000 industrial firms with largest volume of sales in Aerospace and Ordnance, 1976; Industrial Research Laboratories of the United States (14th Edition), 1975.

Table C.8 Ten Most Important Centers of Research and Development in the Office, Scientific and Measuring Equipment Industries, 1976

Rank[a]	# of Firms with Research Labs in SMSA	# of Research Labs	# of Research Labs with Employment Disclosed	Employment Disclosed Total
1 Greater N.Y.[b]	9	14	7	794
New York[c]	(6)	(8)	(1)	(8)
Nassau Suffolk	(1)	(1)	(1)	(16)
Bridgeport	(4)	(4)	(4)	(133)
Paterson	(1)	(1)	(1)	(637)
2 Rochester	3	6	6	5,134
3 Greater L.A.[d]	7	8	2	825
Los Angeles	(3)	(4)	(1)	(425)
Anaheim	(4)	(4)	(1)	(400)
4 Philadelphia	6	7	5	1,157
5 Boston	5	8	4	609
6 Chicago	5	7	3	360
7 Minneapolis	4	7	6	925
8 San Jose	4	4	1	215
9 San Diego	2	3	0	-
10 Dallas	1	1	1	246
10 Erie	1	1	1	108

Note: Based on a survey of the 49 Fortune 1000 in the office, scientific and measuring equipment industry.

[a]Rank as shown in Table 5.10.
[b]New York, Nassau Suffolk, Bridgeport and Paterson combined.
[c]Includes IBM research facilities with undisclosed, but very large employment figures.
[d]Los Angeles and Anaheim combined.

Source: Fortune 1000 industrial firms with largest sales in Office, Scientific and Measuring Equipment, 1976; Industrial Research Laboratories of the United States (14th Edition), 1975.

Table C.9 Rankings of Most Important Production Centers According to Value Added per Production Worker in the Motor Vehicle and Parts, Electrical Appliance and Electronics, Aerospace and Ordnance, and Office, Scientific and Measuring Equipment Industries, 1977

Motor Vehicle & Parts

SIC 371

Rank[a]	10 SMSAs	VAPPW[b]
1	Greater S. Francisco (San Francisco)	82,134 *
2	Cincinnati	80,076
3	St. Louis	75,964
4	Milwaukee	65,693
5	Columbus	58,185
6	Lima	55,182
7	Dayton	54,650
8	Detroit	53,423
9	Akron	53,421
10	Dallas	51,154
Lowest ranking center		21,714

Electrical Appliances & Electronics

SIC 365-366

Rank	10 SMSAs	VAPPW
1	Dallas	71,203
2	Ft. Lauderdale	70,909
3	Greater L. Angeles (Los Angeles) (Anaheim)	67,109 * *
4	Miami	56,929
5	Chicago	56,081
Lowest ranking center		27,200

SIC 367

Rank	7 SMSAs	VAPPW
1	Greater S. Francisco (San Jose)	57,546 *
2	Tampa	47,692
3	Phoenix	42,808
4	Boston	40,505
5	Greater L. Angeles (Los Angeles)	35,517 *
6	Ft. Lauderdale	33,625
7	Miami	33,000
Lowest ranking center		22,714

Office, Scientific & Measuring Equipment

Aerospace and Ordnance

SIC 372-376

Rank	7 SMSAs	VAPPW
1	Greater S. Francisco (San Jose)	120,000 *
2	Dallas	88,408
3	Greater L. Angeles (Los Angeles)	82,000 *
4	Boston	66,574
5	St. Louis	61,330
6	Greater New York (Nassau Suffolk) (Bridgeport)	61,175 * *
7	Seattle	55,833
	Lowest ranking center	23,000

SIC 38

Rank	10 SMSAs	VAPPW
1	Rochester	135,803
2	Erie	75,437
3	Boston	64,392
4	Greater S. Francisco (San Jose)	57,216 *
5	Philadelphia	53,684
6	Detroit	51,350
7	Greater New York (Paterson) (New Brunswick)	48,917 * *
8	Buffalo	48,777
9	Chicago	48,551
10	Minneapolis	45,173
	Lowest ranking center	26,846

SIC 357

Rank	5 SMSAs	VAPPW
1	Dallas	126,533
2	Greater S. Francisco (San Jose)	105,138 *
3	Minneapolis	88,987
4	Boston	85,697
5	San Diego	75,411
	Lowest ranking center	12,538

aRanks as shown respectively in Table 5.7 through 5.10.
bValue added per production workers (in dollars). Asterisk indicates most important SMSA in given greater metropolitan area.

Source: Census of Manufactures, 1977.

Special Cases

Because of sharp differences in characteristics of value added between SIC 367 and SIC 365–366 (Electrical Appliances and Electronics) and between SIC 357 and SIC 372–376 (Office, Scientific, and Measuring Equipment), the two industries were treated slightly differently by establishing not one, but two independent rankings of centers according to value added. In these two industries, we established upper-tier arrays of production centers by simply merging the upper tier listing of each of the 100 sets of rankings. For SIC 357, we used the upper half of the array because of the small number of observations available (10 places in all).

Notes

1. This directory includes "independent" research laboratories, as well as the research labs of major industrial firms. Here, we included only the research labs of the Fortune 1000 of the four industries studied.

APPENDIX D

Location of National Headquarters, Divisional Head Offices and Regional Sales Headquarters of Selected Large Corporations

Table D.1 Location of National Headquarters, Divisional Head Offices and Regional Sales Headquarters of Selected Large Corporations, 1976

		National Headquarters Fortune 500 1976	National Headquarters Fortune 500 1959	National Headquarters 2nd Fortune 500 1976	National Headquarters Fortune 150 1976	Divisional Headquarters Fortune 650 1976	Regional Sales Headquarters Sample Fortune 650 1976
DIVERSIFIED SERVICE CENTERS							
National Nodal							
New York	1	100	137	62	23	1,173	4
Los Angeles	1	21	17	18	6	558	3
Chicago	1	44	50	46	16	780	6
San Francisco	1	14	13	14	6	329	3
Regional Nodal							
Philadelphia	1	11	21	13	3	252	3
Boston	1	9	6	12	3	225	4
Dallas	1	8	8	19	4	161	5
Houston	1	10	1	12	6	327	3
St. Louis	1	12	16	7	4	220	5
Baltimore	1	2	1	6	3	116	4
Minneapolis	1	13	6	10	7	232	3
Cleveland	1	18	19	16	3	259	4
Atlanta	2	4	0	9	4	102	3
Miami	2	2	0	4	3	68	1
Denver	2	3	4	3	3	131	3
Seattle	2	2	2	0	0	62	2
Cincinnati	2	3	4	5	2	94	4
Kansas City	2	2	4	4	3	75	5
Phoenix	2	2	0	2	0	48	1

City							
Indianapolis	2	3	4	1	0	65	3
New Orleans	2	2	1	0	1	65	2
Portland	2	6	1	3	2	78	4
Columbus	2	1	1	5	0	80	4
Subregional Nodal							
Memphis	3	2	0	1	0	50	2
Salt Lake City	3	0	0	3	1	28	0
Birmingham	3	1	2	3	0	27	1
Nashville	3	1	1	1	0	65	0
Oklahoma City	3	1	2	1	0	50	1
Jacksonville	3	1	0	1	1	36	0
Syracuse	3	2	2	2	1	46	2
Richmond	3	3	4	3	2	37	1
Charlotte	3	1	0	3	1	41	1
Omaha	3	2	2	2	1	30	4
Mobile	4	1	0	1			0
Little Rock	4	0	0	0			0
Shreveport	4	0	0	0			0
Des Moines	4	0	0	1			0
Spokane	4	0	0	0			0
Jackson	4	0	0	1			1
SPECIALIZED SERVICE CENTERS							
Functional Nodal							
Detroit	1	15	15	8	4	306	4
Pittsburgh	1	14	21	11	2	200	2
Newark	1	6	8	5	2	145	3
Milwaukee	2	11	7	7	0	138	4
San Jose	2	1	1	2	0	44	1
Hartford	2	4	2	4	0	78	1

(continued on next page)

Table D.1 (continued).

	National Headquarters Fortune 500 1976	National Headquarters Fortune 500 1959	National Headquarters 2nd Fortune 500 1976	National Headquarters Fortune 150 1976	Divisional Headquarters Fortune 650 1976	Regional Sales Headquarters Sample Fortune 650 1976
Rochester	3	4	2	1	0	44	1
Louisville	3	0	0	5	0	26	2
Dayton	3	4	3	5	0	69	0
Bridgeport	3	23	3	12	3	156	0
Toledo	3	7	6	1	0	83	0
Greensboro	3	5	3	2	2	61	0
Akron	3	4	4	2	2	67	0
Allentown	3	1	2	1	1	24	0
Tulsa	3	4	2	2	0	73	0
New Brunswick	3	2	1	3	2	73	0
Jersey City	3	0	2	3	0	24	0
Wilmington	3	3	3	0	5	82	0
Paterson	4	3	2	4			1
Knoxville	4	0	0	0			0
Wichita	4	2	2	3			0
Fort Wayne	4	1	2	0			0
Peoria	4	1	2	0			0
Kalamazoo	4	1	1	0			0
Government-Education							
Washington	1	2	0	2	5	119	3
Sacramento	3	0	0	0	0	13	2
Albany	3	1	2	1	0	27	0

Raleigh-Durham	4	0	0	0			0
Fresno	4	0	0	0			0
Austin	4	0	0	1			0
Lansing	4	0	0	0			0
Oxford-Ventura	4	0	0	1			0
Harrisburg	4	3	0	1			0
Baton Rouge	4	0	0	0			0
Columbia, S.C.	4	0	0	0			0
Utica	4	0	0	0			0
Trenton	4	0	0	0			0
Madison	4	1	0	0			0
Stockton	4	0	0	0			0
Education-Manufacturing							
New Haven	3	4	2	2	0	57	0
Springfield	3	0	1	2	1	32	0
Tacoma	4	1	1	0			0
South Bend	4	0	1	1			0
Ann Arbor	4	0	0	3			0
PRODUCTION CENTERS							
Manufacturing							
Buffalo	2	1	5	1	0	62	1
Providence	3	2	2	2	0	61	0
Worcester	3	2	2	2	1	54	0
Gary	3	0	0	0	1	17	0
N.E. Pennsylvania	3	0	0	0	0	16	0
Grand Rapids	3	1	0	2	0	44	0
Youngstown	3	0	0	2	0	16	0
Greenville	3	1	0	2	0	40	0
Flint	3	0	0	1	0	6	0

(continued on next page)

Table D.1 (continued)

		National Headquarters Fortune 500 1976	National Headquarters Fortune 500 1959	National Headquarters 2nd Fortune 500 1976	National Headquarters Fortune 150 1976	Divisional Headquarters Fortune 650 1976	Regional Sales Headquarters Sample Fortune 650 1976
New Bedford	4	0	0	0			0
Canton	4	2	2	3			0
Johnson City	4	0	0	0			0
Chattanooga	4	1	0	2			0
Davenport	4	1	1	1			1
Beaumont	4	0	0	0			0
York	4	0	0	1			0
Lancaster	4	1	1	0			0
Binghamton	4	0	1	0			0
Reading	4	1	0	1			0
Huntington	4	1	2	0			0
Evansville	4	0	0	0			0
Appleton	4	2	1	1			0
Erie	4	1	1	2			0
Rockford	4	1	1	0			0
Lorain	4	0	0	0			0
Industrial-Military							
San Diego	2	1	2	2	1	26	1
San Antonio	3	3	0	1	0	30	1
Norfolk	3	0	0	2	0	16	0
El Paso	4	0	0	1			0
Charleston, SC	4	0	0	0			0
Newport News	4	0	1	0			0

Lexington	4	0	0	0			0
Huntsville	4	0	0	0			0
Augusta	4	0	0	1			1
Vallejo	4	0	0	0			0
Colorado Springs	4	0	0	1			0
Pensacola	4	0	0	0			0
Salinas	4	0	0	0			0
Mining-Industrial							
Tucson	4	0	0	0			0
Bakersfield	4	0	0	0			0
Corpus Christi	4	0	0	0			0
Lakeland	4	0	0	0			0
Johnstown, PA	4	0	0	0			0
Duluth	4	0	0	0			0
Charleston, WV	4	0	0	1			1
CONSUMER-ORIENTED CENTERS							
Residential							
Nassau-Suffolk	1	1'	3	6	2	81	1
Anaheim	2	1	1	4	0	121	1
Long Branch	4	0	0	0			0
Resort-Retirement							
Tampa	2	1	0	2	1	38	2
Riverside	2	1	0	1	0	24	1
Ft. Lauderdale	3	1	0	0	0	10	0
Honolulu	3	1	1	1	1	46	1
Orlando	3	1	1	0	0	19	1
West Palm Beach	4	0	0	0			0
Albuquerque	4	0	0	0			0
Las Vegas	4	0	0	0			0

(continued on next page)

Table D.1 (continued)

	National Headquarters Fortune 500 1976	1959	National Headquarters 2nd Fortune 500 1976	National Headquarters Fortune 150 1976	Divisional Headquarters Fortune 650 1976	Regional Sales Headquarters Sample Fortune 650 1976
Santa Barbara	4	0	0			0
UNITED STATES	500	500	500	150	11,477	128

Note: The Fortune 150s include the Fortune 50 largest transportation, 50 largest retailing and 50 utility companies. The Fortune 650s include the Fortune 500 industrials and the Fortune 150s. The "Divisional Head Offices--Fortune 650" column includes a full count of all the head offices of all the divisions of the Fortune 650. The "Regional Sales Headquarters -- Sample of Fortune 650" column includes all the regional sales headquarters of an 8-firm sample of the Fortune 650. The 8 firms included in the sample are: Continental Group, Clark Oil, Deere & Co, Burroughs Corp, Exxon, Procter & Gamble Corp, Chrysler and AT&T. Information on Chrysler comes from The Chrysler Corporation Financial Situation, Hearings Before the Subcommittee on Economic Stabilization, US House of Representatives, 96th Congress, 1979, Part 2: Appendix. Information on AT&T comes from the Directory of Corporate Affiliation, 1976. Information on remaining 6 corporations comes from Large Corporations and Urban Employment, Subcommittee on the City, US House of Representatives, 95th Congress, February, 1978. The distribution of the national headquarters of the Fortune 150s and the divisional head offices of the Fortune 650s is not tabulated for size 4 SMSAs (blank cell).

Source: Fortune 1976 and 1959 (national headquarters); Directory of Corporate Affiliations, 1976 (divisional headquarters); various sources (regional sales headquarters -- see note), 1976.

APPENDIX E

Industrial Specialization of the Complexes of National Headquarters and Divisional Head Offices of Selected SMSAs

The industrial specialization of the complexes of national headquarters and divisional head offices of the 40 selected nodal and functional nodal centers shown in Table 6.8 was identified on the basis of the industry of specialization of the Fortune 650s present in these SMSAs either through their national headquarters or through divisional head offices.

The list of Fortune 650 firms with national headquarters in each of the 40 SMSAs was drawn from Fortune; that of Fortune 650 firms not locally headquartered but present through divisional head offices, from the *Directory of Corporate Affiliations*. To identify the industrial specialization of these Fortune 650 firms, we used Fortune's 28 industry classifications of the 500 largest industrial firms, with three additional classes for transportation, retailing, and utilities. In cases where a Fortune 650 was present in an SMSA through divisional head offices only, and where such divisions operated in an industry entirely different from that of its parent, every effort was made to account for such a presence in the proper industrial grouping.

To measure industrial specialization of these complexes of corporate offices, we proceeded with a simple tally of Fortune 650 present in these SMSAs in each industrial grouping giving a score of 2 to those firms present through their national headquarters, and a score of 1 to those firms present only through divisional head offices. For example, this procedure indicated in the food industry the presence in Omaha of 2 Fortune 650 firms through their national headquarters and 3 Fortune 650 firms through divisional offices yielding a total score of 7 $[(2 \times 2) + 3]$. Patterns of concentration were them examined to simplify the somewhat unwieldy 31 (28 plus 3) industry classification by observing which major

Table E.1 **Measurement Criteria for Strength of Industrial Specialization of Complexes of National Headquarters and Divisional Head Offices in Selected SMSAs, Eleven Broad Industry Groups, 1976**

	Measurement Criteria for Strength of Specialization of Complexes in Size 1 and 2 SMSAs		
	Strong	Medium	Weak
Foods and Beverage (77)[a]	5 or more	4	3 or less
Retail Transportation and Utilities (150)	9 or more	6 to 8	5 or less
Paper Products and Construction Materials (46)	5 or more	4	3 or less
Printing, Publishing and Broadcasting (15)	3 or more	2	1 or less
Metal Manufacturing (35)	3 or more	2	1 or less
Metal Products, Ind. & Farm. Equipt, Transp. Equipt. (111)	11 or more	7 to 10	6 or less
Electrical Appl., Electron., Office, Scientific Equip (59)	9 or more	6 to 8	5 or less
Petroleum, Chemical and related (95)	8 or more	5 to 7	4 or less
Pharmaceutical and Cosmetics (25)	5 or more	4 or 3	2 or less
Tobacco (5)	3 or more	2	1 or less
Textile, Apparel and Furniture (27)	4 or more	3	2 or less

Note: Table shows scores needed by the complex of national headquarters and divisional head offices in given SMSA to qualify as "strong," "medium" or "weak" in each of the eleven broad industry groups. Scores are determined for each SMSA with a simple tally of Fortune 650s present in the SMSA in a given industrial grouping giving a score of 2 to those firms that are present through their national headquarters and a score of 1 to those firms that are present only through divisional head offices (see text).

Measurement Criteria for Strength of Specialization of Complexes in Size 3 and 4 SMSAs

Strong	Medium	Weak
4 or more	3	2 or less
7 or more	4 to 6	3 or less
4 or more	3	2 or less
3 or more	2	1 or less
2 or more	-	1 or less
9 or more	5 to 8	4 or less
7 or more	4 to 6	3 or less
5 or more	4	3 or less
4 or more	3	2 or less
2 or more	-	1 or less
3 or more	2	1 or less

[a]Number in parenthesis indicates the number of Fortune 650 in each of the 11 broad industry groups.

Source: Fortune, 1976; and Directory of Corporate Affiliations, 1976.

industry groups tended to cluster in the same SMSAs and to establish criteria of strength for each cluster of industries.

This resulted in a simplified 11-industry classification and in the identification of criteria of strength (Strong, Medium and Weak) for each of these 11 groups. Criteria are shown in Appendix Table E.1. It will be noted that criteria are less stringent for smaller places than for larger ones.

APPENDIX F

Location of Major Commercial Banks, Life Insurance Companies, Accounting Firms, and Advertising Agencies

Table F.1 Location of the Headquarters of the Top 250 Commercial Banks, Headquarters of the Top 50 Life Insurance Companies, Field Offices and Partners of the Big Eight Accounting Firms and Headquarters and Field Offices of the Top 200 Advertising Agencies, 1976

		Top 250 Commercial Banks		Top 50 Life Insurance		Big Eight Accounting		Advertising Headquarters		Field Offices of Nonlocal	
	SMSA Size	#	Deposits $ Billions	#	Accounts $ Billions	# Field Offices	# Partners[a]	Top 50	Next 150	Top 50	Next 150
DIVERSIFIED SERVICE CENTERS											
National Nodal											
New York	1	20	198.9	7	88.1	8	767	37	59	13	nt
Los Angeles	1	5	26.9	1	2.6	8	341	1	5	29	10
Chicago	1	9	40.2	3	4.1	8	516	4	12	20	8
San Francisco	1	7	86.6	0	0	8	203	0	3	19	12
Regional Nodal											
Philadelphia	1	12	18.2	2	4.6	8	172	0	6	3	6
Boston	1	5	9.9	2	19.0	8	151	0	4	6	5
Dallas	1	5	10.6	0	1.5	8	218	2	0	4	2
Houston	1	5	7.9	0	0	8	216	0	2	6	5
St. Louis	1	3	3.4	1	1.0	8	110	1	1	1	1
Baltimore	1	4	4.9	0	0	8	63	0	3	1	3
Minneapolis	1	3	4.0	2	2.2	8	128	1	4	4	2
Cleveland	1	5	8.4	0	0	8	159	0	8	1	1
Atlanta	2	4	5.6	0	0	8	109	0	5	8	5
Miami	2	1	1.4	0	0	8	98	0	0	5	3
Denver	2	3	2.2	0	0	8	100	0	0	5	5
Seattle	2	5	8.7	0	0	8	81	0	1	3	3

Cincinnati	2	4	2.6	2	3.5	8	70	0	0	1	3
Kansas City	2	3	1.7	1	0.8	8	90	0	2	2	5
Phoenix	2	3	5.9	0	0	8	50	0	0	4	2
Indianapolis	2	3	3.7	1	0.8	7	56	0	2	1	0
Portland	2	2	5.2	0	0	8	61	0	0	4	2
Columbus	2	3	2.5	1	1.0	8	68	0	1	2	2
Subregional Nodal											
Memphis	3	3	2.3	0	0	7	42	0	0	2	0
Salt Lake City	3	3	2.2	0	0	6	34	0	1	0	0
Birmingham	3	2	1.8	1	1.3	8	54	0	0	0	0
Nashville	3	3	2.8	1	2.6	5	35	0	0	0	0
Oklahoma City	3	2	1.6	0	0	8	47	0	0	2	0
Jacksonville	3	0	0	0	0	7	29	0	1	2	1
Syracuse	3	0	0	0	0	6	31	0	1	1	1
Richmond	3	3	2.2	1	1.1	7	45	0	0	1	0
Charlotte	3	2	4.9	0	0	8	62	0	0	1	1
Omaha	3	1	0.5	1	1.2	7	46	0	0	1	0
Mobile	4	1	0.2	0	0	3	8				
Little Rock	4	0	0	0	0	3	8				
Shreveport	4	0	0	0	0	2	6				
Des Moines	4	1	0.2	2	5.3	5	30				
Spokane	4	1	0.2	0	0	1	6				
Jackson	4	2	0.3	0	0	3	14				
SPECIALIZED SERVICE CENTERS											
Functional Nodal											
Detroit	1	7	14.1	0	0	8	157	3	2	9	3
Pittsburgh	1	4	11.7	0	0	8	112	1	0	2	4

(continued on next page)

273

Table F.1 (continued)

	SMSA Size	Top 250 Commercial Banks #	Deposits $ Billions	Top 50 Life Insurance #	Accounts $ Billions	Big Eight Accounting # Field Offices	# Partners[a]	Headquarters Top 50	Next 150	Field Offices of Nonlocal Top 50	Next 150
Newark	1	5	4.0	2	47.5	8	126	0	3	1	1
Milwaukee	2	3	3.1	1	8.6	8	136	0	2	1	1
San Jose	2	0	0	0	0	7	59	0	0	1	1
Hartford	2	2	3.2	5	35.3	7	73	0	1	0	0
Rochester	3	1	0.4	0	0	7	35	0	1	1	0
Louisville	3	3	2.3	1	0.8	6	58	0	2	0	0
Dayton	3	1	0.6	0	0	4	25	0	0	1	1
Bridgeport	3	3	1.4	0	0	2	9	0	1	0	0
Toledo	3	1	0.6	0	0	8	57	0	0	1	1
Greensboro	3	1	2.9	2	2.1	3	15	0	1	0	0
Akron	3	1	0.7	0	0	4	24	0	0	0	1
Allentown	3	2	1.1	0	0	2	4	0	0	0	0
Tulsa	3	2	1.5	0	0	6	73	0	0	0	0
New Brunswick	3	0	0	0	0	0	0	0	0	0	0
Jersey City	3	1	0.6	0	0	0	0	0	0	0	0
Wilmington	3	3	1.8	0	0	2	20	0	0	0	0
Paterson	4	1	0.2	0	0	0	0	0	0	0	0
Knoxville	4	1	0.2	0	0	0	0	0	0	0	0
Wichita	4	1	0.2	0	0	4	17	0	1	0	0
Fort Wayne	4	1	0.2	1	3.5	3	8	0	0	0	0
Peoria	4	0	0	0	0	2	10	0	0	0	0
Kalamazoo	4	0	0	0	0	0	0	0	0	0	0

Government-Education											
Washington	1	7	5.3	0	0	8	183	0	1	7	2
Sacramento	3	0	0	0	0	6	26	0	0	0	0
Albany	3	2	0.4	0	0	3	18	0	0	0	0
Raleigh-Durham	4	1	1.1	0	0	3	19				
Fresno	4	0	0	0	0	0	0				
Austin	4	1	0.2	0	0	5	15				
Lansing	4	1	1.4	0	0	0	0				
Oxnard Ventura	4	0	0	0	0	0	0				
Harrisburg	4	2	0.5	0	0	4	11				
Baton Rouge	4	2	0.5	0	0	2	6				
Columbia, S.C.	4	3	0.6	0	0	4	9				
Utica	4	1	0.2	0	0	0	0				
Trenton	4	1	0.2	0	0	0	0				
Madison	4	0	0	0	0	0	0				
Stockton	4	0	0	0	0	0	0				
Education-Manufacturing											
New Haven	3	0	0	0	0	5	48	0	0	0	0
Springfield	3	0	0	1	6.4	1	8	0	0	0	0
Tacoma	4	0	0	0	0	0	0				
South Bend	4	0	0	0	0	4	15				
Ann Arbor	4	0	0	0	0	0	0				
PRODUCTION CENTERS											
Manufacturing											
Buffalo	2	3	10.9	0	0	7	44	0	0	0	0
Providence	3	3	3.2	0	0	6	37	0	0	1	0
Worcester	3	1	0.4	1	1.7	2	17	0	0	0	0
Gary	3	0	0	0	0	0	0	0	0	0	0

(continued on next page)

Table F.1 (continued)

	SMSA Size	Top 250 Commercial Banks		Top 50 Life Insurance Accounts		Big Eight Accounting		Headquarters		Field Offices of Nonlocal	
		#	Deposits $ Billions	#	Accounts $ Billions	# Field Offices	# Partners[a]	Top 50	Top Next 150	Top 50	Top Next 150
N.E. Pennsylvania	3	0	0	0	0	1	1	0	0	0	0
Grand Rapids	3	0	0	0	0	4	22	0	0	0	0
Youngstown	3	0	0	0	0	2	4	0	0	0	0
Greenville	3	0	0	0	0	4	20	0	1	0	0
Flint	3	0	0	0	0	0	0	0	0	0	0
New Bedford	4	0	0	0	0	0	0				
Canton	4	0	0	0	0	0	0				
Johnson City	4	1	0	0	0	0	0				
Chattanooga	4	0	0.2	0	0	3	12				
Davenport	4	0	0	0	0	0	0				
Beaumont	4	0	0	0	0	0	0				
York	4	0	0	0	0	0	0				
Lancaster	4	1	1.0	0	0	0	0				
Binghamton	4	0	0	0	0	0	0				
Reading	4	1	1.1	0	0	0	0				
Huntington	4	0	0	0	0	0	0				
Evansville	4	0	0	0	0	0	0				
Appleton	4	0	0	0	0	0	0				
Erie	4	0	0	0	0	0	0				
Rockford	4	0	0	0	0	0	0				
Lorain	4	0	0	0	0	0	0				
Industrial-Military											
San Diego	2	0	0	0	0	7	51	0	0	1	3

Center										
San Antonio	3	2	1.2	0	0	4	34	0	1	0	0
Norfolk	3	1	1.7	0	0	3	14	0	0	1	0
El Paso	4	1	0.2	0	0	0	0				
Charleston, SC	4	0	0	0	0	0	0				
Newport News	4	0	0	0	0	2	5				
Lexington	4	1	0.2	0	0	0	0				
Huntsville	4	0	0	0	0	0	0				
Augusta	4	0	0	0	0	0	0				
Vallejo	4	0	0	0	0	0	0				
Colorado Springs	4	0	0	0	0	0	0				
Pensacola	4	0	0	0	0	0	0				
Salinas	4	0	0	0	0	0	0				
Mining-Industrial											
Tucson	4	0	0	0	0	3	8				
Bakersfield	4	0	0	0	0	0	0				
Corpus Christi	4	0	0	0	0	3	8				
Lakeland	4	0	0	0	0	0	0				
Johnstown, PA	4	0	0	0	0	0	0				
Duluth	4	0	0	0	0	0	0				
Charleston, WV	4	1	1.2	0	0	0	0				
CONSUMER-ORIENTED CENTERS											
Residential											
Nassau-Suffolk	1	1	1.6	0	0	6	27	0	0	0	1
Anaheim	2	0	0	1	1.7	3	14	1	0	1	1
Long Branch	4	1	0.2	0	0	0	0				
Resort-Retirement											
Tampa	2	0	0	0	0	8	51	0	0	1	3
Riverside	2	0	0	0	0	0	0	0	0	0	0

(continued on next page)

Table F.1 (continued)

SMSA Size	Top 250 Commercial Banks		Top 50 Life Insurance Accounts		Big Eight Accounting		Headquarters of Nonlocal		Field Offices of Nonlocal	
	#	Deposits $ Billions	#	Accounts $ Billions	# Field Offices	# Partners[a]	Top 50	Next 150	Top 50	Next 150
Ft. Lauderdale	3	0	0	0	0	5	17	0	0	0	1
Honolulu	3	2	2.1	0	0	7	58	0	1	1	0
Orlando	3	0	0	0	0	5	22	0	0	0	1
West Palm Beach	4	0	0	0	0	2	3				
Albuquerque	4	1	0.2	0	0	4	16				
Las Vegas	4	0	0	0	0	0	0				
Santa Barbara	4	0	0	0	0	0	0				

Note: The distribution of headquarters and field offices of Top 200 Advertising firms is not tabulated for size 4 SMSAs (blank cells).

n.t.: not tabulated.
[a] Partners, managers, directors and principals.

Source: Moody's Financial Manuals (Top 250 commercial banks); Fortune (Top 50 Life Insurance); Individual Directories of Arthur Andersen, Arthur Young, Coopers & Lybrand, Enrst & Ernst, Haskins & Sells, Peat Marwick Mitchell, Price Waterhouse, Touche Ross (Big Eight Accounting Firms); Advertising Age; and Directory of Advertising Agencies (Top 50 and Next 150 Advertising Agencies).

APPENDIX G

Location of Research Laboratories, 100 Largest Four-Year Colleges and Universities, and Medical Schools

Table G.1 Location of Industrial Research Laboratories, 100 Largest Four-Year Colleges and Universities, and Medical Schools, 1976 and 1959

| | SMSA Size | # of Industrial Research Laboratories | | 100 Largest 4-year Colleges and Universities | Medical Schools | |
		1975	1956	1977	1974	1959
DIVERSIFIED SERVICE CENTERS						
National Nodal						
New York	1	507	538	8	7	6
Los Angeles	1	317	356	5	2	3
Chicago	1	385	389	2	6	5
San Francisco	1	118	94	2	1	1
Regional Nodal						
Philadelphia	1	176	204	2	5	5
Boston	1	263	189	3	3	3
Dallas	1	57	38	2	1	1
Houston	1	96	31	1	2	1
St. Louis	1	67	65	0	2	2
Baltimore	1	60	55	1	2	2
Minneapolis	1	51	48	1	2	2
Cleveland	1	115	123	1	1	1
Atlanta	2	35	18	1	1	1
Miami	2	15	5	0	1	1
Denver	2	59	23	1	1	1
Seattle	2	33	20	1	1	1
Cincinnati	2	42	43	1	1	1
Kansas City	2	38	37	1	2	1
Phoenix	2	33	7	1	0	0

Indianapolis	2	30	36	1	1	1
New Orleans	2	9	8	0	2	2
Portland	2	20	17	1	1	1
Columbus	2	34	22	1	1	1
Subregional Nodal						
Memphis	3	6	11	1	1	1
Salt Lake City	3	22	7	1	1	1
Birmingham	3	12	9	0	1	1
Nashville	3	6	5	0	2	2
Oklahoma City	3	3	8	1	1	1
Jacksonville	3	4	2	0	0	0
Syracuse	3	18	24	1	1	1
Richmond	3	16	12	1	1	1
Charlotte	3	14	8	0	0	0
Omaha	3	3	7	0	2	2
Mobile	4	4	3	0	1	1
Little Rock	4	2	3	0	1	1
Shreveport	4	1	0	0	1	0
Des Moines	4	7	6	0	0	0
Spokane	4	1	2	0	0	0
Jackson	4	0	1	0	1	1
SPECIALIZED SERVICE CENTERS						
Functional Nodal						
Detroit	1	98	108	1	1	1
Pittsburgh	1	91	65	1	1	1
Newark	1	186	203	1	1	0
Milwaukee	2	71	62	1	1	1
San Jose	2	82	22	1	1	1

(continued on next page)

Table 6.1 (continued)

	SMSA Size	Industrial Research Laboratories 1975	# of Industrial Research Laboratories 1956	100 Largest 4-year Colleges and Universities 1977	Medical Schools 1974	Medical Schools 1959
Hartford	2	57	43	1	1	0
Rochester	3	36	34	0	1	1
Louisville	3	18	15	1	1	1
Dayton	3	34	32	0	0	0
Bridgeport	3	121	67	0	0	0
Toledo	3	23	24	2	1	0
Greensboro	3	15	10	0	1	1
Akron	3	25	17	2	0	0
Allentown	3	21	19	0	0	0
Tulsa	3	21	25	0	0	0
New Brunswick	3	40	38	1	1	0
Jersey City	3	22	59	0	0	0
Wilmington	3	20	17	1	1	0
Paterson	4	34	34	0	0	0
Knoxville	4	8	3	1	0	0
Wichita	4	12	3	1	0	0
Fort Wayne	4	12	6	0	0	0
Peoria	4	3	4	0	0	0
Kalamazoo	4	7	10	1	0	0
Government-Education						
Washington	1	212	60	2	3	3
Sacramento	3	6	0	2	1	0
Albany	3	23	25	0	1	1

City						
Raleigh-Durham	4	17	5	2	2	2
Fresno	4	3	0	1	0	0
Austin	4	18	3	1	0	0
Lansing	4	4	5	1	1	0
Oxnard-Ventura	4	3	2	0	0	0
Harrisburg	4	6	8	0	1	0
Baton Rouge	4	11	6	1	0	1
Columbia, S.C.	4	4	1	1	1	0
Utica	4	7	4	0	0	0
Trenton	4	41	18	0	0	0
Madison	4	16	9	1	1	1
Stockton	4	2	1	0	0	0
Education-Manufacturing						
New Haven	3	30	47	0	1	1
Springfield	3	12	19	1	0	0
Tacoma	4	3	9	0	0	0
South Bend	4	11	9	0	0	0
Ann Arbor	4	29	6	2	1	1
PRODUCTION CENTERS						
Manufacturing						
Buffalo	2	51	73	1	1	1
Providence	3	29	27	0	1	0
Worcester	3	30		0	1	0
Gary	3	7	15	0	0	0
N.E. Pennsylvania	3	7	10	0	0	0
Grand Rapids	3	13	16	0	0	1
Youngstown	3	7	14	1	0	0
Greenville	3	10	3	0	0	0

(continued next page)

Table G.1 (continued)

	SMSA Size	# of Industrial Research Laboratories 1975	# of Industrial Research Laboratories 1956	100 Largest 4-year Colleges and Universities 1977	Medical Schools 1974	Medical Schools 1959
Flint	3	2	2	0	0	0
New Bedford	4	0	0	0	0	0
Canton	4	6	10	0	0	0
Johnson City	4	0	0	0	0	0
Chattanooga	4	5	10	0	0	0
Davenport	4	5	5	0	0	0
Beaumont	4	0	0	0	0	0
York	4	0	0	0	0	0
Lancaster	4	0	0	0	0	0
Binghamton	4	0	0	0	0	0
Reading	4	0	0	0	0	0
Huntington	4	0	0	0	0	0
Evansville	4	0	0	0	0	0
Appleton	4	0	0	0	0	0
Erie	4	0	0	0	0	0
Rockford	4	0	0	0	0	0
Lorain	4	0	0	0	0	0
Industrial-Military						
San Diego	2	52	18	1	1	0
San Antonio	3	7	7	0	1	0
Norfolk	3	6	3	0	1	0
El Paso	4	0	0	1	0	0
Charleston, SC	4	0	0	0	0	1

Newport News	4	0	0	0	0	0
Lexington	4	0	0	1	1	1
Huntsville	4	0	0	0	0	0
Augusta	4	0	0	0	1	1
Vallejo	4	0	0	0	0	0
Colorado Springs	4	0	0	0	0	0
Pensacola	4	0	0	0	0	0
Salinas	4	0	0	0	0	0
Mining-Industrial						
Tucson	4	11	1	1	1	0
Bakersfield	4	0	0	0	0	0
Corpus Christi	4	0	0	0	0	0
Lakeland	4	0	0	0	0	0
Johnstown, PA	4	0	0	0	0	0
Duluth	4	0	0	0	1	0
Charleston, WV	4	0	0	0	0	0
CONSUMER-ORIENTED CENTERS						
Residential						
Nassau-Suffolk	1	103	65	1	1	0
Anaheim	2	60	17	1	1	0
Long Branch	4	13	10	0	0	0
Resort-Retirement						
Tampa	2	14	3	1	1	0
Riverside	2	21	0	0	1	0
Ft. Lauderdale	3	9	1	0	0	0
Honolulu	3	15	3	1	1	0
Orlando	3	4	2	0	0	0
West Palm Beach	4	8	2	0	0	0

(continued on next page)

Table 6.1 (continued)

	SMSA Size	# of Industrial Research Laboratories		100 Largest 4-year Colleges and Universities	Medical Schools	
		1975	1956	1977	1974	1959
Albuquerque	4	10	4	1	1	0
Las Vegas	4	0	0	0	0	0
Santa Barbara	4	0	0	0	0	0
UNITED STATES		6,661	4,834	100	113	84

Source: Industrial Research Laboratories, 1975 and 1956; U.S. National Center for Education Statistics, Education Statistics, 1977; Journal of American Medical Association, November Issues, 1960 and 1977.

Bibliography

Abramovitz, Moses, "Manpower, Capital and Technology," in *Human Resources and Economic Welfare. Essays in Honor of Eli Ginzberg*, edited by Ivar Berg, New York: Columbia University Press, 1972.

Advertising Age, New York: Various Issues.

American Banker, "Survey of Edge Act Subsidiaries," February 1977.

American Banker, "Survey of Loan Production Offices," July 18, 1975.

American Medical Association, *Directory of Residency Training Programs*, 1974–75 and 1959–60.

American Medical Association, *Journal of the American Medical Association*, November issues, 1960 and 1975.

Berry, Brian J. L., *Geography of Market Centers and Retail Distribution*, Englewood Cliffs, N.J.: Prentice-Hall, 1967.

Berry, Brian J. L. and William L. Garrison, "The Functional Basis of the Central Place Hierarchy," *Economic Geography*, Vol. 34, 1958.

Bluestone, Barry and Bennett Harrison, *The Deindustrialization of America*, New York: Basic Books, 1982.

Blumberg, Philip I., *The Megacorporation in American Society*, Englewood Cliffs, N.J.: Prentice-Hall, 1975.

Chandler, Alfred, *The Visible Hand: The Managerial Revolution in American Business*, Cambridge, Mass.: Harvard University Press, 1977.

Clark, Colin, *The Conditions of Economic Progress*, London: MacMillan, 1940.

Cohen, Robert, "Employment Consequences of Structural Changes in the Auto Industry," mimeograph, New York: 1981.

Cohen, Robert, *The Impact of Foreign Direct Investment on U.S. Cities and Regions*, Research Commissioned by the U.S. Department of H.U.D., Washington, D.C.: U.S. Government Printing Office, 1979.

Cohen, Robert, "The Internationalization of Capital and U.S. Cities," Ph.D. Dissertation, New York: New School for Social Research, 1979.

Cohen, Robert, *Lending by Transnational Banks and Other Financial Institutions to Transnational Corporations*, New York: U.N. Center on Transnational Corporations, 1977.

Conservation of Human Resources, *The Corporate Headquarters Complex in New York City*, New York: Conservation of Human Resources, 1977.

Directory of Corporate Affiliations, Skokie, Ill.: National Register Publishing Co., 1977.

Dunn, Edgar S., *The Development of the U.S. Urban System*, Baltimore: The Johns Hopkins University Press, 1980.

Dunn, Edgar S., "A Flow Network Image of Urban Structures," in *Regional Studies*, 1971.

Federal Reserve Board of the United States, *Report of Assets, Liabilities, and Income of Commercial and Mutual Savings Banks*, 1976 and 1960.

Fisher, A. G. B., *The Clash of Progress and Security*, London: MacMillan, 1935.

Forbes, "Whatever Happened to Akron," November 22, 1982.

Fortune, "500 Largest Industrial Firms," various years.

Fortune, "Second 500 Largest Industrial Firms," various years.

Fortune, "50 Largest Retailing, Transportation and Utility Companies," various years.

Fuchs, Victor, "The Service Industries and U.S. Economic Growth Since World War II," Working Paper #211, National Bureau for Economic Research, Stanford: 1977.

Fuchs, Victor, *The Services Economy*, New York: National Bureau for Economic Research and Columbia University Press, 1968.

Goldstein, Harold, "Recent Structural Changes in Employment in the United States," Working Paper, New York: Conservation of Human Resources, Columbia University, 1981.

Goldstein, Harvey A., Nancy A. Paulson, and Edward M. Bergman, "Models of Industry Employment Change for Labor Market Areas and States," Mimeograph, New York: Center for the Social Sciences, Columbia University, 1981.

Gordon, David, "Capitalist Development and the History of American Cities," in William Tabb and Larry Sawers, *Marxism and the Metropolis,* New York: Oxford University Press, 1978.

Greenfeld, Harry, *Manpower and Growth of Producer Services,* New York: Columbia University Press, 1966.

Hoover, Edgar M. and Raymond Vernon, *Anatomy of a Metropolis,* Cambridge Mass.: Harvard University Press, 1959.

Industrial Research Laboratories of the United States, 14th Edition, New York: R.R. Bowker Company, 1975.

Industrial Laboratories of the United States, 12th Edition, Washington: National Academy of Sciences, 1956.

Knight, Richard V., "The Cleveland Economy in Transition: Implications for the Future," Working Paper, Cleveland: Cleveland State University, College of Urban Affairs, 1977.

Marshall, Alfred, *Principles of Economics,* 9th Edition, London: MacMillan & Co. Ltd, 1961.

Moody's, Industrial Manuals, various years.

Moody's, "300 Largest U.S. Commercial Banks," various years.

Moody's, "50 Largest U.S. Life Insurance Companies," various years.

National Science Foundation, *1974 Characteristics of the National Sample of Scientists and Engineers, Part 3: Geographic,* NSF Publication #76-330, Washington, D.C.: Government Printing Office, 1977.

Perry, David C. and Alfred J. Watkins, editors, *The Rise of the Sunbelt Cities,* Beverley Hills, Calif.: Sage Publications, 1977.

Pred, Allan, "Major Job Providing Organizations and Systems of Cities," Commission on College Geography, Resource Paper No. 27, Washington, D.C.: Association of American Geographers, 1974.

Pred, Allan, *City Systems in Advanced Economies,* New York, N.Y.: Halsted Press, 1977.

Quante, Wolfgang, *The Exodus of Corporate Headquarters from New York City,* Praeger: New York, 1976.

Sale, Kirkpatrick, *Power Shift: The Rise of the Southern Rim and Its Challenge to the Eastern Establishment,* New York: Random House, 1975.

Sears, Carl and Robert G. Hawkins, *Foreign Firms in New York City: A Survey Study,* Occasional Papers in Metropolitan Business and Finance, #1, New York University, Solomon Brothers Centers for the Study of Financial Institutions, 1979.

Singlemann, Joachim, *From Agriculture to Services,* Beverly Hills, Calif.: Sage Publications, 1979.

Stanback, Thomas M., Jr., *Understanding the Service Economy,* Baltimore: The Johns Hopkins University Press, 1979.

Stanback, Thomas M., Jr. and Richard V. Knight, *Suburbanization and the City,* Montclair, N.J.: Allanheld, Osmun & Co., 1975.

Stanback, Thomas M., Jr. and Richard V. Knight, *The Metropolitan Economy,* New York: Columbia University Press, 1970.

Stanback, Thomas M., Jr., Peter J. Bearse, Thierry J. Noyelle, and Robert A. Karasek, *Services/The New Economy,* Totowa, N.J.: Allanheld, Osmun & Co., 1981.

Stanback, Thomas M., Jr. and Thierry J. Noyelle, *Cities in Transition,* Totowa, N.J.: Allanheld, Osmun & Co., 1982.

Standard and Poor's, Industrial Manuals, various years.

Standard Directory of Advertisers, Skokie, Ill.: National Register Publishing Co., 1977.

Standard Directory of Advertising Agencies, Skokie, Ill.: National Register Publishing Co., 1977.

Sternlieb, George and James W. Hughes, editors, *Post Industrial America: Metropolitan Decline and Inter-Regional Job Shifts,* New Brunswick, N.J.: Center for Urban Policy Research, 1975.

Thompson, Wilbur R., "Economic Process and Employment Problems in Declining Metropolitan Areas" in George Sternlieb and James W. Hughes, *Post Industrial America: Metropolitan Decline and Inter-Regional Job Shifts,* New Brunswick, N.J.: Center for Urban Policy Research, 1975.

Thompson, Wilbur R., *Introduction to Urban Economics,* Washington, D.C.: Resources for the Future, Inc., 1965.

U.S. Civil Aeronautics Board, *Statistics of Passenger Air Traffic,* various years.

U.S. Civil Service Commission, *Federal Civilian Workforce Statistics. Annual Report of Employment by Geographic Areas,* 1976 and 1966.

U.S. Department of Commerce, Bureau of the Census, *Census of Manufacturers,* 1939, 1948, 1958, 1967, 1972, and selected state data for 1977.

U.S. Department of Commerce, Bureau of the Census, *Census of Retail Trade,* 1939, 1948, 1958, 1967.

U.S. Department of Commerce, Bureau of the Census, *Census of Wholesale Trade,* 1972.

U.S. Department of Commerce, Bureau of the Census, *Enterprise Statistics, Part II: Central Administrative Offices and Auxiliary Establishments,* 1972, 1963.

U.S. Department of Commerce, Bureau of the Census, *Statistical Abstract of the United States,* Washington, D.C.: Government Printing Office, 1980.

U.S. Department of Commerce, Bureau of the Census, *Current Population Reports,* Series P-25.

U.S. Department of Commerce, Bureau of Economic Analysis, *Survey of Current Business,* July 1978.

U.S. Department of Commerce, Bureau of Economic Analysis, *The National Income and Product Accounts of the United States, 1929-74 Statistical Tables,* Washington, D.C.: Government Printing Office, 1977.

U.S. Department of Commerce, Bureau of Economic Analysis, *Personal Income in State and Local Areas, 1970-1975,* Washington, D.C.: U.S. Government Printing Office, 1976.

U.S. Department of Commerce, Bureau of Economic Analysis, *County Business Patterns,* 1959, 1969 and 1976.

U.S. Department of Housing and Urban Development, *The 1980 President's National Urban Policy Report,* Washington, D.C.: Government Printing Office, 1980.

U.S. Department of Labor, Bureau of Labor Statistics, *Employment and Earnings, State and Local Areas,* 1959, 1969, 1976.

U.S. Federal Communication Commission, *Statistics of Communication Common Carriers,* various years.

U.S. Federal Reserve Board, *Flows of Funds,* Washington, D.C.: Federal Deposit Insurance Corporation, various years.

U.S. House of Representatives, Committee on Small Business, *Conglomerate Mergers: Their Effect on Small Business and Local Communities,* 96th Congress, Washington, D.C.: Government Printing Office, 1980.

U.S. House of Representatives, Subcommittee on the City, *Large Corporations and Urban Employment,* 95th Congress, Washington, D.C.: U.S. Government Printing Office, 1978.

U.S. National Center for Education Statistics, *Education Statistics,* various years.

U.S. Office of Management and Budget, *Standard Industrial Code of the United States,* Washington, D.C.: Government Printing Office, 1973.

U.S. Senate, Subcommittee on Reports, Accounting and Mergers, *The Accounting Establishment,* 95th Congress, Washington, D.C.: Government Printing Office, March 1977.

Watkins, Alfred J., *The Practice of Urban Economics,* Beverly Hills, Calif.: Sage Publications, 1980.

Westaway, John, "The Spatial Hierarchy of Business Organizations and its Implications for the British Urban System," *Regional Studies,* #8, 1974.

Wilson-Salinas, Patricia, "Subemployment and the Urban Underclass," Working Paper, Austin: Graduate Program in Community and Regional Planning, University of Texas, 1980.

Index

Italicized page numbers refer to material in tables.

THE AUTHORS

Thierry J. Noyelle is Research Scholar at the Conservation of Human Resources Project, Columbia University. He is coauthor of *Services/The New Economy* and *Cities in Transition*.

Thomas M. Stanback, Jr. is Professor of Economics at New York University and Senior Research Scholar at the Conservation of Human Resources Project. He is the author of *Understanding the Service Economy* and coauthor of *The Metropolitan Economy: The Process of Employment Expansion, Suburbanization and the City*, *Services/The New Economy* and *Cities in Transition*.

EC
AS
WW

073JMK

Noyelle